URBANIZATION IN ISRAEL

Urbanization in Israel

Elisha Efrat

CROOM HELM
London & Canberra

ST. MARTIN'S PRESS
New York

©1984 Elisha Efrat
Croom Helm Ltd., Provident House, Burrell Row,
Beckenham, Kent BR3 1AT

Croom Helm Australia Pty Ltd, 28 Kembla St,
Fyshwick, ACT 2609, Australia

British Library Cataloguing in Publication Data

Efrat, Elisha
    Urbanization in Israel.
    1. Urbanization — Israel
    I. Title
    307.7'6'095694   HT147.I/

    ISBN 0-7099-0931-4

All rights reserved. For information, write:
St. Martin's Press, Inc., 175 Fifth Avenue, New York, NY 10010
Printed in Great Britain
First published in the United States of America in 1984

Library of Congress Cataloging in Publication Data

Efrat, Elisha.
    Urbanization in Israel.

    Bibliography: p.
    Includes index.
    1. Cities and towns — Israel. 2. Urbanization — Israel.
3. Israel — Social conditions. 3. Israel — Social conditions. I. Title.
HT147.17E38   1984   307.7'6'095694   83-24718
ISBN 0-312-83523-X (St. Martin)

Printed and bound in Great Britain

CONTENTS

LIST OF FIGURES

LIST OF TABLES

INTRODUCTION

This book deals with the urban geography of Israel, and its purpose is to analyze the fundamentals and processes of the development of both old and new towns in the country on the background of Jewish settlement trends since the end of the last century until today. A comprehensive approach is taken in the description of the dominance of the settlement phenomenon which rapidly grew in Israel during the last 35 years. This issue is important to study because the rate of urbanization in that country is quite high, and by the year 2000 it is estimated that most of its population will live in towns.

Urban development in Israel could not build on old traditions. Prior to the <u>Bilu</u> (1) settlers, in the eighties of the last century, the number of Jews in the country was not large, and they were concentrated in four towns: Jerusalem, Tiberias, Safed and Hebron. According to the 1922 census, ca.80% of the total Jewish population of 86,000 lived in these four towns, half of them in Jerusalem. According to the 1948 census, 80.4% of the total population of 750,000 lived in cities and other urban settlements, of these 30% in Tel Aviv-Jaffa and 14.5% in Jerusalem. Today the ratio of urban to total population is one of the world's highest, reaching 85.6%, an indication significant geographical and demographic developments such as Israel had not previously known.

The aim of this book is to consider the main processes that have characterized urban settlement in Israel and the factors that have determined the present pattern of urban settlement.

In the past, most of the settlement research in Israel dealt with the agricultural sector, while little was written about the characteristics and processes of urban settlements. Research about urbanization in Israel from a geographic, economic and

social perspective only began in the mid-1960s by
academic and governmental institutions. This research was the outcome of the drastic changes which
took place as a result of the mass construction of
housing for the rapid absorption of immigration, security needs, and the distribution of the population.
The reconstruction of ancient towns, the establishment of more than 30 new towns, the development of
modern transportation arteries, together with the
desire to preserve the landscape and to establish an
equilibrium between the old and new - all of these
activities needed comprehensive survey and urban research.

This book contains sixteen chapters which present the main urban problems of Israel. The first
three chapters analyze the historic distribution of
towns in Israel, a focal point from which the urban
processes evolved, the attitudes towards town establishment as viewed by the "Fathers" of Zionism, and
the social processes that occurred as a result of
urbanization. The next six chapters show the patterns of town development in the context of the urban nodes of Jerusalem, Tel Aviv and Haifa, in the
metropolitan and conurbation areas, in the ancient
towns and those that grew out of the agricultural
Moshavot (2), and in the desert town of Beer Sheva.
The tenth chapter describes the new towns in the
country as a drastic change in the overall urban
process of Israel. This subject is presented by a
chapter on Ashdod, the largest development town in
Israel, one on Elat, a very unusual development
town, and by one on Arad, which represents a modern
approach to the issue of populating new towns. The
last three chapters of the book deal with additional
aspects of urbanization: The Arab town in Israel in
the administered areas, and historical and architectural processes in town building. The analysis and explanation of all of these topics are accompanied by
maps and illustrations which are an integral part of
the geographical description. A detailed and up-to-
date bibliography at the end of the book enables
scholars to broaden their knowledge concerning the
different aspects of the urban geography of this
issue.

NOTES

1.   'Bilu' are the initials of a Hebrew slogan
in the meaning of: The House of Jacob, let's go! It
was the slogan of the first Zionist immigrants from
Russia, Rumania and Poland who came to the land of

Israel.

2. Moshavah (pl. Moshavot) is the Hebrew term for a village of the regular European type, with land, buildings, farming installations, all privately owned.

Chapter One

THE DEVELOPMENT AND DISTRIBUTION OF TOWNS IN THE
LAND OF ISRAEL

The existence of towns in the Middle East long pre-
cedes their establishment in Europe. The world's
most ancient town is assumed to be Jericho, founded
6000 years before Christ.
    During the following Millenia towns appeared
throughout the region, particularly along the Fertile Crescent - the fertile and temperate zone that
stretched from Mesopotamia to Egypt. By the Greek
and Roman periods, the development of towns extended to Europe as well. Such towns were usually gar-
rison towns, offering protection behind their walls,
particularly during time of war, to the resident and
local surrounding population and functioning as hubs
for marketing and trade. Royalty and those that
directly served it, generally resided in the towns.
Economically their populations were engaged primarily in subsistence agriculture; they lacked the high
degree of occupational specialization and economic
interdependence so characteristic of modern urbanization. These attributes began to appear in the Middle East, with the Moslem era in the 7th century,
with the establishment of the renown cities of Bagh-
dad, Cairo, Damascus and Constantinople - all of
which are to this day - and, in Europe, during the
Crusador period beginning in the 12th century. With
the exception of those cities just mentioned above,
other Middle Eastern towns, despite their early origins, did not achieve the size or diversity of many
eventually later established in Europe. Still they
were of particular importance in the region, owing
to their status as centers of administrative, economic and social activity.

THE HISTORY OF TOWN DEVELOPMENT AND DISTRIBUTION IN THE LAND OF ISRAEL

Israel is unique in that it contains both very ancient and new towns. Some, such as Jerusalem and Nazareth, have existed since before the common era; others were founded as little as twenty years ago. The establishment and existence of urban settlements throughout various locations and historic periods have been strongly interrelated with the natural, political and economic events of the country. Through the centuries, towns experienced alternating periods of prosperity and depression. They flourished when conditions in the country were peaceful and settled, and declined during periods of war, invasion and incursions of nomadic desert tribes.

Until the 20th century, in general, the towns of Israel remained small. They did not have sufficient economic base or agricultural hinterland for intensive growth and development. Their economies relied mainly on trade and commerce, serving as market towns for nearby farming villages and as trading points along caravan and shipping routes. Due to Israel's position within the center of the Fertile Crescent, already in ancient times, the country served as a passageway for various nomadic peoples wandering from region to region through the land. Major travel routes developed including the Via Maris (1) and the Mountainous Route (2), along which travellers and goods-laden caravans crossed the country, enroute to Europe, Africa and elsewhere. Most towns existed along such routes, where they could profit from trade with travelling merchants and peddlers and through the provision of hostelries and supplies.

Over the centuries, whenever the country's population felt threatened, they tended to concentrate in the towns, which offered greater security. The depredation of desert nomads and sea robbers induced many people to move to towns or large villages. Populations in the areas of towns such as Hebron, Beer Sheva and Gaza, were particularly vulnerable to nomadic attack, due to their location within the zone separating the cultivatable areas of the country from the barren arid and semi-arid regions of the south and east. With the encroachment of the desert varying according to the yearly rainfall - further north during years of low rainfall, receding southward in seasons of greater precipitation - the border zone was an area of frequent tension between the local agricultural settlements and the desert nomads, who drove their flocks into the zone during times of low rainfall and did not hesitate to take from the crops and property of the villagers.

Due to the constant struggle for power among nations of the Middle East, war was a common phenomenon. On numerous occasions, Israel became a battleground, as a result of internal conflict, enemy attack, or the meeting of foreign armies within its borders. Even the largest towns were not immune to the plunderings of powerful armies, marching along the major roads. Towns on the flat coastal plain were more easily destroyed as they were prone to attack from both land and sea, and lacked material barriors of protection. Hill towns had greater defensibility as the material surroundings could be used to advantage; building towns on hilltops assured enemies of an ascenting attack, and there was always a plentiful supply of stone building materials. For these reasons, in periods of danger and insecurity, hill towns were favored while coastal towns declined.

To maintain control of the land, once gained, ruling governments generally erected fortresses and fortified cities along important routes. Ramparts and center walls reflected the protective, primary function of the early towns. By Roman times, the country abounded in such urban settlements, but most subsequently suffered destruction. Roman rule was followed by that of the Byzantines, whose civilization during the 5th and 6th centuries CE was also of a predominantly urban character; many churches and other buildings date to this period. By the decline of the Islamic Empire beginning in the 8th century, however, the Arabs were still in the process of transition from a nomadic to a settled way of life: they were not attracted to an urban environment and founded mainly villages. The Crusaders enlarged and fortified a number of towns during the time of their conquests in the 12th century, and left behind many fortresses and churches, the ruins of which scatter the country to this day. They were followed by Mamelukes and Turks, who showed little interest either in the towns or the development of the country's economy.

The distribution of urban settlement in the Land of Israel, through the time of Turkish rule, was generally characterized by three longitudinal axes, with a chain of towns in the coastal plain, another along the mountain watershed and in the Jordan Valley, and one chain in the northern part of the Negev. A number of distinguishable geographical

3

phenomena of town distribution in Israel during this time are discussed as follows:(Figure 1.1)

1. Most of the ancient towns whether located on the coast, mountains, or in the valleys remained situated on their historical sites and through to the 19th century, did not expand beyond their original boundaries; thus urban sprawl, near or on their peripheral areas, did not occur. For example, Gaza, Jaffa and Acre on the coastal plain and Hebron, Jerusalem and Nazareth in the mountains, remained within their original boundaries throughout their history, during periods of growth and prosperity as well as in times of adversity and depression.

2. Almost all of the towns were located on primary travel routes. The mountain towns were established on both sides of the Mountainous Route. Most coastal towns developed where geographical conditions fostered the building of small harbours; these towns served as ports for maritime transportation and nodes for the distribution of, to and from the interior of the country. Other coastal towns were located along the historical Via Maris. The distance between one town and the next along either the coast or mountains demonstrates the towns strong relationship to their travel routes. It is apparent that the distance between coastal harbor towns resulted from the possibility of being able to travel from one town to the next within a single day. This relationship applies to the primary harbors of Gaza, Jaffa, and Acre, and others to the north and south beyond the borders of Israel, and also to the secondary, smaller harbors of Ashqelon Ashdod-Yam, Rishpon, Caesarea, Dor, Atlit and Shiqmona, the intervals reflect distances negotiable within a day by various types of sailing vessels. Even the distance between the towns of Beer Sheva, Hebron, Jerusalem, Ramallah, Nablus and Jenin are surprisingly more or less equidistant, spaced at 20-25 miles (32-40 km.) intervals readily traversed by caravans or pedestrians in one day.

3. Towns have also been established on sites

4

Figure 1.1: Towns in the Land of Israel (1947)

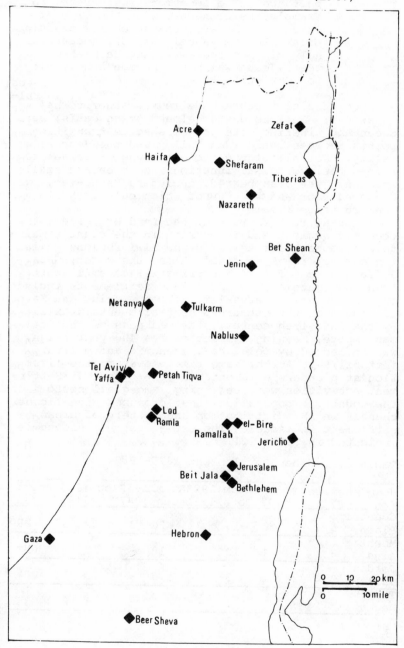

which have some historic or religious importance. The location of Nazareth, for
example, is connected with the life of
Jesus, and Safed, because of its association with the Kabbalists (3), because a
holy city to the Jews, and Bethlehem,
where Jesus was born, became a holy city
for Christianity.

Various special factors have led to other towns'
locations: Jericho was developed on an oasis; Bet
Shean and Tiberias were established as transition
points between the Jordan Valley and the Jezreel
Valley. Not all of the ancient towns of Israel retained their original functions. Most became smaller
and many just disappeared, including Yavne-Yam,
Caesarea, Dor and Shiqmona of which only archeolog-
ical remnants remain.
　　During Turkish rule of the Land of Israel, the
economic neglect and insecurity in the country maintained support for towns in the hill regions while
the coastal towns declined. Along the coast, Gaza,
Jaffa and Acre functioned primarily as small port
towns and gateways to the inland settlements including the towns of Jerusalem, Hebron, Nablus and Safed
all found on the country's central mountain axis.
By the late 19th century, the weakness of the Ottoman Empire, meaning the end of its 400 year reign,
was reflected by political, economic and military
instability. At the same time, however, the first
Zionist pioneers were enterin the country. Settlement activities were beginning, among all sectors of
the country's population, that produced significant
changes in the distribution and pattern of urban
settlement in Israel. The extent of this growth is
indicated in Table 1.1.

Table 1.1: Urban Development 1875-1982

Region	Before 1875	to-1876 tal1922	Accm. Total	1923 1931	Accm. total	1932 1947	Accm. Total	1948 1982	Accm. Total	
Coastal Plain	5	5	8	13	7	20	2	22	3	25
Mountains	8	8	4	12	-	12	-	12	1	13
Jordan Valley	2	2	1	3	-	3	-	3	1	4
The Negev	-	-	1	1	-	1	-	1	2	3

PRE-STATE URBAN DEVELOPMENT

In the years prior to World War I many of the Jewish
immigrants settled in existing towns, particularly
Jaffa. Others founded rural settlements - including
the first Moshavot (Jewish agricultural villages),
many of which urbanized in later years. In 1909, Tel
Aviv was founded as a suburb of Jaffa (it was granted local authority in 1921). In Judea and Samaria,
Tulkam, El-Bire and Beit Jala received town status
from the Turkish authorities as did Bet Shean in the
Jordan Valley.

World War I brought an end to the Ottoman Empire, and British Mandate period began. Significant
British development activity occurred including the
establishment of Haifa as a major port and industrial site. With the improved security of British rule
the years 1923 and 1931 saw a substantial growth in
coastal urbanization. New urban centers were added,
especially in the vicinity of Tel Aviv, including
Ramat Gan, Bene Beraq, Bat Yam, Givatayim, Herzliyya
and slightly to the north, Netanya.

Between 1931 and 1947, which marked the end of
the British Mandate, the coastal plain became quite
developed. Urbanization of Moshavot began. Tel Aviv
became a flourishing town, no longer dependent of
Jaffa, and received municipal status in 1934. Nahariyya and Holon were added to the list of new urban
communities. By the end of the Mandate period, the
number of towns in the coastal plain was 22, in contrast to 12 in the mountainous regions, with the
coast continuing to hold the greater potential for
further urban growth. (Table 1.1)

BRITISH URBAN DEVELOPMENT ACTIVITY

During the Mandate period, the British objectives
were not to improve the spatial distribution of
towns in the country; what was done was no more than
the selective development of existing urban infra-
structures and the advancement of particular settlements according to the security, strategic and economic interests of the Mandate authorities. In
their limited activities, however, they brought a
European standard of planning skills and an aware-
ness of urban issues.

Among their activities, the British were interested in developing Haifa as a large harbor in the
eastern part of the Mediterranean and therefore encouraged investments in the building of a harbor, in

its installations, and in reclaiming land for an industrial zone near the harbor. They were also interested in developing administration and services in Jerusalem and expressed this objective by building public institutions and residential neighbourhoods for British personnel. Other towns of interest to them were: Beer Sheva as the capital of the Negev, Jaffa as the second harbor in the country, and Gaza as the southern-most harbor along the coastal plain. Administrative and security objectives also gave impetus to settlements such as Ramla and Lod as transportation nodes, Lod for its airport and railway operation center, Ramla as the hub of interurban bus service, and Nahariyya and Netanya as recreational centers.

URBAN DEVELOPMENT DURING STATEHOOD

Since the establishment of the State of Israel in 1948, there has been a distinct change in the pace of urbanization in the country. The early decades of the State have seen the rapid development of new towns in every region. This has occurred despite that, at the inception of the State there was no policy within the new government as to an approach for urban development. During the pre-State era, the emphasis of the Zionist settlement organizations had been directed almost entirely toward agricultural rural settlements. The needs of the State, however, posed the necessity for a comprehensive approach to settlement in Israel, with particular focus on urbanization. The primary factors that forced this re-evaluation and change of policy were:

1. The mass immigration that occurred in the years immediately following statehood, resulting in a pressing housing shortage which only urban settlement could solve;
2. the desire to create a series of medium-sized towns, dispersed throughout the country to function in an intermediary capacity between the large cities and small agricultural villages; and
3. the need to populate underpopulated areas, particularly along the border, as a means of securing the State's territory.

The recognition of urban settlement as a solution for Israel's rapidly populating regions did not immediately lead to the establishment of new towns;

instead, population was added first to those already
in existence, including Lod, Ramla, Bet Shean and
Beer Sheva. As they reached the point of saturation,
immigrants were directed to Maabarot (4) erected
alongside veteran Moshavot. Some of the Maabarot
were later dismantled as immigrants were transferred to permanent housing elsewhere; others developed
into permanent annexations of the Moshavot, as at
Rishon Leziyyon, Rehovot and Hadera. The remainder
eventually became independent self-supporting settlements, of which Or Aqiva and Yehud are examples.

There then began a period of establishing development towns, first small towns such as Sederot,
Ofaqim, Ramat Yishai and Netivot, and later larger
towns, including Bet Shemesh, Qiryat Malachi, Qiryat
Ono, Dimona and Maalot. By the late 1950s and 1960s
a new approach was adopted to establish full-fledged
cities; Ashdod, Elat, Arad and Karmiel were begun
during this period.

Numerous new towns and urban centers were created as a result of these activities. Suburbs also,
especially in the areas surrounding Tel Aviv and
Haifa, expanded substantially and are expected to
remain a focus of further urban development. The
impact has been a substantial alteration of the pre-
State structure and distribution of urban settlement
in the country.

The arrival of numerous immigrants greatly affected urban growth. The vast majority had been
urban dwellers in their country of origin and it was
predictable that most would gravitate toward an urban life in Israel as well. The concentration of
immigrants in urban settlements led to the continual
growth of new and established towns and suburbs. The
tendency of many immigrants to remain in the town at
their port of arrival was particularly experienced
by Tel Aviv and Haifa where most immigrants first
entered Israel. Both cities became far more populated than the interior towns of the country, including Jerusalem, to which fewer immigrants came. The
continued expansion of urban centers in the coastal
plain was accompanied by economic growth as well, in
agriculture, industry and commercial services. This
enabled an availability of employment, and goods and
services that increased the attractiveness of the
coastal chain of towns, between Nahariyya in the
north, and Ashqelon in the south, and resulted in
further immigrant settlement in the plain.

In an examination of changes in urban distribution in Israel since statehood, the development of
the Tel Aviv conurbation is prominently apparent. As

Tel Aviv's economy, based largely on the activities of private enterprise, and population grew, the city expanded. Suburban neighborhoods developed and surrounding agricultural settlements urbanized. These communities gradually evolved into one sprawling urban unit, creating a conurbation that stretches from Herzliyya and Ramat HaSharon in the north, to Rishon LeZiyyon in the south, and to Bene Beraq and Givatayim on the east side.

In contrast, the mountain towns of Judea, Samaria and the Galilee were unable to develop as quickly, because of topographical conditions rendering construction difficult, their distance from the main centers of the population and economic activity and their lack of large scale industry. Most of the mountain towns, therefore simply maintained their size and did not participate in the growth occuring in other parts of the country. Two exceptions to this situation are the cities of Jerusalem and Beer Sheva. Despite its location in rugged terrain, high in the Judean Hills, Jerusalem has become a large city. This has been largely due to the institutional and economic support of the government which designated Jerusalem as the capital of Israel, as has been the case during the time of the Jewish Commonwealth 2000 years previously, and the seat of Parliament. The institutions of religious organizations especially educational, have also had an impact on population growth, as has the establishment of some light industry. As a result of the 1967 Six Day War, the political border with Jordan, that divided the city since statehood, was eliminated as a limit to urban expansion, West Jerusalem was reunited with East Jerusalem and the municipal boundaries were later extended over a large area, to allow for future metropolitan development. Since 1967, the growth of population and neighbourhoods has far outspaced the previous rate.

Beer Sheva has become one of the largest cities in Israel, achieving growth beyond original expectations, despite its rather isolated location on the edge of the Negev desert. With government emphasis to further development in the Negev region, Beer Sheva has gained from its location in the northern part of the desert along the major north-south routes that lead from the central population areas of the country into the Negev. The city also had the advantage of an existing urban infrastructure from Turkish and British efforts in developing the town during the past century. These factors have contributed to a rate of development that surpasses

that of other Negev towns, such as Elat, Mitzpe
Ramon, Yiroham and Arad.

Overall, the geographic distribution and development of towns in Israel is still in a stage of
crystallization. The urban maturity of the Tel Aviv
conurbation, the city of Haifa with its port and
industries along the bay, and Jerusalem as the government capital contrast with most of the development towns established since 1948 that are still
neither villages nor quite towns. Urbanization in
Israel is continuing rapidly as is evident in such
towns as Ashdod, Ashqelon, Upper Nazareth and
Dimona which, despite their recent establishment,
have quickly attained urban character. It can be
expected that urbanization will remain the primary
settlement trend in Israel's future.

NOTES

1. 'Via Maris' is an ancient route between
Egypt and Mesopotamia which entered the Land of
Israel from Northern Sinai, ran along the Coastal
Plain through the Irron, Jezreel, Bet Shean and
Kinnarot Valleys, and then over to the Golan Heights
toward Damascus. Its meaning is: 'Sea Road'.
2. 'Mountainous Route' is an ancient route,
which after crossing the Sinai Peninsula, entered
the Land of Israel at the Qadesh Barnea oasis, ran
through Beer Sheva, climbed to Hebron, Bethlehem and
Jerusalem, and then continued to the rift valleys of
Samaria and Nablus, into the Jezreel Valley. From
there it turned northwest, where it reached the Sea
of Acre.
3. 'Kabbala' is a stream in Jewish mysticism
which originated in the 11th and 12th centuries in
Southern France and Spain. It is also called 'The
Secret Wisdom'. Its main fundamentals are: the
explanation of interrelationship between God and the
world, the creation of the world, and the finding of
ways to achieve perfection in morality and spiritual
life. Safed was during hundreds of years the center
of the Kabbalists.
4. 'Maabarah' (pl. Maabarot) is a Hebrew term
for a transition camp, many of which were built in
the years 1948-1950, in order to supply temporary
housing for immigrants who came at those years to
Israel.

Chapter Two

URBANIZATION IN THE LAND OF ISRAEL DURING THE PRE-
STATE PERIOD OF ZIONIST SETTLEMENT

It is doubtful whether the Zionist movement had any
favourable inclination towards urban development
during the period of settlement in the Land of Israel from the late 1800s until the establishment of
the State of Israel in 1948. The original Zionist
settlement ideology was not concerned with the establishment of towns as a means of populating the
country. Zionism was based on a very pragmatic ideology whose aim was to establish a new society in
the Land of Israel. Cultural and material means were
needed to establish this aim and they were found in
the framework of an ideology which emphasized the
return to the soil and the establishment of a society of farmers and laborers thus changing the traditional occupation of Jews from services and commerce to agriculture.

URBANIZATION IN THE EYES OF THE ZIONIST FOUNDING
FATHERS

The founding fathers of the Zionist movement from
the end of the last century onwards, did not advo-
cate the foundation of new cities in the Land of
Israel, although there were some exceptions to this
rule. Herzl, for example, in his vision of the Jewish State, visualized Haifa as a modern Jewish city,
based on industry and its seaport.(1)
     The BILUs, the early pioneers who came to this
country from Russia at the end of the last century,
preferred the towns or, at least, an urban way of
life. However, their limited means and the lack of
available institutional financing did not permit the
founding of new towns. Instead, they settled in the
existing towns or founded small Moshavot or settlements, such as Petah Tiqva, Nes Ziyyona, Rishon

Le Ziyyon and Rosh Pinna. These had in common a few semi-urban features but there was no organized body with the initiative and the means to encourage the urban development of the new settlements.

A major change in the character of the country's settlement pattern took place with the advent of the pioneer settlers the Halutzim (2), before and immediately after the First World War. They held the belief that a country can only be won by the conquest of the land through agricultural labor, and that the main settlement effort should therefore be directed towards working the land and not towards occupations typical of an urban way of life. The village should influence the town and not visa-versa. One of the aims of the leaders of the Yishuv (3) was to prevent as far as possible, the drift of new immigrants to the towns, and at the same time, to establish rural centers as a counterweight to existing towns. Great efforts were made to develop new types of farming communities, both collective settlements such as the Kibbutz (4) and co-operative settlements, such as the Moshav (5). They were eminently suited to the settlement policies of that period, and combined development of the agricultural economy with free competition in the open market. In the course of time, the achievements of the Jewish farmer in Israel placed him in the front rank among the farmers of the Middle East.

As was expected, the emphasis placed on agricultural settlements did not encourage urban development. The problems of the towns were recognized but little was done to find solutions for them, as life in the towns continued to follow traditional patterns. The year 1909, though, saw the founding of the Ahuzat Bayit quarter on the northern outskirts of Jaffa. The objective of its founders was at first limited to building a European-style suburb to enjoy improved standards of building construction, density and sanitation than that found within the city. It was planned along the lines of the Garden City, which had become popular in Europe at the beginning of the century. Later, this suburb became the nucleus of the city of Tel Aviv and the starting point for the purchase of more land, the construction of additional residential quarters, land speculation, and intensive building, which has marked the ever accelerating growth of Tel Aviv. In spite of this conspicuously urban phenomenon, the utterances of the Zionist leaders of that period contained but few references to the problems relating to the towns of Israel. It can indeed be said

13

that the founding of Tel Aviv was the only instance of a significant urban development in the early part of the century.

During this time, as the pace of immigration grew, so did the proportion of those choosing urban settlement, as it was less costly and quicker to achieve, and required much less land than agricultural settlement. Yet, even knowing these facts did not bring about a change in the attitude toward urbanization on the part of the Zionist organizations. After World War I, there were discussions about urbanization, as it was assumed that immigration to the Land of Israel would increase and urban centers would be needed for settlement purposes; but because the expected increase did not materialize, agricultural settlements remained the basis for immigrant absorption.

It should, however, be pointed out that the Zionist settlement institutions could not dictate settlement sites to incoming immigrants, who were free to choose their own place of residence. Institutional funds for land purchases from Arab landowners were also limited. Without a comprehensive plan identifying priorities for Jewish settlement locations, a dichotomy arose between institutional national capital and private capital in the acquisition of settlement lands. Land in urban areas or in areas of intensive agriculture, particularly those suitable for citrus fruits, were acquired by private enterprise, whereas land in remote regions was bought by the Jewish National Fund (JNF).(6) In general, urban centers expanded on privately owned land under speculative conditions, while national capital could only assist immigrants to settle in the peripheral areas and in the agricultural sector. With the passage of years, this brought about a situation whereby towns and suburbs with high population potentials were created on private land while smaller agricultural settlements in peripheral areas were developed largely on national land.

Throughout the settlement period, the rural settlements provided the source of biological and political renewal of the population in the country, influencing life in the towns. The political influence of members of the Kibbutzim was disproportionate to their number in the Jewish population. Economically and socially, the Kibbutzim were so well organized that they could distribute their agricultural products through their own institutions without the mediation of local small towns in order to reach the large city. The service sector carries

14

no economic weight in the Kibbutzim which apparently
is a reaction to the fact that services and commerce
were principle occupations in the Diaspora. This of
course, is contrary to the norms of modern urban development where the proportion of employees in commerce and services increases as the economy of an
urban settlement expands. However, there were experiments to develop light industry in the agricultural sector in order to diversify their means of
sustenance. In those times it was quite easy to advance and succeed in such ventures as technology was
underdeveloped in the towns; small projects in light
industry thereby became accepted as a very important
basis in the agricultural sector.

The overwhelming influence of the agricultural
settlements is quite surprising in view of the comparatively large number of Jews living in towns who
continually outnumbered those living in villages.
The number of Jews engaged in agriculture gradually
increased during the period of Zionist settlement
but it never exceeded one quarter of the total Jewish population of the country. The proportion of
rural settlers out of the total Jewish population
was: 14% before 1914; 18% in 1922; 20% in 1927; and
23.7% for the period of 1934 to 1936. On the eve of
the establishment of the State of Israel (in 1947)
the rural population was 25.6% of the total Jewish
population of 645,000. The situation was paradox-
ical - a minority, consisting of the members of the
agricultural Kibbutzim led the country politically,
economically and socially while the majority, who
lived in the towns, occupied a secondary position
and were alloted only a small position of the national resources. This policy left its mark on developments in the Jewish population during the Mandatory period and even during the first years of the
State of Israel. Matters connected with urbanization and the foundation of new towns did not receive
the attention which they deserved. Urban development,
in contrast to rural settlement, was largely left to
its own devices without the benefit of an overall
plan or national directives. The growth of towns
was governed by waves of immigration, which resulted in a steep use of housing costs.

URBANIZATION DURING THE TIME OF THE BRITISH MANDATE

During the time of the British Mandate, Jewish urban settlement did not occur under the auspices of
the official Zionist organizations. The only ex-

ception was the experiment of Afula, established in
1925 in the center of the Jezreel Valley. This settlement was found by members of the Fourth Aliyah
(7) comprising mainly small merchants from Poland,
who wanted to continue their way of life in this
country in light industry and commerce. The agricultural settlements around Afula's periphery, especially the Kibbutzim, were well organized, socially and economically and boycotted the towns from the
beginning. They did not use the services Afula provided, which they would bypass due to their own network of distributional, education, cultural and
other services. For many years, Afula had difficulty
in developing a viable economy based on services and
industry. Not a village, nor quite a town, after
twenty five years of existence, its population numbered just 2,500. It was only in 1974 that Afula at
last received town status.

During the 1930s, urban growth was given a
boost with the immigration of Jews from Germany.
Many of them could not accept an agricultural way
of life and instead, applied their knowledge and
capital towards industrial development and thereby,
the enlargement of urban centers in the country.

Urbanization began to occur in the veteran
Moshavot that had been established mainly in the
coastal plain prior to World War I. Originally established as agricultural settlements, most continued to have some residents occupied in agriculture,
yet, with the introduction of light industry and the
influx of immigrants, much of their populations
turned to occupations in commerce or industry, and
the levels of available services and housing densities increased. Petah Tiqva, Rishon Le Ziyyon, Rehovot, Hadera and Kefar Sava are all examples of
Moshavot that have become towns. Suburbs such as
Ramat Gan, Bene Beraq and Herzliyya, which were established during the 1920s and 1930s, experienced
rapid urban advancement due to a large extent, to
their proximity to Tel Aviv. They quickly developed
as nodes for industry and commerce and as dormitory
towns for the population of the Tel Aviv area.

A factor in the rapid metamorphosis of Moshavot
into towns was also the largely middle class economic background of their inhabitants. Their orientation was far more prone to urbanization, in contrast
to that of the Kibbutzim and Moshavim whose ideological opposition prohibited such a development. This
is supported by the fact that, out of the agricultural sector, only from Moshavot did urban settlements develop.

Urbanization in the Tel Aviv area was manifested by the construction of many housing projects. These projects were initiated in the 1930s by various companies and organizations which had specific interests in such urban development. Less-costly outlying land was used to provide inexpensive housing for laborers, allowing for a concentration of manpower for citrus work. Middle class people sought suburban homes around urban centers, and religious groups were interested in establishing homogenious suburbs and neighbourhoods for their members. Over time, these trends created a mosaic of neighbourhood units populated by different groups. Eventually, when the municipal borders of towns were enlarged, such suburbs and housing projects were incorporated into the enlarged municipal boundaries, resulting not in an organic town but rather a heterogeneous conglomeration of neighbourhoods. Towns such as Holon and Bat Yam are examples of this phenomenon.

In sum, urban growth during the pre-State settlement period in Israel was largely haphazard and sporadic. The official Zionist bodies did not have particular interest in urban settlement in the country and, therefore gained no experience in urban planning and development. Urbanization during the period occured independently in the private enterprise market place. The lack of a planned prototype of a Jewish town and minimal knowledge of such urban issues as size, structure, architectural style, community diversity and social needs added further complication to the pressing limitations of time and material resources when urban development became essential with the inception of statehood. As such, the rapid urban development that occured during the early decades of the State has been characterized by much trial and error, and adjustment to urgent and unexpected needs.

NOTES

1. E. Cohen, The City in the Zionist Ideology (Institute of Urban and Regional Studies), Jerusalem, 1970).
2. 'Halutz' (pl. Halutzim) is a Hebrew term for the Jewish and Zionistic pioneers who came at the beginning of the present century to the Land of Israel on farmland and to create new settlements.
3. 'Yishuv' is a Hebrew term which indicates the Jewish community in the Land of Israel before the establishment of the State of Israel in 1948.

4. A 'Kibbutz' is a communal settlement established on national or state property. Everything
else there is collectively owned by the members. The
basic principle in that form of settlement is that
every member gives to the community to the best of
his abilities and receives from it according to his
needs. All the members' needs - food, clothing, furniture, education, health care, entertainment, recreation - are fully met by the community.
5. The 'Moshav' is a small holders' settlement.
Each settler works there his separate plot of land,
lives in his own household and draws income from his
farm's produce. This independence is limited by
four basic principles: 1. Each member receives national land but no larger than he and his family can
work alone; he may not divide the lot between several heirs. 2. The settler himself must carry out
the work and hire labour only with the consent of
the Moshav authorities. 3. Mutual aid and responsibility between all members. 4. Joint marketing of
produce, joint purchasing of farming and even household appliances.
6. A Jewish and Zionist organization founded
by Prof. Z.H. Shapiro in 1901 with the aim to buy
land in Palestine for Jewish colonization, and to
reclaim land for potential agricultural settlement.
Land purchased by the Jewish National Fund remains
forever the property of the whole nation and cannot
be sold to private farmers.
7. The fourth wave of immigration of Jews to
the Land of Israel between the years 1924-1931. This
wave included about 80,000 people.

Chapter Three

SOCIAL AND DEMOGRAPHIC FACTORS OF THE IMMIGRANT ROLE
IN ISRAEL'S URBANIZATION

In reviewing the history of the settlement activities of the Zionist movement in the last chapter we
have seen that little organized urbanization took
place during the pre-State period largely as a result of the Zionist ideological concentration on
agricultural settlement, and the lack of capital and
control of immigrant distribution in the country
that might otherwise have encouraged planned urban
development. By the end of the British Mandate, the
settlement structure of Israel consisted primarily
of the three main towns of Tel Aviv, Haifa, and
Jerusalem, countered by numerous small agricultural
settlements. Planned urbanization began to occur
only after statehood, due to the necessity of accomodating the mass influx of immigrants that arrived
during the early years and settling in the underpopulated areas of the State.
     The backgrounds of the immigrants, economically,
socially, religiously and ideologically, strongly
influenced their absorption in the country, especially regarding their choice of settlement mode and
the character they imparted to their new communities.
The inclination of many immigrants, however, in
choosing their settlement site and type were heavily
swayed by the policy of the government and the
Jewish Agency to direct immigrants to newly developing regions rather than to the existing large towns.
This policy was known as The Distribution of the
Population.

LANDS OF ORIGIN OF THE IMMIGRANTS

There was considerable differentiation between the
arriving groups of Jewish immigrants depending on
their country of origin. Accordingly, the immi-

grants can be roughly divided into three main groups: Eastern European, Western Europeans, and those from Islamic countries.

In Eastern Europe, Jews were generally occupied as small merchants and peddlers or engaged in various services. They were not farmers and therefore did not reside in agricultural villages, nor did they choose the large cities as home. In many cases, both alternatives were forbidden to Jews by the ruling government. Instead, they gathered in their own communities, creating townlets that were both semi-urban and semi-agricultural in character. Many Jews served as middlemen between the rural villages and the cities, merchandizing and transporting crops and goods; others engaged in functions needed within their own communities. Their communities were generally segregated from the bulk of the Eastern European population, in order to maintain their traditional Jewish lifestyle and to protect themselves from the frequent hostility exhibited towards them by the general populace, often as a result of government incitement; this was true even when Jewish communities were established in large cities, where they would congregate in neighbourhoods segregated from the rest of the city.

The Jews of Western Europe were much more integrated in the general community life. They were also not farmers, centuries prohibiting this occupation to Jews had sifted out any inclination towards the profession, even when restrictions were removed. The cities and towns of Western Europe were far more developed, economically and culturally, than those of Eastern Europe; they were also larger in size. The Jewish population, much of which had received higher education, participated in this growth and were engaged mainly in the profession and in administration, commerce and banking.

The Jews of Islamic countries were mostly concentrated in the large towns; 70-90% lived in towns with populations greater than 100,000 people. Economically, there was a sharp contrast within the Jewish population, between a small wealthy elite and the bulk of Jews who were quite poor. This attribute parallels that of the general Arab urban population, in a society that was socially and economically underdeveloped in contrast to the situation in Europe.

SETTLEMENT MODE CHOICE OF IMMIGRANTS

The Jews who immigrated to Israel during the mid-19th century came primarily for religious reasons, to live in the Holyland; they joined the Jewish population living in the four cities sacred to Judaism: Jerusalem, Safed, Tiberias and Hebron. Their way of life was similar to that Eastern Europe, engaged in small-scale commerce; a portion of the community relied on contribution from Jews overseas for support.

The early Zionist settlement, from the late 1880s until World War I, emphasized agricultural development. These Jewish pioneers were ideologically bent on rebuilding the Jewish national homeland and establishing a productive agricultural sector to support it. Immigrants coming during the time between the World Wars also held a positive ideology towards Jewish nationhood, though many preferred urban settlement; this was true too of those who came to Israel, despite other alternatives, during the early Hitler years. It was largely Europeans that comprised the self selected immigration of this pre-State era.

The immigration that occured during the dozen years that followed the start of World War II resulted more from necessity than ideological choice. Many of those who successfully escaped the European Holocaust arrived in Israel, as did refugees who had survived the war period, though most had also to avoid British restrictions on immigration into the country. In the first years of the State's existence, Jews from Arab countries fled to Israel en mass from government retribution in their former home countries.

One of the early actions of the Israeli government was to pass the Law of Return, guaranteeing every Jew the right to settlement and citizenship in Israel. Immigration has continued at varying rates, since that time, some (such as Russians) coming as a result of oppression, and others (including North Americans) out of free choice and a desire to participate in the development of the Jewish State.

STATISTICAL EXAMINATION OF THE IMMIGRANTS

Within a period of 80 years, immigration to Israel increased the population size by a factor of sixty. From the establishment of the State until 1981 about 1.7 million immigrants arrived in the country, compared with one half a million during the previous thirty years of the British Mandate. During the

mass immigration of the first four years of statehood, almost seven hundred thousand immigrants
arrived, as shown in Table 3.1. The proportion of
immigrants to the existing population reached its
peak in 1949 when 266 immigrants arrived for every
1,000 inhabitants. These statistics are phenomenal
due not only to the high level of immigration but
also to the ability of the small existing population
to absorb and integrate so many newcomers into the
country.

Table 3.1: Jewish Immigrants Between 1948-1981

Period	Number of Immigrants	Annual Average
1948-1951	684,201	171,000
1952-1954	51,193	17,000
1955-1957	160,961	54,000
1958-1960	72,393	24,000
1961-1964	220,323	55,000
1965-1968	72,276	18,000
1969-1972	172,372	43,000
1973-1981	244,731	27,000

Source: Statistical Abstract of Israel.

The immigration of the first years included most of
the Holocaust refugees who had been left homeless
and waiting in camps in Europe, and in British
transition Camps in Cyprus. Almost the entire Jewish populations of Yemen and Iraq immigrated en mass
in 1949 and 1950. Waves of newcomers from North
Africa, Rumania, Poland and elsewhere followed. By
1981, 25% of the world Jewish population was located
in Israel, as compared to just 6% prior to the establishment of the State. Of the immigrants who
arrived during the years 1948-1981, 44% originated
from Asia and Africa, while 54% came from European
and American countries.

AGE DISTRIBUTION OF IMMIGRANTS

An examination of the age distribution of the immi-

22

grants who entered Israel from 1948 to 1981 reveals that 31% were under the age of 14, 64% were of working age (15-64), and 5% were 65 or older. When controlling by place of origin, the parallel figures for Asia and Africa were: 40% under the age of 14, 57% in the age bracket 15-64, and 3% age 65 or older; for the same categories of European and American immigrants, the statistics were: 22%, 72% and 6% respectively. Entire families had come from Africa and Asia, which is apparent from the relative normalcy of their age distribution, although the low proportion of elderly seems to indicate a lower age of life-expectancy and that some elderly were left behind. The European distribution indicates the large numbers of young adults arriving without families, and also gives evidence of the impact of the Holocaust: very few Jewish children were born during the years 1940-1945 in Europe.

Forty-one percent of those immigrants who arrived between 1955 and 1964 from Europe and America were wage earners as opposed to only 24% of those from Asia and Africa, a factor of the larger family size among the latter groups. Occupationally, among wage earners from Asia and Africa only 7% were professionals (e.g. doctors, lawyers) in contrast to 22% of those from Europe and America. Of Asian and African immigrants, 11% were merchants and salesmen, and 47% were engaged in light industry, whereas 6% and 40% are the parallel figures for Europeans and Americans.

The usual source of population growth in most countries is the natural birthrate; in Israel however, almost two thirds of its growth has been the result of immigration. Immediately following statehood, the Jewish population in Israel totalled 650,000 people with a non-Jewish population of 156,000. During the first 33 years of the State, the Jewish population grew to 3.3 million and the non-Jewish population reached 654,000, including the addition of the population of East Jerusalem, a growth rate of 5.0 and 4.2, respectively. The growth rate was a result of immigration more than the natural birthrate. From 1951, which marked the end of the mass immigration of the State's first four years of existence, until 1967, the Jewish birthrate remained relatively constant at approximately 35,000 births per year. Since 1968, however, the natural growth rate has increased, reaching 46,000 for the year 1981.

IMMIGRANT ROLE IN ISRAEL GOVERNMENT, ECONOMIC AND SOCIAL POLICY

With the establishment of the State of Israel, the government was forced to begin planning settlement, economic and social policies and activities on a comprehensive scale, as opposed to the relatively narrow agricultural emphasis of the Zionist movement during the pre-State era. The mass influx of immigrants during the first years placed severe pressures on the government to quickly provide the housing and the social and economic structure for their integration into the country. As such, the immigrants became an integral part of the governments' efforts to solve the deficiences of past policies, particularly in developing the industrial and service sectors of the economy and the urbanization promoted by those economic sectors.

Where massive economic restructuring has taken place elsewhere in the world, involving large population transfers and requiring transitions in the economic activities of the populace, the retraining of farmers for an urban lifestyle was the primary objective; this can be seen in the recent history of Greece, following World War I, and of Pakistan, upon its separation from India. The situation has been much to the contrary in Israel, starting from the early pioneers, former urban dwellers who chose an agricultural lifestyle on ideological grounds. Later immigrants, many who had been involved in small-scale urban commerce or non-producing services in their countries of origin, had to be retrained for positions as farmers, and industrial and public workers. Occupational training was an important factor in the economic development of the State, and one of the foci of immigrant absorption activities, remaining so to this day. The influx of immigrants, the emphasis of immigrants, the emphasis for economic development in industry and services, and the retraining of immigrants to serve in the newly developed occupations gave particular impetus to urbanization in Israel. The establishment of commercial and industrial centers and sufficient housing and social-cultural services for the population in them, all within relative proximity, results, of course, in an urban environment.

Town development in Israel was undertaken in two primary ways. The evolution of agricultural settlements into urban centers was an approach that took hold already in the pre-State period, as light industry and higher density housing were established,

24

owing to private investment and the desirable coastal location of the settlement, close to the main cities of Tel Aviv and Haifa. This trend has continued unabated during the existence of the State, many such villages have become fully recognized towns.

The State of Israel has also approached new urbanization through the establishment of new towns throughout the country. During the pre-State years, as the cities of Tel Aviv, Haifa and Jerusalem expanded, they became nodes of economic and administrative activity in relation to the numerous agricultural settlements surrounding them. There were, however, few towns with the economic capacity to function as intermediary nodes between the villages and larger cities. The objective of the Israel government was to establish medium-sized towns to fill in the nodal settlement hierarchy envisioned for the country. Such towns have been well established in other countries of the world. In England, for example, 60% of the population reside in medium-sized towns, as does approximately 40% in Australia. In Israel only 18% lived in such towns prior to 1948, this figure has reached 35% following the establishing of many new towns in every area of the country, bringing the proportion of urban settlement in Israel to 86% of the population - one of the highest rates in the world.

Nonetheless, the following factors have been of particular concern in relation to the establishment of development towns in Israel:

1. The Kibbutzim, early in the century, established a strong relationship with the developing major cities, distributing agricultural products and obtaining desired materials and services through direct contact with the cities. This relationship has expanded over the years, particularly as the consumption level of the Kibbutzim has reached a high standard. The establishment of medium-sized towns has had little effect on altering the situation; their objective of functioning as intermediaries between the cities and Kibbutzim is currently not being achieved.

2. Approximately 80% of Israel's population is concentrated along the coastal strip, while the Galilee, the Negev and much of the mountain areas are sparsely populated. This unbalanced spatial structure concentrates the majority of industries and

services in the coastal plain, while access to goods and services in the other
areas are more difficult to acquire. A
primary objective in establishing new
towns is the development of industrial
and service sectors throughout the country, thereby improving the accessibility
to goods and services. The employment
provided by economic development, along
with the provision of social and cultural facilities, is expected to provide incentive to attract residents to the new
towns, achieving a more balanced redistribution of the population. To date,
there has been modest success; some towns,
such as Arad, have been growing rapidly,
while others have stagnated.

Chapter Four

JERUSALEM - THE CAPITAL OF ISRAEL

Throughout its long history, the city of Jerusalem,
a capital built on the hills, has had to contend
with physical and human factors which decisively influenced its development, its period of prosperity
and of adversity, the growth of its population and
its economic structure. There are not many capitals
in the world today that are located in the hills;
easier terrains are generally favoured. Jerusalem
represents, therefore, an exceptional geographic-
urban phenomenon: an unusual and difficult physical
background against which functions a capital city
which is, at the same time, a religious focus for
many peoples having an interest in its status, its
appearance and its planning.
      Below we shall examine the city of Jerusalem
from the point of view of its geographical features,
the fluctuation of its size and population throughout its history, its particular structure based on
quarters, its status as a national capital, the land
uses and the different concepts that have guided its
planners from the end of the 1st World War until the
present day.

THE PHYSIOGRAPHIC BACKGROUND

Jerusalem's status and importance throughout the
course of its long history has been determined by
its location on the crest of the Judean hills, at
the intersection of the north-south and east-west
trunk roads. The geographical location of the city
is also related to the morphological structure of
the Judean hills. These form a continuous mass,
whose crest is not broken by valleys, while ravines
and valleys abound in both the eastern and western
slopes. The unbroken nature of the plateau on which

27

Jerusalem is located, has contributed to the city's becoming a center and stronghold, whose domination extended over a very wide area.

For most of its history, Jerusalem has been a seat of government. This can be understood in the light of the topographical conditions and the position of the city astride the natural junction of two main traffic arteries. It is not possible to traverse the Judean hills without crossing the plateau on which Jerusalem is situated. The north-south road must also follow the plateau, and its alignment must lie within fairly narrow limits, since any significant deviation to the east or to the west, would bring it up either against canyons or against steep ravines. The Hebron - Bethlehem - Jerusalem - Ramallah - Nablus - Jenin trunk road has always been a major importance and passes through Jerusalem at the point where it intersects another trunk road, leading from the Coastal Plain to Transjordan. It is not surprising, therefore, that no city of similar importance arose in antiquity, either to the west or to the east of Jerusalem.

The original site of Jerusalem lay on a slope, 1-2 miles (2-3 km.) east of the watershed, a not inconsiderable distance, in view of the primitive transport facilities of the period. The area of ancient Jerusalem, the so-called Fortress of Zion, never exceeded 450 acres until the middle of the 19th century. The difficult topography and the small area of agricultural land available in the Qidron Valley and in the vicinity of the Spring of Gihon, would have severely limited the development of the city, had it to depend only on its own resources. However, the fact that Jerusalem was chosen to be the capital, ancient tradition, enabled it to draw on the resources of the entire country, which flowed into the capital as revenues connected with taxes, pilgrimage and foreign trade.

The original site of ancient Jerusalem lay at the lowest part of the Temple Mount ridge, and a precipitous slope descended from it to the Qidron Valley. The successive stages of the city wall served the purpose of complementing the natural topography where necessary for the defence of the town. The population of Jerusalem depended at first for its water supply on the Spring of Gihon. Further development of the town was dependent on the construction of rainwater cisterns and of conduits bringing water from more distant sources.

THE BOUNDARIES OF THE CITY

The boundaries of Jerusalem, which had originally
lain east of the watershed, expanded in spite of the
topographical limitations, and eventually crossed
the watershed. Table 4.1 shows the relative areas
of the eastern and western sections of the city at
different periods:

Table 4.1: Relative Areas of Jerusalem, East and
West of the Watershed

	East of the Watershed	West of the Watershed
Ancient Jerusalem	100%	0%
End of 19th Century	41%	59%
1921-1947	21%	79%
1948-1952	14%	86%
1953-1966	12%	88%
1967-1973	48%	52%
1974-1981	40%	60%

At the beginning of the British Mandate, the municipal boundary of Jerusalem enclosed an area of 3,180
acres, 95% of which lay outside the Old City. With
the expansion of the Jewish population, it became
necessary to extend the city boundaries and the town
planning area reached 11,000 acres towards the end
of the Mandate. The 1948 war led to a radical
change. The city was divided into a western and an
eastern sector, the former under Israeli, and the
latter under Jordanian jurisdiction. The boundary
between the two sections was the armistice line,
which had been the line occupied by the opposing
forces at the end of the hostilities.
    The area of the Israel section of Jerusalem,
after its western boundary had been moved some distance westwards, reached 6,440 acres. It was clear
even then, that this area would not be sufficient
for the growing needs of the city, which had become
the capital and the political centre of the state,
and in 1952 the western boundary was moved still

further westwards, bringing the city's area to 9,250
acres. After the 1967 war, which brought about the
reunification of both parts of Jerusalem, there followed a renewed growth of the eastern section, and
a more balanced relation was achieved between the
areas on both sides of the watershed. The united
city now occupies an area of 27,125 acres.

THE POPULATION

Over a long period of time, the population of Jerusalem remained small and fairly stable. Under Ottoman rule, between the 16th and 19th centuries,
Jerusalem was not more than a small townlet. From
the middle of the 19th century, as a result of Jewish immigration and the growing interest shown by
Christian European countries, Jerusalem began to
emerge from its long stagnation, its population increased and numerous religious building, pilgrim
hostels and other public institutions were erected
in the city. While the population at mid-century
did not exceed 11,000,towards the end of the century it began to rise rapidly, as shown in Table
4.2. (1)

Table 4.2:   The Population of Jerusalem 1838-1946

Year	Total Population	Jewish Population
1838	11,000	3,000
1845	15,000	6,000
1865	18,000	9,000
1877	36,000	13,000
1893	58,000	28,000
1910	68,000	50,000
1922	62,578	33,971
1931	90,578	51,264
1946	165,000	100,000

The trend of the Jewish population growth during
these years shows the following characteristics:

    1.   Average annual growth of 1,513 between

30

the years 1838 and 1910.

2.   Marked decrease between the years 1910
and 1922, mainly on account of the 1st
World War.

3.   Until the 1st World War, the growth of
the Jewish population was far greater in
Jerusalem than in the rest of the country.
Thus, the number of Jews in Jerusalem increased from 3,000 in 1838 to 50,000 in
1910, i.e., 16.7 times, while the parallel
increase in all other parts of the country
was from 11,000 to 68,000, i.e., only 6.2
times.

4.   Between 1931 and 1946 there was a marked
rise in the Jewish population, the average annual increase being 3,249.

5.   The proportion of the Jewish to the total
population in Jerusalem rose continually
during most years up to 1910. It then
dropped, but started to rise again with
the beginning of the Mandate, reaching
60.6% in 1946.

Table 4.3 shows the Jewish population of Jerusalem
and its rate of growth during the period 1948-1981,
as compared with parallel figures for the whole of
the country.

The trend of the Jewish population growth during
these years, comparatively to the growth in the whole
country, shows the following characteristics:

1.   The average annual growth for the whole
country during the period from 1948 to
1965 was 11.6% compared to 7.3% for
Jerusalem.

2.   Until the 1967 War, the growth of Jerusalem generally lagged behind that of the
rest of the country. The exception was
the year 1950, which marked the return to
Jerusalem of many of its inhabitants who
had left during the 1948 War.

3.   After 1957 there was a more or less
steady annual population growth of about
2-3%, due partly to natural increase, and
partly to internal migration.

4.   To the extent that there were higher
rates of population growth, they were due
either to large waves of immigration, or
to the deliberate policy of stimulating

Table 4.3: The Jewish Population in Jerusalem
Between 1948-1981

| Year | Jerusalem | | The Whole Country | |
	Population	Rate of Annual Growth (%)	Population	Rate of Annual Growth (%)
1948	83,984	--	872,700	--
1949	103,000	22.6	1,173,900	34.5
1950	121,000	17.5	1,370,100	16.7
1951	137,000	13.2	1,577,800	15.1
1953	143,000	2.2	1,699,400	3.8
1955	146,000	1.0	1,789,100	2.6
1957	152,000	2.0	1,976,000	5.2
1959	160,000	2.6	2,088,700	2.8
1961	165,000	1.5	2,179,500	2.2
1963	178,000	3.9	2,430,100	5.7
1965	189,000	3.1	2,599,000	3.5
1967	266,000	36.4*	2,766,300	4.2
1969	283,100	3.2	2,919,200	2.8
1971	301,300	3.2	3,095,100	2.8
1973	326,400	4.2	3,307,500	3.4
1974	344,200	5.4	3,318,100	0.3
1975	355,500	3.3	3,493,200	1.8
1977	376,000	2.6	3,653,200	1.9
1979	398,200	3.0	3,836,200	2.5
1981	415,000	1.9	3,977,900	1.1

* United Jerusalem after the Six Day War.

the development of Jerusalem.
5.   In 1967 the city was reunited, and the
        sudden rise of 36.4% between 1966 and
        1967 reflects the inclusion of the Arabs
        of East Jerusalem in the total population
        figure.

THE QUARTERS OF JERUSALEM

Jerusalem's quarters are one of its most distinctive
features. In no other Israel town is there such a
clear-cut division into quarters along well defined
geographical and demographical lines. Nowhere else
do we find that the inhabitants identify themselves
with their quarter to such a degree, even to the
point that one can often guess at a person's character according to the quarter in which he lives.
The creation of the Jerusalem quarters is generally
attributed to the topographical structure, in which
heights alternate with valleys. The latter were
originally used for agriculture, and later as traffic arteries, parks and public open spaces. The
houses that were built on the heights, separated by
the valleys, formed a mosaic pattern of quarters,
which followed the city's topography. Other circumstances that contributed to the distinctive character of these quarters were connected with sociolog-
ical factors, differences in the way of life of
various sections of the population, political-en-
vironmental conditions, etc.
        The older quarters of Jerusalem beyond the Old
City walls were not the result of conventional planning. They developed in the course of generations,
and they reflect the personalities of their founders
and their inhabitants, who, as a rule, had a common
origin and formed a closely knit social group.
Their material background did not play a significant
role, as they were not seeking economic advantage or
prestige. In contrast to the modern practice of
planning a quarter and then settling it with inhabitants of heterogeneous background, who have to undergo a process of social re-education before they
can adapt themselves to their new surroundings, the
old Jerusalem quarters were founded by people of
small means, having a more or less similar background. Their main motive in building their quarter
was to live in close proximity to each other, and
not amongst the Moslem and Christian population of
the Old City. Their motivation was contrary to that
often seen in modern cities, where the tendency is

to move to isolated and exclusive residential sections, with their social and environmental advantages.

Over 30 residential quarters were built in Jerusalem up to the 2nd World War, starting with the oldest quarters, such as Mishkenot Sha'ananim, Nahlat Shiv'a, Mea She'arim, Yemin Moshe and the Bukharian Quarter, and ending with the newer quarters of Rehavia, Bet Hakerem, Talbiyeh and Talpiyot. Not only Jews, but also Arabs and others, developed a pattern of residential quarters. Christian communities found land purchase easier, as they enjoyed the political backing of the churches and religious orders. Both Russians and Germans built extensively outside the Old City walls. The Russians developed the Russian Compound as a centre for pilgrims from their country, while the Germans built the German Colony in a distinctive architectural style. Other quarters, such as Baq'a, Abu Tor and Musrara were also built with the object of enabling people of similar background to live near each other within a heterogeneous city. It is usual for people to settle in communities with those of backgrounds similar to their own. If we note the differences of nationality, ethnic affiliation, language, religion and way of life, we can understand the manifold motives that led to the establishment of a large number of quarters. The Jews, in particular, are noted for their tendency to live among themselves and to refrain from mixing with their neighbours. The strength of the communal bond among Jews is rooted in religion and tradition. Some Jews are so extreme in their communal segregation, that they isolate themselves even from the rest of the Jewish people. This extreme religious orthodoxy may lead to the construction of special residential quarters for the community, which are built according to a similar conservative and unchanging architectural pattern.

The first Jews who, in the sixties of the last century, left the old City and founded the quarters of Mishkenot Sha'ananim and Yemin Moshe, were motivated by the need for land that they could build on and develop. These quarters were built parallel to the Old City Wall, and planned so that they could be defended against an attack from any side. (2) The pattern of life in these quarters resulted in a closely-knit social fabric, whose economy was largely based on assistance from abroad. Mea She'Arim and Nahlat Shiv'a were established some time later, and were of a similar character. The distances between the quarters depended on the availability of pur-

34

chasable land. The foundation of each quarter was organized and promoted by a leading personality around whom the settlers rallied. Their layout was patterned on that of a small Jewish town and centered around the synagogue, the ritual baths, the religious school and the market. The streets are narrow, and the densely built houses cluster around interior courtyards. At the beginning of the 1st World War there was already a fairly large number of such quarters, all of them not far from the Old City and mostly situated on both sides of the Jaffa Road, which is the main access to the Old City from the west.

Most of the Jews who arrived in Jerusalem after the 1st World War, were not particularly religious, and did not keep strictly to the Jewish religious observances. They came to settle in Jerusalem as a matter of choice, and as they did not fit in well with the older religious inhabitants, they preferred to live in the new quarters which were then being built. These newcomers did not follow the pursuits of the older population, and their economy was based on commerce, industry, building and other trades. They created a demand for more spacious dwellings, better planned neighbourhoods, educational and cultural institutions, and all other facilities expected in a modern city. With an increasing population, the area of the new quarters grew, while the old quarters became more and more congested. The new quarters copied, with certain alterations, the architectural style prevalent in Europe during the twenties and thirties, while the old quarters continued to develop in their traditional style, unaffected by the new trends.

After the establishment of the State of Israel, many new quarters were built by government and other public initiative, with the object of furthering the growth of the city. At the same time, private building entrepreneurs engaged in the construction of higher class residential buildings and quarters, and there began a migration of old-timers to the new quarters in the central and western parts of the city. The buildings which they vacated in the old quarters were usually taken over by their orthodox neighbours.

JERUSALEM AS A CAPITAL CITY

The 1948 War of Independence and its aftermath were a time of crisis for Jerusalem. The unusual and

artificial geographical-urban conditions created by
the war imposed the need to modify at short notice
the urban plan of the city, the road network, the
main access routes and the social and economic
basis of the population. Jerusalem had become a border town, and as such had to struggle for its existence. This was a crisis from which Jerusalem has not
yet fully recovered, and its effect will probably
be felt for many years to come, as the changes that
were forced on the city left profound traces that
are not easily effaced. It will be useful, therefore, to examine Jerusalem's status as a capital in
the light of past approaches to the planning and
building of the city, and to draw conclusions regarding its position today and its prospects for the
future.

The plan of according Jerusalem an international status was not realized owing to the objection of
both commanding parties, and the end of the 1948 war
left a divided city, each half having become a border town. By decision of the Israel government, the
Israel part of Jerusalem was declared the capital
of the new state, with all the functions implied by
this status. This establishment of a fait accompli
ran counter to the views of many countries who objected to such a step for political, and perhaps
also for religious reasons. The geographical conditions too, did not seem at the time to favour such
a decision. The economy of Jerusalem had been destroyed and a large number of its inhabitants had
left during the war. Jerusalem was no longer near
the center of the country, but at the end of an artificial corridor. There were no adequate urban services, and certainly not of a standard required in a
capital. Jerusalem could not compete with Tel Aviv,
which had become the social, cultural and commercial
center of the country. It had no international
links with the outside world, and no buildings to
house the offices of the government and of other
administrative institutions. There was no economic
hinterland, and no industrial, commercial or civic
centers that would justify Jerusalem's existence as
the country's capital.

In spite of all these unfavourable conditions,
the government decided on a number of unconventional
measures with a view to developing Jerusalem and
making it self-supporting. The influx of capital was
encouraged, new immigrants were directed to the capital, crafts and industries were developed in order
to provide employment. Making Jerusalem the capital
of the state was a political stop, which had to be

translated into practice by taking immediate and far reaching steps affecting planning and building, employment and the economic structures of the population. Jerusalem is an example of a town developed through government initiative in spite of unfavourable geographical conditions and artificial boundaries. The will to develop Jerusalem under such adverse conditions can only be understood in the light of the special relationship which has always bound the Jewish people to this city.

PLANNING AND CONSTRUCTION OF WESTERN JERUSALEM

Proper planning begun only after the British conquest of Jerusalem by General Allenby. On December 9, 1917 he announced the military government's intention to preserve and maintain the places holy to the three religions, and in 1948 he commissioned an engineer from Alexandria, by the name of McLean, to draw up the first town plan. As no topographic map was available, McLean's outline plan was of little value, but the building regulations issued at his instigation by the military governor of Jerusalem remain relevant to this day. The main provisions were: 1. preservation of the sky-line of the eastern mountain range; 2. a 35ft limit on the height of buildings; 3. a ban on industrial construction within the city; 4. a ban on all construction around the Old City walls; 5. limited construction on Mount Scopus and the Mount of Olives, and in the Valley of Qidron; 6. the exclusive use of stone for the construction of roofs which in all public buildings must be dome-shaped.

These provisions, designed to preserve the special character of Jerusalem, caused the city to develop mainly to the west and south west, in view of the restrictions imposed on construction in the Old City and its immediate neighbourhood. Generally, McLean's object, rather than to solve local problems, was to lay down general town planning guide-lines. The Old City was regarded as the architectural but not as the functional core of the city, and was separated from the newer sections by open green belts. McLean wanted Jerusalem to grow to the north, the west and the south, with only little development in the eastern part, where he was aware of the climatic and topographical limitations. He also adopted the principle of urban dispersal and proposed two main urban axes, the one to the north-west and the other to the south-west of the Old City. His guide-lines were followed in most of the subsequent town plans worked out by Geddes, Ashby, Holliday and Kendall.

In Geddes' plan of 1919 the Old City was regarded as a separate entity and the Mount of Olives and the holy sites were made into open spaces so as to preserve their ancient character. The main stress was laid on the northwards and eastwards expansion of the city and McLean's two nodes, conceived of as a counterweight to the Old City, were abandoned. Instead, a civic centre was provided for on the longitudinal axis of Jaffa Road, Jerusalem's main street, while the Hebrew University was located on Mount Scopus, east of the Old City. Thus, while McLean had favoured the southeastern expansion of the city, Geddes envisaged its growth towards Mount Scopus in the east.

In 1922 Ashby drew up a more detailed plan. For the first time the city boundaries were fixed, running through Shu fat, Isawiye, El'Ezeriye, Mar Elias and Sharafat; and the planning space was subdivided by uses and building regulations into four main zones - the Old City, open spaces and parks in the valleys, industry and crafts near the main traffic arteries, and residential areas.

In 1930, Holliday published another outline plan, again based mainly on uses and building regulations. For the first time, however, an attempt was made to incorporate Jerusalem in a country-wide plan. The roads were classified, with a ring road surrounding the city and linking it to the national road network. This plan, which was again largely based on former concepts, remained in force for many years and determined the shape of the city until 1944, when it was replaced by Kendall's outline scheme. In this scheme, the concepts of all the previous plans, and particularly of Holliday's plan of 1930, came to full expression and fruition.(3) According to Kendall, Jerusalem was destined to become a major communications centre straddling two main intersecting traffic arteries, as well as an administrative center and a meeting ground for the British, Jews and Arabs in the country. His object was to plan the city as a capital with administrative, political and scientific-educational rather than industrial functions. The existing road network remained the basis for the new scheme, but greater emphasis was placed on Holliday's by-pass roads. The light industry zones were surrounded with green belts, and park space were extended. Six residential areas were laid out, each having a standard building density. A clear distinction was made between the

different religious and ethnic communities, with
most of the Jewish quarters in the west and most of
the Arab neighbourhoods in the south and east. Much
attention was paid to the preservation and embell-
ishment of the skyline. The concept of neighbourhood units was also further developed. (Figure 4.1)
 From this series of outline plans we may see
that during the Mandatory period satisfactory provisions were made to ensure an adequate architectural design, to conserve the landscape and topography of the city and to maintain its ancient and holy
sites. The Old City was regarded as the principal
architectural element which also influenced the
planning of the newer parts of the town. Use was
made of the fact that the topography of Jerusalem
lends itself to the construction of neighbourhood
units, and much weight was given to the height and
depth of the buildings to preserve its peculiar
character. Strict architectural requirements were
imposed, and care was taken not to break up the
skyline. In addition to the requirement that buildings should be properly set into the hillside, there
was a stringent regulation that they should all be
made of stone so as to present a solid and dignified
appearance. Throughout an organic architectural
approach was adopted. Although the style might vary,
all buildings merged well into the landscape and became an integral part of it.
 In 1948, with the establishment of the State of
Israel, Jerusalem became a border city, divided between Jews and Arabs, who were both opposed to its
internationalization. (4) Despite this irrational
state of affairs, or perhaps because of it, unconventional steps were taken on both sides of the
armistice lines to promote the development of what
had virtually become two towns. In 1949, Rau worked
out a new outline plan for the Israeli sector. It
was based on creating a new urban ring and shifting
the centre of gravity westwards from the Old City
by setting up a new, artificial urban node. In this
new plan necessity was very much the mother of in-
vention. (Figure 4.2) In the past the city had been
spreading to the west, mainly because the eastern
mountain range from Mount Scopus to Gethsemane was
declared public open space and put out of bounds
for construction. Now that the western part was cut
off from the central business district, this direction remained the only outlet for expansion. At
the same time the Jewish sector had become a national capital and as such had to accomodate a reasonable number of inhabitants, public institutions,

Figure 4.1: Outline Scheme of Jerusalem (1944)

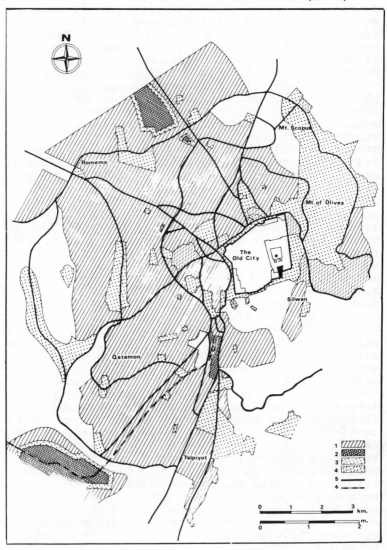

1. Residential Zone   2. Industrial Zone
3. Public or Private Open Space 4. Cemetery
5. Main Road   6. Railway Line

parks and public spaces. The size of the city was, moreover, determined by security considerations. As a border city, it had to be big enough to be able to defend itself. The population for 1985 was thus set at 250,000. It was also necessary to set up industries to provide employment in more than just administrative work. In line with the city's international functions, a central site was allocated to public buildings and institutions.

Needless, however much effort was put into this plan, it could not overcome the fact that the bisected city was not a sound well-integrated organism. While in the Western section detailed town plans and strict building regulations were enforced, a much laxer attitude was adopted in the Eastern section, and this tended to aggravate the dichotomy. The new detailed plan for the Western section also bore insufficient account of the possible reintegration of the city, especially as far as the communication arteries were concerned. Owing to the shift from east to west, the connection with the Old City, a principal element in all former town plans, was severed. The new urban node, with its government buildings and university campus, became a geographic and architectural but not a functional center, and many function were left at their former site, on the periphery of the new town. (5)

Moreover, even with optimal planning many problems could not be solved within the existing municipal boundaries. The available land reserves were not sufficient for further public construction, or for accomodating the future population of the city which was eventually expected to increase to 250-300,000.

Thus the planning concepts adopted in West Jerusalem were a direct result of the unnatural conditions imposed on the city. Since the commercial center was displaced to the west, Jerusalem had to develop in an ox-bow shape, with the central business district at the top and the residential neighbourhoods along the two flanks - the old residential quarters near the border in the east and the new residential quarters in the west.

The various public buildings - the university campus, the government buildings - were located in the central space. According to the new outline scheme, the city was supposed to develop along the western spurs of the Judean hills area roughly suitable for urban development and encroach on the east into the terrain set aside for open space at the western edge of the pre-1948 outlay. At a later stage the Jerusalem Corridor also came to be includ-

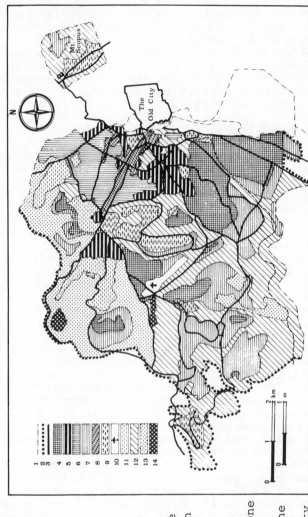

Figure 4.2: Outline Scheme of Jerusalem (1955) – The Western Part

1. Armistice Line
2. Planning Boundary
3. Main Road
4. High-Density Residential Zone
5. Mid-Density Residential Zone
6. Low to Mid-Density Residential Zone
7. Low Density Residential Zone
8. Commercial Zone
9. Public Institutions
10. Local Airport
11. Industrial Zone
12. Public Open Space
13. Nature Reserve
14. Cemetery

ed in the town planning space. The idea was to set
up additional engineering works, communication centers, industries, and defence installations in the
western hills, as far as 6-7 miles (9.6 - 11.2km)
away from the city, without building up the intervening space. At the same time it was intended to
promote the agricultural development of this mountainous hinterland. (6)

PLANNING AND CONSTRUCTION OF EAST JERUSALEM

After the War of 1948 the West Bank of Palestine was
annexed by what was then the Emirate of Trans-Jordan.
This implied a complete change in the geographical
status of East Jerusalem. Under the British, Jerusalem had been the commercial and economic center
of Judea, Samaria and Trans-Jordan. It had provided
the main outlet to the Mediterranean via the routes
leading through it to Jaffa and Haifa, by which all
supplies were conveyed to the city. Jerusalem also
served as a major purchasing centers for the Arab
population. With the annexation of the West Bank
it ceased to be a central city and major market
place, and became a border city, an economic backwater, with all supply lines directed towards Amman
which derived its goods from Aqaba and Beirut. The
Old City merchants, previously the wholesalers and
suppliers of the East Bank of the Jordan river, now
became dependent on importers in Amman. Consequent-
ly many of them moved to the business centers in the
East Bank. This economic subordination to the East
Bank also affected the city's physical development
and gave it an eastward orientation. It began to
spread in directions which are undesirable from the
town planning point of view, towards the eastern
flanks of the Temple Hill, to the Valley of Qidron,
the Judean desert and the busy route to Jericho and
Amman, as well as along the traffic arteries to the
north and south. Here again there was not much scope
for natural expansion as only about one sixth of the
original planning space was available. (Figure 4.3)
In the east and southeast the terrain was highly unsuitable for urban development, so that building
took place mainly along the saddle of the Jerusalem
Hills, on both sides of the Jerusalem-Ramallah Road.
Little development took place towards the south, as
the direct connection with Bethlehem was severed.
The winding road subsequently built on the eastern
flanks of the Jerusalem Hills was hardly conducive
to urban construction.

Figure 4.3: Outline Scheme of Jerusalem (1966) –
            The Eastern Part

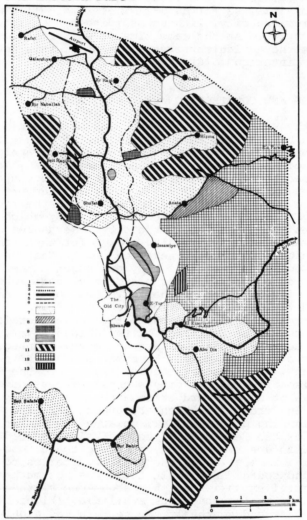

1. Armistice Line 2. Boundary of Eastern
   Jerusalem   3. Planning Boundary
4. Main Road   5. Road
6. Proposed Main Road
7. Residential Zone
8. Industrial Zone 9. Light Industrial Zone
10. Public Open Space 11. Agricultural Area
12. Afforestation Area 13. Cemetery

Most of Jerusalem's Arabs had always lived in
the Old City. Great efforts were made to improve
their living conditions and raise the standard of
public services. Since there was not enough space
for commerce and trade, new areas formerly assigned
to residential uses in the north of the city were
converted to this purpose. Local public transportation facilities still left much to be desired and
the increase in the private vehicle fleet was not
matched by a corresponding expansion of the road
network in and around the city.

The Government of Jordan eventually decided to
incorporate an area of 34,750 acres, from the 'Atarot airfield in the north through Ein Fara in the
east down to the village of Sur Bahir in the south,
in a new outline scheme, whose main land uses were:
residential buildings along the mountain ridge to
the north; agriculture in the valleys; heavy industry - near 'Anata. It also included arterial roads
to Amman, Ramallah and Bethlehem. In the east a continuous wooded area was envisaged running eastward
from the Mount of Olives. The residential areas
were divided into neighbourhood units of 1,000 acres
each, comprising the vicinity of 'Atarot airport,
Er-Ram, Beit Hannina, Shu'fat, 'Anata, Beitunia,
Abu-Dis and Sur Bahir. These units were supposed
to include service and industrial centers, parks,
residential buildings and the like. In the north two
parallel roads were planned, so that the existing
Ramallah road would have become an internal artery.
As the industrial zone in Wadi Goz was insufficient,
a new one was located near the railway station which
was easily accessible from the south and the west.
The Mount of Olives was designed as a public open
space, a site for religious institutions and a
nature reserve. New olive and cypress trees were to
be planted there to ameliorate the landscape. It
was further intended to rehabilitate the archaeological site of Tel el Ful, north of Jerusalem, and
the old Roman road running next to it.

Very little detailed planning was, however,
done. It was not easy to plan the rural areas incorporated within the new outline scheme because of
the highly fragmented land titles which made comprehensive planning, especially for public uses, practically impossible. In adapting to the new conditions dictated by the armistice lines, both West and
East Jerusalem were forced to abandon their natural
economic centers in the west and expand to the west
and east, respectively and to the north and south.
The new town plan conceived under these circumstan-

ces for East Jerusalem was thus based on urban dispersal along the mountain ridge and the development
of new settlement nodes on the flat mountain spurs.
These nodes were to be linked by means of a main
north-south artery, by-passing the Old City. In
addition, an eastern traffic artery to Trans-Jordan
was designed. This meant ribbon development along
the mountain ridge, with the main city area of East
Jerusalem, having several outlying sub-centres with
residential and service functions. The entire development was designed as a ring encircling the
Israeli part of Jerusalem from the east, while linking the north and south of the West Bank and connecting the two with Amman.

LAND USES

Although Jerusalem's area today exceeds 27,000 acres,
it is still far from being fully built up. There is
also a lack of balance in the distribution of land
uses, which, as in other towns are the result of
historical, economic, social and political developments, as well as of a deliberate planning process.
     With the exception of the supply of water,
which resulted in the foundation of ancient Jerusalem east of the watershed, where natural wells were
found, though subsequent knowledge permitted the
consolidation of the water supply within the walls
of the Old City, topography was by far the most important single factor in determining the land uses.
The mosaic pattern of hills and valleys led naturally to agriculture and traffic arteries concentrating
in the valleys, while the hills, which were unsuitable for any other purpose, were used for building.
This led to the later development of separate quarters, each with its special distinctive character.
     The residential areas and the traffic arteries
spred out from the focal point of the Old City in a
north-western, western and south-western direction,
advancing slowly from lower to higher ground until
the watershed was reached, and on from there according to the local topographical conditions.
     The drive for a progressive urban development
outside the Old City limits, was mainly due to the
initiative of the British mandatory government, who
planned the expansion of the town by setting out new
roads and areas for new dwelling quarters and other
urban functions. These plans found expression in a
succession of Town Planning Schemes. However, in

contrast to the rapid development of Tel Aviv and
Haifa, the pace of construction in Jerusalem was
much slower, due to the city's special character and
the functions assigned to it. Geographically Jerusalem is distant from the main economic centres of
the country, and is furthermore hilly with difficult
accessibility. Therefore, it did not attract industrial investors to the same extent as the coastal
towns. If it was considered desirable to attract a
particular industrial enterprise to Jerusalem, artificial incentives had to be offered in the form of
subsidies, or other preferential treatment.

Jerusalem, with its religious character and
Holy Places, has always been a city of pilgrimage,
and this has furthered tourism, the hotel industry
and the construction of religious buildings. At the
same time, the religious character of the city has
had a restraining influence on the development of
sites with historical, architectural or religious
associations. The special sentiments attached to
Jerusalem and its traditions, are to a certain extent antagonistic to an active and modern urban development, similar to that experienced by the coastal towns. Jerusalem has witnessed interesting experiments in blending old and new architectural
styles, but this in itself does not bring about
economic prosperity. The building of new churches,
convents and mosques did not bring in its wake new
residential construction or additional investments.
As a rule, the construction of a new religious building was accompanied by the appropriation of a large
plot of land, for use as garden or private open
space, and serving to isolate the building from its
neighbours. The growing number of such sites as the
Russian Compound, the Abyssinian Church, the Notre
Dame Convent, the Ratisbonne Convent and the Terra
Sancta property, has created numerous enclaves within the continuous texture of the city. The land
transactions carried out from time to time by convents do not always take account of the current land
prices as determined by the supply and demand in the
free market, and thus have created a number of fro-
zen land assets within the dynamic development of
the city, which have subsisted up to this day. (7)
The need of premises for government and other administrative buildings has been another factor influencing land use, both during the Mandate and
after the establishment of the State of Israel. Many
such buildings were constructed, both within and
outside the old central business district, either in
the form of separate buildings, or as part of the

government functions, did not enable it to compete with the industrial towns, and slowed down its development.

The heterogeneous character of Jerusalem's population was another factor that hindered the city's development. The mixed population of Jews and Arabs had always been a source of tension, mainly on political grounds, and led in time to the physical separation of residential quarters, place of work, business districts and public and religious institutions. The Arab population, which had always constituted a majority in and near the Old City, established itself mainly in the eastern part of Jerusalem, while the Jews, who had started to move out of the Old City during the second half of the 19th century, developed the western quarters of the town. The separation between the residential and business districts of both communities created a series of boundary zones, in which there was little urban development. The Jewish population, too, was far from homogeneous. The differences between the ways of life of the traditional orthodox and the modern liberal Jew, were reflected in the character of the residential quarters which they built, from the crowded courtyards of Mea She'arim to the garden suburbs of Bet Hakerem and Talpiyot, or the European quarters of Rehavya and Talbiyeh. Each group with a common way of life, did its best to preserve the special character of its quarter, and this tendency militated against the rapid development of the city as a uniform single planning unit. On the other hand, it is this diversity that has given Jerusalem its distinctive character, though at the expense of a modern and rapid development.

One of the most striking features of the spatial developments of the fifties in Jerusalem was the siting of the Hebrew University campus at Giv'at Ram, to the west of the old town planning boundary, and in the geographical centre of the new city area. Opposite Giv'at Ram were sited the Knesset (8), the Government Centre and the Israel Museum, the whole complex of buildings being surrounded by gardens and public open spaces. A system of roads to be built in the valleys, will complete the ox-bow shape, planned to extend from the Convention Hall in the north, along the quarters lining Herzl Avenue to the west, the old Jerusalem quarters to the east, and the quarters bordering the Refa'im Valley to the south.

In the thirties the central business district moved westward, along the Jaffa Road. The traditional commercial centers in the Old City was replaced by the triangle bound by Jaffa Road, Ben Yehuda Street and King George Avenue, and the adjacent streets and passages. The greater part of the businesses, banks and places of entertainment are to be found in this area, in which one third of the city's working population is employed. (9) Other concentrations of employment are to be found in the Government the Hebrew University, the various industrial zones and the Hadassah Medical Centre. Of all the Jerusalem working force, about 80% are employed in the western, and the remainder in the eastern sector. Although neighbourhood commercial centers have been built, mainly in the southern quarters, most business is still carried out in the central commercial district. The abolition of the barrier between the two sections of the city strengthened the ties with the Old City, which had always been the historical center of Jerusalem, and lessened, although only slightly, the rate of business and building expansion in the western quarters.

As regards the present trends in land uses, it can be said that the central business district along the Jaffa Road is so dominant, and its influence on shopping patterns at all levels is so marked, that no alternative is in sight, the more so as the geographical center of the city is a residential area. The result is that businesses continue to concentrate in this central business distirct, while the population tends to move more and more to the southwestern and western residential suburbs.

PLANNING AND CONSTRUCTION OF THE REUNITED CITY

The post 1967 boundaries, especially when compared with those of the divided sections, appear to be eminently satisfactory. The new eastern boundaries are the same as during the British Mandate, while the western boundaries are those fixed by the new outline plan. The present boundaries thus comprise the eastern crest - the Mount of Olives and Mount Scopus - the Old City and the village of Silwan, as well as the villages of Sur Bahir, Beit Safafa and Shu'fat, and the narrow urban strip running north via Shu'fat to the 'Atarot airfield. The city thus has a total area of 27,125 acres, about three times its former size. The new boundary lines were determined mainly by the desire to set up a single geographic entity, create a geographic security belt, secure direct access to 'Atarot airport - the only one in the Judean-Samarian massive - and include as little of the rural Arab population as possible.

The new boundaries of Greater Jerusalem with their totally different geographic-urban layout present the town planner with a fresh challenge. Instead of a marginal city lying on the eastern end of a narrow corridor Jerusalem once again straddles the road running along the mountain ridge with free access from north to south and from east to west. It is no longer confined in its growth to one single direction and now disposes of considerable land reserves for a big population and for the countrywide functions of a national capital. It is no longer a blind alley, and new traffic arteries can now be developed to connect it with the road system of Judea and Samaria. A comprehensive town plan can now be drawn up, preserving the unique archaeological, historical and architectural character of the Old City while incorporating the holy places in the overall design. Instead of encroaching upon the rural area of the Jerusalem corridor in the west, the city now has scope for further expansion to the east. Here, on the margin of the desert, there are big, populous villages which can be integrated within the city while maintaining their characteristic appearance. As against these advantages there is the ribbon development north of Shu'fat and east of E-Tur to contend with, as well as the scattered layout of the entire eastern section. (Figure 4.4)

Serious attention must also be given to the demographic problem, which will have a major impact on future development trends. The Jewish population, which amounted to 200,000 at the beginning of 1967, was originally expected to grow to 250,000 by 1985. With the change in boundaries another 66,000 Moslem and Christian inhabitants have been added - about a quarter as many as there were before. Some 25,000 live in the Old City and the rest are spread over the neighbouring villages. This population which has a big natural increase might grow to 140,000 by 1985 and to 180,000 by 2,000. This means that the population target for 1985 has already been reached and that by 2000 a population of about 450,000 - 500,000 may be expected. Accordingly the previous planning concepts must obviously be overhauled. Now the order of the day is to build and plan a big city with a considerable growth potential, perched high on the mountains but nevertheless called upon to fulfill major national and country-wide functions. In view of the new demographic structure of Jerusalem, its extended boundaries and increased area, profound physical changes are likely to take place which may

50

Figure 4.4: Outline Scheme of Re-United Jerusalem (1967)

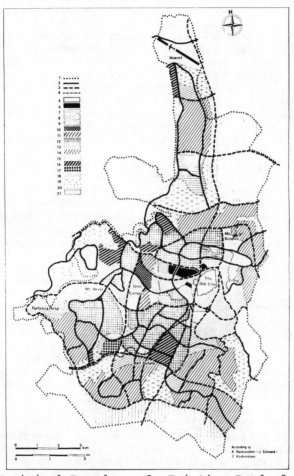

1. Municipal Boundary 2. Existing Road 3. Proposed Road 4. Railway Line 5. The Old City
6. Central Business District 7. Commercial Zone
8. Institutions 9. University Campus 10. Administrative Institutions 11. Cultural Institutions
12. High-Density Residential Zone 13. Mid-Density Residential Zone 14. Low to Mid-Density Residential Zone 15. Low-Density Residential Zone 16. Industrial Zone 17. Sub-Center 18. National Park
19. Public Open Space 20. Nature Reserve 21. Communication Center

determine its character for many generations to come.
Many of the functions originally designed for the
Jerusalem corridor will be relocated in the city.
New residential areas will be set up and additional
public institutions will be erected, probably on
Mount Scopus and in the vicinity of Government
House. New industrial zones will be established. The
environs of the Old City which continue to be a
center of attraction for tourists and visitors will
be revamped in a style appropriate ot its landscape.
The longitudinal axis joining East and West Jerusalem will presumably become a center of commerce
and tourism and turn into a major traffic artery.
    Thus it is obvious that quite different plan-
ning concepts must be applied from those that were
in force during the past twenty-five years. With
the removal of the political barrier between the two
parts of the city it has become glaringly evident to
what extent the city's development had been affected
by the unnatural conditions imposed upon it. Now
that the natural physical conditions have been re-
stored, more national trends can begin to operate,
especially as the city boundaries are now bigger
than ever before. The original idea of a business
    integrated with the existing centers round the
Old City, and restricted development to the west,
has been revived. Thus, the city will resume its
traditional course. Already the artery running parallel to the Old City walls has become a main road,
where lively trade and tourist traffic are about to
develop. The city will also continue to grow in its
natural north-south direction, along the mountain
ridge, rather than towards the Valley of Soreq in
the west. As a united city, it is likely to become
the main urban center of Judea and Samaria, so that
Ramallah in the north and Bethlehem in the south,
which are intimately associated with Jerusalem, will
become satellite towns. Its central position on the
lateral axis from Tel Aviv in the west to Jericho
and 'Amman in the east is also bound to affect its
development.
    Guidelines for a new master plan were laid down
in 1977. It was recommended to restrain the growth
of the main city center, but to further the development of modern shopping and office centers in outlying neighbourhoods. In order to preserve the city's
architectural character, limitations on high-rise
building and the requirement of stone facing for all
buildings are to be rigorously applied.
    While in the southwest residential building
continued after 1967 on a fairly large scale and

vacant lots elsewhere were often used for new construction, the main effort was directed to the new
areas of the city in the north and south, beyond the
former armistice line. First was the large Ramot
Eshkol quarter, which adjoins the older northern
border streets. It was followed by the Givat
Shapiro quarter, which creates a direct link with
the Hebrew University compound on Mount Scopus.
Later came four large development areas in the outer
circumference: Ramot Allon in the northwest, Neve
Ya'aqov in the northeast, Giloh in the south, and
East Talpiyot in the southeast. (Figure 4.5)

The Hebrew University has seen the return of
its original campus atop Mount Scopus, where an intensive restoration and building program was launch-
ed in 1968. Other institutes of learning, as
Christian theological seminaries, are in the construction or planning stage in various parts of the
city.

The capital is attracting now increasing numbers of industrial enterprises, particularly of the
electronics and other science-intensive branches,
for which new areas were set aside in the south and,
principally, at Atarot in the north.

While the pre-1967 blueprint for commercial
development called for expansion only westward, the
emphasis shifted back to the center after the city
was reunited. A highly ambitious project for a
commercial center west of Jaffa Gate, with some
underground thoroughfares and parking space, is under discussion. On the other hand, the development
plans of secondary commercial centers in the suburbs were favorably considered.

The advisability of a large conurbation centered on Jerusalem is a debatable point. Most experts
hold that such a development should not be encouraged, so as not to spoil the landscape on the approaches to the city, of singular beauty and great spiritual significance to mankind. In the long run,
however, it may prove difficult to prevent an at
least partial amalgamation of satellite towns like
Bethlehem or Ramallah with the capital city on which
their economy is largely dependent. The solution
appears to lie in detailed planning and landscaping,
protecting skylines, open spaces and scenic vistas.

Related to this issue is the debate on thicken-
ing the Jerusalem circumference at a diameter of
dozens of miles, where new satellite towns were proposed. Some planners, however, prefer preserving the
region's rural character and advise concentrating
development efforts more within Jerusalem's present

Figure 4.5: Dispersion of Greater Jerusalem

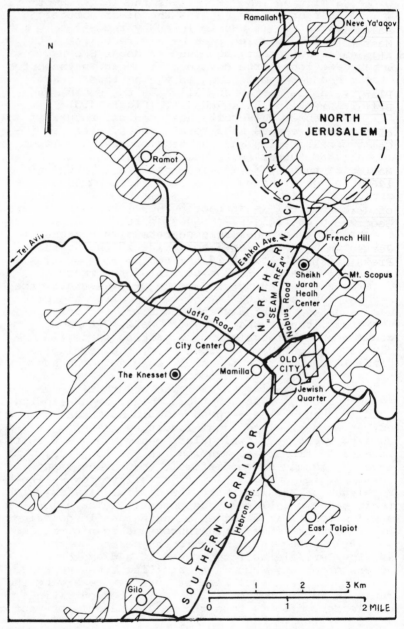

municipal boundaries.

NOTES

1.   D.H.K. Amiran, The Development of Jerusalem 1860-1970 (Urban Geography of Jerusalem,
Massada Press, Jerusalem, A Companion Volume to the
Atlas of Jerusalem, 1973), pp. 20-52.
2.   Ibid.
3.   H. Kendall, Jerusalem - The Holy City
Plan, Preservation and Development during the
British Mandate 1918-1948 (London, 1948)
4.   E. Efrat, Patterns in Urban Development
of Modern Jerusalem (Tijdschrift voor Econ. en Soc.
Geog., Rotterdam, 1964), pp. 223-229.
5.   J. Dash and E. Efrat, The Israel Physical
Master Plan (Ministry of the Interior, Jerusalem,
1964), 91 pp. + plates.
6.   E. Efrat, The Hinterland of the New City
of Jerusalem and its Economic Significance (Economic
Geography, 40, 3, 1964), pp. 256-260.
7.   A. Shachar, The Functional Structure of
Jerusalem (Urban Geography of Jerusalem, Massada
Press, Jerusalem, A Companion Volume to the Atlas of
Jerusalem, 1973), pp. 76-90.
8.   A Hebrew Term for the Israeli parliament.
9.   A. Shachar, ibid.

Chapter Five

TEL AVIV AND THE CONURBATION

In describing and analysing the urban development of
Tel Aviv, it will be discovered that the physical
geographical features were of much less importance
in influencing the city's growth as was the case
with Jerusalem. Tel Aviv is an example of a town
built on a lowland which, as a result of intensive
construction sprawled over a large area, has created
anew its own urban geographical features that have
been the framework for ever continuing inner development.

TEL AVIV'S GEOGRAPHICAL SETTING

Tel Aviv's origins are associated with Jaffa, a town
which was established hundreds of years ago. Jaffa
is based at the edge of an underground geological
ridge which stretches into the sea, creating a natural bay containing many abrasive rocks. This bay
has attracted settlers since ancient times. Sailors,
looking for a coastal point to land at, found that
the Jaffa bay offered good anchoring conditions.
Jaffa developed as a densely populated port town on
the small hill opposite the bay and functioned as a
gateway to the interior of the country. Main roads
led from Jaffa to Jerusalem and elsewhere; by the
end of the 19th century, it was served by the railroad as well. At this time, Jaffa was a center of
commercial and economic activity employing Jewish
and Arab residents and Christian Pilgrims; as the
bridge to the country, numerous immigrants were attracted to the town, increasing the community's
population.
     The area surrounding the Jaffa hill is compris-
ed of level plains, separated by sandstone ridges,
that lie parallel to the coastline. The erosional

impacts of the Ayalon river and its tributaries, as they crossed the plains towards the sea over the centuries, created sandstone-banked river beds, swamps, and flat plains in which good soil accumulated. The town of Jaffa, however, did not expand into the periphery of the hill, and remained bounded by sand dunes lying to the north-east and citrus groves which had been developed to the south and east.

By the end of the 19th century, Jewish immigrants began to establish new neighbourhoods adjacent to the existing Jewish section of the city. Neve Tsedek was begun in 1887, and Neve Shalom followed in 1890, becoming a home for Jewish settlers originating from a variety of nations. Other neighbourhoods were built during later years. By the beginning of the 20th century, the Jewish population of Jaffa totalled to approximately 3,000 people, accounting for a fifth of the town's population.

The city of Tel Aviv began with the founding of the neighbourhood of Ahuzat Bayit in 1909, on sand dunes just northeast of Jaffa. It is doubtful whether its founders had any vision or intention of creating a city as vast as is Tel Aviv today. Jews from European countries established Ahuzat Bayit to escape from the conditions of high density and low sanitation found in the oriental town of Jaffa. Their objective was the creation of a <u>Garden City</u> suburb, a concept then popular in Europe and the United States as a response to the polluted dirty and noisy cities of the industrial revolution. The idea entailed the construction of quiet residential areas on the outskirts of the cities where urban dwellers could reside surrounded by well-tended vegetation. It was on this model that Ahuzat Bayit appears to have been created. It was built according to a grid system of parallel streets, forming rectangular land parcels on which small, generally single-storey houses were constructed. It offered a living environment that was found to be quite convenient and comfortable by its early residents, unaware that their neighbourhood was to eventually become the central core of the largest conurbation in Israel.

It should be stressed, though, that Ahuzat Bayit was not situated at a prime geographic location. It was not located very close to the sea nor to agricultural areas which were the economic foundations of the Jaffa vicinity. Nor was it established at the Yarqon River, the major waterway of the area that might have served as a focus for urban

development. Instead, Ahuzat Bayit was built in the
heart of the sand dunes, perhaps because of the a-
vailability of purchasable land there, or due to its
proximity to Jaffa as an employment center or to the
main roads that provided accessibility to Jerusalem,
Petah Tiqva and Nablus. Maintaining relationships
with the interior settlements of the country was
more important to Jewish settlement objectives, at
that time, than a seaward focus. From its inception,
Tel Aviv concentrated on an inland orientation and
did not develop as a coastal town in reference to
the sea; this later made it difficult for the city's
harbor to function, as neither sufficient land area
for port related economic development nor adequate
transportation facilities to the port were available.

Tel Aviv's location is not favourable from a
climate point of view either. Situated lower than
Jaffa and further from the sea; the city does not
benefit from the cool sea breezes; temperatures and
humidity levels are high during the summer months,
which makes it uncomfortable to live in the city.
The average annual temperature is 20°C (68°F), while
the average temperature in August, the warmest month,
is 25°C (77°F). However, the annual average humidity is about 70%, decreasing from the east side of
the city to the west, which marks Tel Aviv as among
the most humid places in Israel.

As Tel Aviv developed, it began to sprawl from
the original core towards the north, along the three
parallel sandstone ridges that extend northwards
from the south, running up to the coastline. Along
the coast is a cliff with an average height of 60ft.
(20 meters). The ridges are located between 1.25-
3.7 miles (2-5 kms) from the sea, broken in places
where the water flow of streams has eroded the
sandstone of the ridges, so that they appear as
series of small hills at heights generally between
75-90 ft. (25-30 meters) above sea level. The eastern sandstone ridge is situated near the western
bank of the Ayalon river bed and reaches a height of
210-240 ft. (70-80 meters). Between the ridges, are
longitudinal valleys. Tel Aviv developed in relation to this topography of ridges and valleys, particularly the street system. Most of the main
streets run longitudinally along the valleys; perpendicular streets followed the openings of gullies
running towards the sea.

The topographical setting of Tel Aviv was covered by sand over the centuries so that the immediate coastal zone, 1.8 miles (3 kms) wide, became
unsuitable for agricultural purposes. The Yarqon

and Ayalon rivers and their tributaries shaped the
topography, as the source of water flows that cut
through the sandstone soil structure. The Ayalon
river at one time reached the sea just north of
Jaffa, but was later pirated by the Yarqon and given
a new waterbed. Today it is desiccated, while
measures have been taken to preserve the flow of the
Yarqon for recreational purposes. (Figure 5.1)
    A swamp that existed near Jaffa, caused by a
tributary which did not have sufficient force to
carve its way to the sea, was once used as an inner
sea, appropriate for small boats to anchor in.
Changes in the Ayalon river system left behind large
evacuated areas with sediment favourable for agriculture, particularly for citrus fruits to the east
and southeast of Jaffa. The Yarqon river also has
changed its original riverbed during periods of geological and historical alteration; its meandering
created a valley 0.6-1.2 miles (40 kms.) and its
depth 12 ft. (4 meters).
    The geographical features of the area, limited
the possible developmental directions of Tel Aviv.
Citrus areas to the southeast were expensive and
generally unavailable for sale. Jaffa bordered on
the south. The Ayalon river in the east and the
Yarqon river in the south formed boundaries; the
immediate sides of the water beds were unsuitable
for construction due to frequency of overflowing
that flooded over the river banks. This left Tel
Aviv little alternative than to develop northwards
towards the Yarqon river across the sand dunes
ridges and valleys of the area.
    Later, as suburban settlements were established
on the higher ridge hills to the east of Tel Aviv,
they were given names appropriate to the topography,
including Ramat Gan, Ramatayim and Ramat HaSharon.
(1)

URBAN DEVELOPMENT AS A RESULT OF CONSTRUCTION TRENDS

From the inception of Ahuzat Bayit, Tel Aviv's population grew, due both to natural increase and the
settlement of Jewish immigrants in the new community.
The number of inhabitants was about 300 in 1910 and
a gradual increase occured until World War I, as
shown in Table 5.1. By 1915 the population had
reached 2,000, but during the war it decreased and
did not return to its previous growth rate until the
beginning of the British Mandate period.
    The first decade of Tel Aviv's existence did

Figure 5.1 Physiographic Factors in the Development
            of Tel Aviv

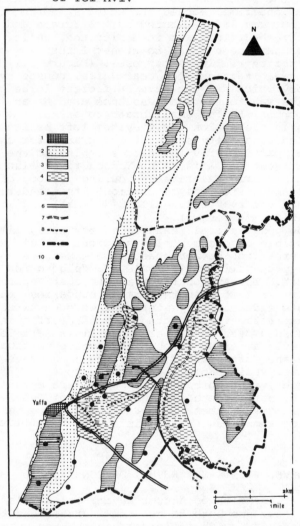

1.	Old Yaffa	2.	Sand Dunes	3.	Sand-stone
	Ridges	4.	Flooding Area	5.	Railway
	Line	6.	Main Road	7.	River
8.	Wadi	9.	Municipal Boundary
10.	Neighbourhood

not show impressive economic development. Its inhabitants worked as clerks, in light industry and various professions. The Zionist settlement movement was occupied almost completely with rural development activities, an emphasis due especially to the influence of the Second Aliyah (2), and therefore the growth of urban areas was not given particular attention. During the 1920s, population growth and urban development accelerated primarily as a result of private initiative, so that the new Jewish town of Tel Aviv emerged distinctly in contrast to the old town of Jaffa.

As Tel Aviv developed its own economic and cultural base, its residents sought political independence as well. They resented paying taxes to the municipalities of Jaffa for which they did not receive services. The riots of 1921 between Arabs and Jews resulted in an animosity that thereafter prevented a functional interrelationship between the two towns; in the same year the British Mandate government gave Tel Aviv the status of a local authority. It's population then numbered 3,600 inhabitants, within an area of no more than 143 hectar.

The inhabitants of <u>Little Tel Aviv</u>, who were mostly engaged in commerce, also exhibited an interest in real estate. Rapid housing construction ensued as land was bought and parcelled; this assisted in the settlement of newly-arriving immigrants and the growth of the city, but it also caused a steep escalation in land prices. The enlargement of Tel Aviv following World War I occured mainly to the north. Growth in other directions was limited by the sea to the west and the surrounding Arab villages: Sumail with its citrus orchards on the east, Abu Kabir in the south, and Manshiye to the southwest. Land unsuitable for citrus groves was also not chosen, as it was more expensive and prone to flooding from time to time as a result of its low-lying flat topography. It was, therefore, the northern sand dunes which were purchased, drained and prepared for construction purposes.

The remnants of the original concept of Tel Aviv as a Garden City disappeared as urban construction aggressively progressed. In one valley between the sand dunes, Rothchild Avenue was aligned; it later became a primary transportation axis within the city. On both sides of the avenue, land was sold for increasingly higher prices. The Arabs, who owned most of the sand dunes, were pleased to sell at the high prices offered by Jews content to have

61

the opportunity to purchase the land. By the mid-
1920s, it was apparent that Tel Aviv was developing
into a substantial town, so real estate speculators
decided to concentrate on building construction.
They built housing along Ha-Yarqon Street, Allenby
Street, Rothchild Avenue and other parallel streets.
New streets were aligned along the longitudinal de-
pressions within the sand dunes, and perpendicular
east-west roads were constructed where openings had
occurred in the sandstone ridges as a result of natural draingage to the sea. Tel Aviv grew tremendous-
ly during the ensuing years due to this intensive
construction activity.

Table 5.1: Population of Tel Aviv Between Foundation
and the World War I

Year	Population
1910	300
1911	550
1912	790
1913	960
1914	1,491

During the 1930s, Jewish immigrants from Central Europe arrived in Israel with considerable capital with which they established industry in Tel
Aviv. An industrial zone was designated beyond the
residential neighbourhoods, and developed along the
main road from Jaffa to Tel Aviv in an area of low
topography. After several years, the residential
communities extended to this zone, so that industrial development had to expand eastwards along new
transportation routes. These new industries generated further urban growth, providing employment that
attracted additional settlers to the area.
The primary transportation routes had a greater
influence than the area's topographical features on
urban growth; much development, particularly industrial plants dependent on adequate transportation
lines for receiving and distributing goods occured
along the primary arteries such as those leading
from Jaffa to Jerusalem and from Tel Aviv to Petah
Tiqva and Nablus. Within the city, streets were

constructed in accordance with the demands of the time, when transportation needs were low, few private automobiles existed, and small buses and carriages were used. The narrow street system of the 1930s remains basically intact as Tel Aviv's present day system. Only a few main arteries have been widened subsequent to their construction, (e.g. Ibn Gevirol and Petah Tiqva Road), as the high density building along both sides of the street has prevented such improvements. As a result, the capacity of the Tel Aviv road system is severely limited.

The Arab riots of 1936-1939 served as a catalyst to Tel Aviv's growth. The Jewish population of Tel Aviv was forced to provide commercial services previously found only in Jaffa with which economic relationships were severed following the riots. This included the establishment of a harbour due to the impossibility of using Jaffa's port. The construction of a harbour near the mouth of the Yarqon river in north Tel Aviv, attracted economic activity to the area; many industrial and commercial operations eventually transferred from Jaffa to the new harbour district, strengthening the city's economic base. In the long run, though, the harbour had a limited impact as there was soon insufficient space for further construction nor adequate transportation routes to serve the harbour.

THE PLANNING ROLE IN TEL AVIV'S DEVELOPMENT

For decades, Tel Aviv developed without the guidance of a master plan, nor any comprehensive planning approach. Until the mid-1920s, the town grew through the successive construction of self-contained neighbourhoods, for each of which a detailed plan had been prepared; this however, did not substitute for a comprehensive plan to coordinate the integration of the neighbourhood units into one urban structure. In the 1930s, the town fathers agreed to the concept of general town planning and invited Sir Patrick Geddes, an English town planner, to prepare an outline scheme for Tel Aviv. Geddes could not alter the development that had already occured, much of it haphazard, speculative market conditions, so his contribution concentrated on northern Tel Aviv which then remained largely undeveloped. He suggested that Tel Aviv develop on the basis of sub-centers of economic activity, focused around squares such as Dizengoff Square, HaMedinah Square and others; this would weaken the tie with Jaffa and encourage

63

growth in the direction of the Yarqon river. In the
north of the city, he planned for higher density
housing of three to four storeys and allowed for a
reasonable amount of setback space between the
buildings; he also recommended specific designs to
improve the aesthetic appearance of building facades.
The fact that the northern areas of Tel Aviv have
achieved, to at least some degree, a pleasant character is primarily attributed to Geddes work.

From the 1930s through the first two decades of
the State, there was no other attempt to confront
the planning problems of Tel Aviv and to prepare a
comprehensive master plan for the city. As a result,
Tel Aviv became a mosaic of disjointed projects,
lacking an overall scheme. The built facts established the defacto design framework for future construction. It is peculiar that Tel Aviv, as the
largest town in Israel, did not receive planning
attention, even during the early years of the State
when there was much concern for planning for other
regions in the country. Though the northern areas
of Tel Aviv did show the benefits of some planning
attention, most of the older sections of the city,
such as Herzl Street, remained unchanged from the
time of their original construction. Only in the
early 1970s was a master plan for Tel Aviv prepared,
after 60 years of the city's existence.

We have seen how Tel Aviv developed despite an
unfavorable geographical location and unsuitable
sandy and hilly topography; however, the necessity
and enthusiasm of the Jewish settlers to establish
the first new Jewish town in centuries was successful though they lacked knowledge of town development
principles. This inexperience was reflected in the
many crucial errors that have occured during the
various growth stages of the city and have remained
duriable features to the present day. At least,
since Tel Aviv reached a population of 100,000 inhabitants, the inner dynamics for continuing growth
have become so ingrained, that correcting past fail-
ures will likely be accomplished only with great
difficulty.

THE CONURBATION

The Tel Aviv conurbation stretches 9 miles (14 kms.)
of Israel's coastline and extends inland for 22.5
miles (36 kms.) This area has become a metropolitan
district and conurbation, during the 74 years since
Tel Aviv's founding, particularly due to its

central location in the coastal plain. Today, the conurbation is the largest urban complex in the country with the highest concentration of population. It is the economic center, with employees in commerce, industry, banking and insurance, and a primary focus of cultural, social and political activity in Israel. As with other large metropolitan areas throughout the world, the urban dynamics of the Tel Aviv conurbation cannot be studied within the framework of the municipal boundaries alone; rather, the city, its surrounding suburbs and the adjoining townships must all be examined as one unit for a complete, accurate picture of urban growth in the area. In addition to Tel Aviv, other towns of the conurbation include Ramat Gan, Bene Beraq, Givatayim, Holon and Bat Yam.

The development of such a large concentration of population is largely due to the many Jewish immigrants to Israel during this century who chose to settle in the Tel Aviv region. As the primary gateway into the country, Jaffa enticed many newcomers to remain as residents, particularly because of the employment and commercial goods and services available in the town as a result of its port function. Tel Aviv could thrive as a suburb of Jaffa due to its proximity to the economic opportunities in Jaffa and the employment available in the surrounding rural settlements, especially in citrus work. This situation formed the basis for continuing population increase and urban development, as a large proportion of immigrants arrived and settled in the Tel Aviv area and contributed investments and employment efforts to the process. Such growth of a port town has not been unique to Tel Aviv; other cities, including New York, Buenos Aires and Sydney, have similarly benefited from mass immigration arriving through their ports. Currently 25% of Israel's population lives in the Tel Aviv conurbation, a proportion which has actually declined since the founding of the State in 1948.

The development of Tel Aviv as a suburban Garden City of Jaffa reflected the desire of the settlers to separate their work place from their living place. As these residential suburbs spread so did the municipal boundaries and the commuting times and distances to work. Tel Aviv was at first built on inexpensive sandy soil, not suitable for agriculture, which permitted the rapid construction of low-density, one-storey buildings on substantial plots of land. Much development also occured along the main transportation routes; as many residences and light industries were constructed alongside the roads in order to take advantage of the better transportation access offered at those sites. By the end of the 1920s and early 1930s, economic development in Tel Aviv allowed the city to gain status as the center of Jewish urban life with no longer a need to fully depend on Jaffa. The investments in industry and commerce of the 4th and 5th Aliyah particularly accelerated the area's urbanization rate as the increased employment opportunities encouraged additional population inflow, and suburban residential construction.

By the time Tel Aviv gained municipal status in 1934, its population had increased to 72,000 inhabitants, in contrast to Jaffa's 65,000 residents. The settlement of Jewish immigrants from Central Europe during the 5th Aliyah (3), significantly increased Tel Aviv's population during the 1930s and the city's economy grew as a result of their investment and occupational activities. The 1936-1939 Arab riots caused a nearly complete severing of relationships between Jaffa and Tel Aviv, focusing the latter to develop all its own economic services, ending any previous reliance on Jaffa; this created additional employment opportunities in Tel Aviv. By the 1940s, the city's population reached beyond 150,000.

Tel Aviv continued to expand, especially among major traffic routes in the city; high quality housing was built along Ben Yehuda and Dizengoff Streets, among others. Residential development occured rapidly in north Tel Aviv, jumping to the north side of the Yarqon river, as well. In the southeast part of Tel Aviv, residential structures of the early years gave way to light industry. The few houses and apartment buildings that remained became the homes of low income groups; structural deterioration in these industrial areas led to the slum-like appearances that remain in evidence today. At the same time, Jaffa expanded southward. Intensive urbanization of the surrounding suburbs and settlements also occured during this period. Suburban neighbourhoods such as Herzliyya and Holon increased in density. Agricultural settlements, including Ramat Gan, Bene Beraq, Nahlat Yitzhak, Givatayim and Bat Yam, became urban nodes. These communities, originally founded on the basis of horticulture, were intended to supply agriculture products (e.g. vegetables and dairy products) to the main city; however, the proximity of Tel Aviv for commercial distributing and purchasing continued to the desirability of the settlements for urban

residential and light industrial development. Their
ample land areas provided construction sites for expansion, in the place of agricultural crops. Industrial strips developed also along main arteries
north of Jaffa and southeast of Tel Aviv, and between Ramat Gan, Bene Beraq and Petah Tiqva. Such
urbanization proceeded at a rapid pace, with all the
settlements depending on an interrelationship with
Tel Aviv, from Bat Yam and Holon on the south side
of Jaffa to the townships on the east and northeast.
    With the abandonment of adjacent Arab villages,
such as Sheik Munis, Salamay and Sumeil, during the
1948 War of Independence, Jewish settlements gained
additional area for expansion. The new Israeli government assumed legal control of all such abandoned
lands which, along with other public lands, the bulk
of property in the country, passed on by the British
Mandate authorities, were used for various settlement projects, particularly in providing for the
tremendous number of immigrants who arrived during
the first years of statehood. Immigration added
greatly to Tel Aviv's population during that time:
in 1946, the population numbered 195,000 inhabitants;
following the first wave of mass immigration in
1946, the population numbered 195,000 inhabitants;
following the first wave of mass immigration in 1948,
the figure was 248,000, and in 1951, 345,000 people.
In response, the government released agricultural
land for construction purposes, particularly between
Tel Aviv and its eastern suburban nodes. This action began a trend of infilling the open areas between the urban settlements of the region, resulting
in today's conurbation with continuous urban development stretching from Holon and Bat Yam on the south,
encompassing Jaffa and Tel Aviv, to Ramat Gan and
Bene Beraq on the east, and beyond the Yarqon River
northwards to Herzliyya and Ramat HaSharon. These
urban boundaries are currently continuing to expand.

CONCENTRIC RINGS OF THE CONURBATION

The structure of the Tel Aviv conurbation is similar
to the classic concentric rings concept. A relatively distinct hierarchy of circles or rings of urban
development is apparent, each ring relatively homogenious internally, yet maintaining a strong relationship to the other rings, and particularly to the
central core of the conurbation.
    In addition to the central core, three general
rings are identified in this chapter. The central

core consists of the Tel Aviv-Jaffa municipality, with the original neighbourhoods forming the nucleus of the conurbation. It is within the core that most of the regions commercial activity occurs. The inner ring is comprised of the surrounding suburban towns of Ramat Gan, Bene Beraq Givatayim, Holon and Bat Yam; these communities are comprised of suburban residential neighbourhoods and local shopping as well as many light industrial plants which required the larger land areas that were available in the inner ring. Urban development is continuous between the core and the inner ring. Beyond this is a developing middle ring, including such settlements as Or Yehuda, Yehud, Savyon, Qiryat Ono, Givat Shemuel and Ramat HaSharon. These serve as sattelite suburbs of Tel Aviv; they have little interrelationship between one another. Located in an agricultural region, they are of low density, comprised of single family villa houses; a few such as Savyon and Ramat HaSharon hold a status of exclusivity. This ring has become attractive to newcomers from the core and inner ring and from other areas of the country. The outer ring is formed by the veteran <u>Moshavot</u> which have developed into independent towns, including Rishon LeZiyyon, Petah Tiqva and Herzliyya, among others. These towns are self-contained urban centers, attracting considerable economic investment and development on their own. The towns, however, have many commuters to employment opportunities within the core, thereby establishing a tie with the Tel Aviv conurbation.

The rings differ from one another in other respects as well. The pace of development is currently slowest in the largely built-up core, increasing in the surrounding suburbs. With the exception of north Tel Aviv, the core's population is older and poorer, as is the quality of housing; the surrounding rings house younger age groups in newer, higher standard living quarters. Residential densities and the degree of urban infill within the urban area decreases towards the east. The core is solidly built up and contains the highest population densities. The density of the inner ring suburbs is lower; along the border of some, urban development is continuous with the core, while open areas distinguish the boundary of other suburban entities. Many single family homes characterize the clearly identifiable communities of the middle ring. The outer ring has the lowest average density rate, as small towns of higher densities are interspearsed within agricultural areas. In the core, population

activities are almost entirely contained within the
municipal boundaries, for work, shopping and other
usual duties. The relationship of the rings to the
core becomes weaker as the distance to the center
increases. Suburban residents may work in the core,
yet do much of their shopping in local or adjacent
suburban shopping centers. The self-sufficient towns
of the outer ring provide employment for most residents, the core may serve a few work commuters and
as a major center of particular commercial and cultural activity. Distinguishing between northern and
southern areas, irrespective of the rings, indicates
the higher densities and solidly built up areas of
such communities as Holon and Bat Yam in the south,
while in the north lower densities and the inclusion
of much open space is in evidence.

THE POPULATION OF THE CONURBATION

In the year 1981, the conurbation numbered 855,100
inhabitants. During the first 30 years of the
State's existence, the conurbation's population grew
by a factor of three; the growth rate since the mid
1950s has been relatively slow in contrast to the
first years of statehood when thousands of immigrants
settled in Tel Aviv and its surroundings. Table 5.2
indicates the extent of population growth in the
conurbation during this period.

Table 5.2: Population in Towns and Urban Settlements
Around Tel Aviv 1948 - 1981

Town or Urban Settlements	1948	1961	1967	1981
Tel Aviv	248,000	386,070	388,000	357,700
Ramat Gan	17,160	90,840	106,800	120,200
Holon	9,560	48,970	75,900	110,300
Bene Beraq	9,300	46,980	64,700	81,500
Bat Yam	2,330	31,960	62,000	114,000
Givatayim	9,630	30,930	40,900	49,900
Yehud	--	6,950	8,100	9,750
Others	2,640	7,810	9,100	10,250

In 1948, the conurbation's inhabitants comprised 34%

of the entire population of Israel. This proportion
has gradually decreased since the 1950s, reading 24%
in 1981. The redistribution of Israel's population
throughout the country has occurred for a number of
reasons. The government's policy to redistribute the
population has led to the development of settlements
and new towns in every region wherein many immigrants have been settled since the beginning of
Statehood. The lack of much vacant land in the conurbation has limited the potential for further construction to accomodate additional residents. The
high cost of housing, as a result, discourages newcomers and forces young adults to seek residence
elsewhere. In real terms, however, the population
is continuing to grow, particularly in the outer
areas of the conurbation.
     Even within the conurbation, there have been
changes in the population proportions of the settlement rings. At the beginning of statehood, 80% of
Tel Aviv's inhabitants lived in the core, but by
1981, only 38.5% did so. The inner ring, surrounding the core, correspondingly increased from 14% of
the population in 1948 to 48% in 1981. These figures seem to indicate that a state of equilibrium
is developing in the conurbation's population distribution. The middle and outer rings have also experienced increase; instead of 12.5% of the population in 1948, 30% resided in those areas in 1981. An
examination of geographical divisions shows a change
in the southern area from 4% in 1948 to 25% in 1981,
and in the east, from 12% in 1948 to 30% in 1981.
A correlation of Tel Aviv's population to distribution over the city's area reveals, as of 1965,
that 47.2% of the population, 185,000 inhabitants,
occupied 24.7% of the land area of central Tel Aviv;
27.2% of Jaffa's and the southern regions' population, 170,000 people, lived on 19.3% of the total
land area, in contrast to the area beyond the
Yarqon River where only 8.6% of the inhabitants
(34,000) lived on approximately 41.3% of the land
area.
     The rate of population growth in the conurba-
tion occurred in waves. During the first twenty
years of statehood, the most rapid development
progressed in the inner ring; in much the same that
urban growth expanded and spilled over from the core
to the inner ring, of current growth patterns continue, the continuous expansion of the built-up environment is likely to extend into the middle ring,
and perhaps the outer ring as well. 50% of the current population growth derives from natural increase,

70

while 25-40% is due to migration within Israel. The
municipality of Tel Aviv has experienced a real decrease in population, as birth rates and the settlement of immigrants is low in the conurbation core,
while death rates are high, indicating the aging of
the area's population. Few potential residents can
afford the high land and housing costs in the central area; rather, newcomers are attracted to the
less expensive and more attractive residential
neighbourhoods of the surrounding rings. Particularly for those seeking their initial settlement area,
whether they originate from the conurbation core or
other areas of the country, the outer regions of the
Tel Aviv metropolitan area offer the most promising
opportunities; such first-time house buyers buy in
the outer ring at a rate three to four times that of
the inner ring.

LAND USE IN TEL AVIV

The most intensively built area of Tel Aviv is found
along the strip extending from Bat Yam in the south
to the Yarqon River in the north, between the coast
on the west and the Ayalon River in the east; the
highest residential density is located within this
urban core. Beyond the Yarqon and Ayalon Rivers,
most of the residential areas are suburban in nature;
the majority of public facilities, open spaces and
utilities are located in the suburban region serving
the entire conurbation. These include the Yarqon
River Park, the exhibition grounds, Tel Aviv University and museums.
    The main streets of the city function as demar-
cations separating commercial, residential and industrial zones. Along the Petah Tiqva Road is the
main industrial zone, a strip running parallel to
the Ayalon River, stretching from the center of Jaffa through the south of Tel Aviv to Nahlat Yitzhak
in the northeast. The industrial zone intersects
with Tel Aviv's central business district (CBD)
which lies to the west of the middle of the industrial strip.
    In the early 1960s, 60% of Tel Aviv's 9,000
factories were located in the main industrial strip,
employing 70% of the city's 5,000 industrial workers.
Most of the factories in the strip are small, each
with just a few employees. Originally, the first
enterprises of the zone dealt with products of daily
consumption and were therefore located so as to be
in close proximity with the central business dis-

trict. Later, as the industrial zone grew, it
expanded into the older residential neighbourhoods
in the south of Tel Aviv, near Jaffa. The small
houses of this area were highly appropriate for
small scale enterprise; due to the deterioration of
age, they were also less expensive to acquire and
taxed at a low rate.

Today, the poorer residential areas are located
in the older neighbourhoods near Jaffa, the better
neighbourhoods are found in the north part of Tel
Aviv where the structures are newer and of a higher
standard of construction. The bulk of residences
are to the northeast of the central business district; there are relatively few residents living in
the CBD itself. Whereas the CBD developed gradually
over a small geographical area in the older part of
the city, residential areas rapidly expanded northwards in response to the high demand for quality
housing, particularly as a result of the influx of
immigrants into Tel Aviv. The sand dunes of the
areas to the north of the city center provided less
expensive land on which such housing could be built.

The Tel Aviv central business district has been
the most stable zone, remaining situated in the
older area of the city. The CBD generally overlaps
with the original section of Tel Aviv, Ahuzat Bayit,
the first suburb built on the outskirts of Jaffa.
The area developed without spatial planning and only
15% of its buildings were constructed for commercial
purposes. Many residential buildings have been altered for commercial purposes. The CBD covers an
area of approximately 1,200 acres, and is bounded
by the following main streets: Herzl, Nahlat Binya-
min, Allenby, Yavne, Yehuda HaLevy, Lillienblum,
Ahad Ha'am and Montefiore. The intensity of land
use decreases towards the northeast and east of the
CBD; the industrial zone is located to the south and
southeast, within the CBD, there is a concentration
of banking, insurance and investment companies,
accounting offices, and entertainment facilities, at
a proportion 25% higher than other types of businesses.

There are other aspects peculiar to Tel Aviv's
development that must be viewed critically from a
planning and geographical perspective. A most obvious phenomenon is the weak relationship of the
city to its coastline. Tel Aviv started as a residential suburb of Jaffa and developed its economic
base through ties with Jaffa and inland settlements.
It established a port only when necessity demanded
one due to the unavailability to Jaffa's and even

72

then insufficient expansion area and access were provided so that the port could not fully develop; today Tel Aviv utilizes the ports at Ashdod and Haifa.
Nor did Tel Aviv build in relation to the coastline,
but rather followed inland geographical features and
major travel arteries. Tel Aviv is not served efficiently by railroad service; though it serves as the
center for traffic from Jerusalem, there is no rail
connection between the southern train station, serving Jerusalem and the south, and the northern station, from which trains run northward to Netanya,
Haifa and Nahariyya. The city also lacks an adequate local airport, to serve intranational air travel without causing adverse impacts to residential
neighbourhoods. Nor has sufficient land area been
allocated for public works projects within the city,
forcing the municipalities to seek tracts of land
beyond the borders of the conurbation for large-
scale public facilities.
     Tel Aviv has other disadvantages as well: an
 uncomfortable climate in summer, poor accessibility
to water sources, a disrupted landscape with little
remaining natural vegetation, a coastline of little
usefulness due to pollution of the water and beach,
and few attractive architectural elements, yet Tel
Aviv is the core of a conurbation with the highest
population concentration in Israel as a result of
its primary advantage - a location in the center of
the country and in the middle of the coastal plain.
As the center of economic social and cultural activities in the country, Tel Aviv has, throughout its
history through to the present time, continued to
hold a magnetic pull, attracting further population
and business to its environs. With the current rate
of urban development in the coastal plain, Tel Aviv
is becoming the center of an urban agglomeration
stretching from Netanya in the north to Holon in the
south, as the number of commuters from outlying suburbs to employment centers is increasing. It remains
questionable whether government policy, to establish
development towns and disperse population concentrations throughout the country, will dissuade the
growth of the Tel Aviv conurbation.
     In summary, it can be stated that the Tel Aviv
conurbation has developed similarly to conurbations
in other parts of the world. Tel Aviv began from a
small settlement. Functioning as a gateway to the
country, thousands of arriving immigrants remained
to settle in the city. This created a need for
rapid housing construction and gave impetus to commercial and industrial development. Real estate

speculation occurred as urban development accelerated. The city shape sprawled, and stretched along primary transportation arteries; construction spilled over from the core into suburban regions, and surrounding agricultural land became urbanized. This growth pattern exhibits features typical to conurbation development.

NOTES

1. 'Rama' in Hebrew means 'height', and 'Giva' means 'hill'.

2. The second wave of Jewish immigrants to the Land of Israel, which took place between 1904-1914. This wave included 35,000-40,000 Jews who came from Russia.

3. The fifth wave of Jewish immigrants to the Land of Israel, which took place between 1932-1940. Most of the Jews came then from Germany after the rise of the Nazi regime. This immigration brought a prosperity to the economic life of the country.

Chapter Six

HAIFA - THE HARBOUR, TOWN AND SUBURBS

Haifa is a harbour town; any analysis of Haifa
should therefore focus on the development of the
harbour and its relationship to the growth of the
town.

NATURAL GEOGRAPHY OF HAIFA

There are few places along Israel's Mediterranean
coast which are suitable for the development of a
harbour and an adjacent town. The sheltered bays at
Haifa and, to a lesser extent, Jaffa are the only
ones of sufficient size to accomodate a modern harbour, exceptions in an otherwise rather smooth
coastline. From Atlit, just south of Haifa, the
coast begins a gentle southward curve and the sea-
shore gradually broadens, narrow in the center of
the Coastal Plain, a wide belt along the Negev
Coast; moving sand dunes lie along much of this
section. North of Atlit, the coastline has re-
treated to the east, beyond the line of the western
most sandstone ridge, leaving indentations of which
Haifa Bay is the most significant. The continental
shelf along the southern coast is quite shallow,
extending seawards for a number of miles; in the
north the shelf narrows and increases in depth. The
600 ft (200 meter) isobath (water depth line) at the
edge of the continental shelf is located 15 miles
(25 kms) off the coast at Ashqelon, 11 miles (18 kms)
from Jaffa, 7.5 miles (12 kms) from Mt. Carmel and
only 3 miles (5 kms) from Rosh Haniqra on the
Israeli-Lebanese border. The slope of the continental shelf, therefore declines gradually from the
southern shoreline, more steeply in the north, resulting in shallow waters along the southern coast
and greater depths along the northern coast. For

the flat-bottomed boats of the past millenia, a
depth of less than three feet was sufficient; to
establish a port, shallow water was even a necessity, in order to construct jetties in accordance
with the skills of the time. The shallow coastal
waters were, therefore, of benefit in the construction of the ancient ports that were spaced along
Israel's seacoast. Modern vessels, however, require
deep water harbours which has led to the obsoles-
cence of the old shallow ports. The water of Haifa
Bay is deep, allowing modern ships to dock close to
shore. This was a primary reason in choosing Haifa
for the construction of a harbour in this century.

Haifa Bay is approximately 7.5 miles (12 kms)
in length and 1.25 miles (2 kms) wide. The bay extends from the cape of Mt. Carmel on the west to
Acre on the east. Near Mt. Carmel, in the southwest
of the bay, the water is 30-36 ft (10-12 meters) in
depth, sufficient for modern shipping vessels. Between Mr. Carmel and Acre begins the Zebulun Valley;
It is the westernmost link in the chain of valleys
separating Galilee from Samaria,has been drained
from a large swamp area in the 1930s, its been separated from the neighbouring Jezreel Valley by the
Shefar'am Hills.(1)Two main streams, the Qishon and
Na'aman, run through the valley to the sea just west
of the center of the bay. As this is a submerged
area of the coast, sand bars would often block the
streams from reaching the sea, in the past, causing
the creation of a swamp adjacent to the bay; during
times of stormy weather, sea water would be driven
into the swamps. This area was therefore unsuitable
for the development of a port, settlement, or extensive agriculture.

Geologically the Zebulun Valley is a rift valley which subsided as the Mt. Carmel block ascended
alongside its southern edge. Mt. Carmel stands out
in the northwest-southeast direction of the fault
lines, in contrast to the north-south alignment of
the sandstone ridges that parallel to the coast. The
sea, being pushed back from the Carmel cape, invaded
the area further north and created a bay - the Haifa
Bay - in the forward areas of the subsided valley.

HISTORY OF DEVELOPMENT AT HAIFA BAY

Until the present century, Haifa was never more than
a small village. Rather, Acre was the primary town
of the bay. The shallow water, along the tiny peninsula on which Acre is situated, was suitable for

the construction of a port during the past centuries
when it would not have been possible in the deep
waters near Mount Carmel. The primary economic basis for Acre, as for other port towns, was trade,
both maritime and land based.

Though founded prior to the common era, Acre
was nearly always secondary in status to Jaffa, as
well as to the port towns beyond Israel's borders.
Its port, in the shallow water on the east side of
the town, was less satisfactory, protected only from
stormwinds coming from the northwest, while vulnerable to those coming from other directions. It held
a minimal role as a trade center and gateway for its
immediate hinterland. Rather, it dealt more with
goods from other Mediterranean ports, such as Venice,
Genoa and Marseilles, because it served as a transfer point for trade between Europe and the East;
European products travelled by ship to Acre where
they transfered to overland caravans enroute to
Arabia, India and beyond. Only with the completion
of the Suez Canal in the later 1880s did sea travel
become possible for the entire trop, without sailing
around the Cape of Africa. As such, Acre remained a
significant port until near the end of the Ottoman
Empire. It thrived during Greek and Roman times,
became the principal port of the Crusaders, and was
revitalized by the Turks in the 17th and 18th centuries. In the 19th and early 20th centuries, however,
it declined due to neglect, as the Ottoman Empire
disintegrated.

Though minor sporadic settlement occurred in
the Haifa area before the common era, the name Haifa
did not appear until Roman times, when a small Jewish settlement and Roman fortress existed at the
city's current site. The Crusaders conquered the
settlement in 1100, after an obstinate defence by
its Moslem and Jewish citizens. Haifa fell to Sal-
addin in 1187, returned briefly to Crusader rule
under Louis IX of France between 1250 and 1265, and
was destroyed by the Mamelukes.   Mt. Carmel was
esteemed as a holy place primarily by Christian
groups. Though Eliyah's cave is located on the
mountain, it did not hold sufficient status to attract either Jewish or Moslem religious settlement;
the Bahai faith, however, chose Haifa as its center,
within the last century. The Carmelites, a Christian order founded during the 12th Century, established a monastary on Mt. Carmel in the 17th Century.
By this time, Haifa was not more than a squalid
fishing hamlet near the Carmel Cape. In the 18th
Century, it was raised by Governor Daher el Amr. He

immediately rebuilt it further east, but even then,
however, he hardly improved its economic position.
Only in the middle of the 19th Century did it begin
to grow slowly, numbering 2,000 inhabitants in 1854,
among the Jews, most of whom originated from Morocco.

In 1869, the German Templars, a Protestant
group, established a colony on the Mt. Carmel slope.
Haifa attracted them with its mild climate, seafront
location, and beautiful mountain and valley land-
scapes. Their choice of a site for the colony was
limited primarily to the lower slopes of Mt. Carmel
as the swamps of the Zebulun Valley and the steep
inclines of much of Mt. Carmel were uninhabitable.
The Templars brought with them a European urban
orientation; their technical and cultural knowledge
enabled them to develop a highly successful urban
settlement and influenced the modernization of Haifa.
The Templars continued to function as an active community until World War II when they were expelled by
the British. The Templar colony was designed by the
architect Jacob Shoumacher. The settlement expanded
so that by the beginning of World War I, it encom-
passed a quarter of Haifa's area. It was noted for
its beautiful layout and cleanliness. The Templars
built and paved many new roads, including the main
road leading to the upper part of Mt. Carmel today,
Rothchild Avenue, and the road to Stella Maris,
part of the Carmelite facilities on the mountain,
both connecting Mt. Carmel with the central port-
area settlement.

In response to the increasing number of Christian pilgrims arriving in Haifa Bay to visit the Holy
Land, the Templars constructed a road from Haifa to
Nazareth, in which is located the Basilica of Annun-
ciation, one of the Christendom's most important
sites, among others in the town. From Nazareth, the
road continues to Tiberias, allowing pilgrims to
more easily visit holy places around Lake Kinneret
(Sea of Galilee). The improved roads enabled vehicular transportation from Haifa to the inland
towns, encouraging higher levels of goods transport
and trade. The Templars developed perhaps the just
tourist industry in the country, providing rental
accomodations in Haifa, and goods and services required by visiting pilgrims.

The Templars were active in establishing agriculture and industry as well in Haifa. Among other
crops, they planted groves of olive trees along the
terraces of the Mt. Carmel slopes. As a result,
they were able to produce oil and soaps; their first
oil factory, constructed in Haifa at the end of the

19th Century, was the forerunner of the Shemen Company operating today. The Nesher Cement Works and other industries also started under Templar involvement. The Templar influence on Haifa's urban development was greater than their numerical proportion within the town's population. The well-designed neighbourhoods of the colony and the opportunities for employment and trade, due to the industrial, commercial and agricultural development of the Templars, attracted new residents to Haifa.

A number of events boosted Haifa's development during the latter part of the 19th and early 20th Centuries. The appearance of steamships was a boom for Haifa as Acre harbour was too shallow for their use. The French were among the first to transfer to Haifa's deep water port, and the Turks built a small jetty there in 1870 to meet the port needs. The prices of port services in Haifa were lowered to lure other maritime traffic as well away from Acre and diminish the latter's importance.

The Ottoman Empire was also responsible for constructing in 1905 the Hijaz-Jizdraelon Valley Railway running from Haifa to Damascus, and continuing to Mecca. This railway line was, of course, of great significance to Muslim pilgrims, and it gave impetus to Haifa's growth. The construction of the railway line required many workers; Haifa served as a development center for the railway and it therefore attracted Arab laborers in Israel and neighbouring countries to relocate in the city to take advantage of the job opportunities offered there. The workers established their homes near the harbour, building generally poor quality houses and shacks, in the areas known today as Wadi Saleeb, Wadi Roshmiya and Wadi Nissnas, extending eastwards from the old central part of Haifa. This began the concentration of the Arab population which exists to this day in the city. When completed, the railroad established Haifa as an important export harbour in the eastern Mediterranean, to which goods arrived from throughout the large hinterland serviced by the railroad. The railroad established not only its station close to the harbour, but also the center for locomotive and wagon railroad carriage repair. The proximity of the railroad encouraged the development of the new factories as well in Haifa, as the railroad provided the transportation of materials and products necessary for industrial operations.

Between the years 1907-1909, the jetty in Haifa's harbour was extended to an approximate length of 1200-1500ft (400-500 meters), in response to the

increasing numbers of ships docking at the port.
Pilgrims comprised much of this traffic; the services they required stimulated employment opportunities in the town, and some of the arrivals added
themselves to the resident population. By this time,
the Turks had recognized the potential of Haifa,
which influenced their activities - though limited -
in further developing the harbour and town, to the
disbenefit of Acre.

The main development of Haifa, and the decline
of Acre occurred during the period of the British
Mandate, especially in the 1920s and 1930s. The
British recognized Haifa's strategic location as a
primary Mediterranean port for the vast hinterland
of the Middle Eastern countries. This was reflected
in the Sykes-Picot Agreement, signed in 1916 during
World War I, as the Ottoman Empire fell; Britain and
France agreed to divide the region into two spheres
of influence, the French in the north, and British
involvement in the south, including the Land of
Israel. England's sphere extended to both Haifa and
the Suez Canal, by which the British hoped to
strengthen their position throughout the entire
Middle East. Their recognition of the importance of
these facilities reflects the centuries of British
maritime experience. Acre was seen to be inadequate
for the construction of a modern harbour, not only
due to its shallow port, but also because its densely built peninsula, including historical and religious buildings, extremely limited the land area
available for the construction of harbour service
facilities and related commercial and industrial
structures. Haifa offered plentiful land area and,
particularly due to its access to the railways,
including the Haifa-Lod-Egypt line built in 1919,
permitted connectors to Syria, Jordan, Iraq and
Saudi-Arabia through the Jezreel and Bet Shean Valleys and to Egypt. Access to such areas as the
Hauran region in Syria and the inland valleys of
Israel, all major agricultural zones, made Haifa a
primary port for agricultural exports.

In the 1930s, the British began projects to
improve and enlarge Haifa's harbour. It is interesting to note that Tel Aviv - 20 years old and a much
larger town - was not considered for such a harbour,
due to Haifa's superior geographical location and
bay. Among the first projects were the construction
of a breakwater in Haifa Bay and the commencement of
Harbour construction, including land reclamation
from the sea, in the bay's southwest corner. A large
new port was completed in 1934. Between 1936-39,

the Kirkuk (Iraq) - Haifa oil pipeline was laid,
followed by the construction of the Haifa Oil Refineries, adding the role of oil exportation to Haifa's port services. The British also developed the
coastline along the bay, providing warehouses and
tank farms, further establishing industrial areas
with railroad access, and stimulating the development of a central business district near the harbour
offering commercial and financial services, particularly those associated with port activities. Haifa
was thereby established as the country's primary
harbour.

JEWISH POPULATION GROWTH IN HAIFA

By 1870, just following the founding of the Templar
colony, Haifa's population had grown to about 3,000
inhabitants; of this only an eighth was Jewish, most
of Eastern (Sephardic) origin such as from Turkey
and North Africa. Though Theodore Herzl noted
Haifa's potential when visiting in 1899, the First
and Second Aliyah (2), comprised of Eastern European
Jews, had only minor impact on the town's population
growth. In 1900, there were 1,500 Jews in Haifa,
and this increased to approximately 3,000 just prior
to World War I. The population growth of Haifa between 1868 and 1914 is shown in Table 6.1.

Table 6.1: Population of Haifa 1868-1914

Year	Population
1868	3,500-4,000
1882	5,000-6,000
1886	7,500
1890	8,500
1902	11,000-12,000
1905	15,000
1909	18,000
1911	20,000
1914	22,000-23,000

Following World War I, however, with the beginning

of British Rule and the active development of the
Haifa harbour, Jewish settlement in Haifa increased
markedly, from the period of the Third Aliyah (3)
onwards. Many Jewish immigrants coming especially
from Central Europe in the 1920s, 1930s and, to a
lesser extent 1940s, arrived by ship at the port,
and then decided to remain in the town. In 1931,
there were 5,000 Jews in Haifa, and by the establishment of the State, the Jewish population total-
ed 70,000 out of Haifa's 140,000 residents.

THE DEVELOPMENT OF HAIFA'S URBAN LAYOUT

Haifa's distinctive topography resulted in the unusual form of the city. Mt. Carmel forms the back-
drop to the harbour area. Much of its slope is
steep, prohibiting a uniform spread of urban growth
from the original town center, as has so often been
the case with town development in level surroundings. Continuous construction was not possible due
to the topography; rather, development occured along
three main tiers. The first tier is the original
central area built along the bay; the second tier,
the Hadar HaCarmel, is located between 148-540 ft
(60 and 180 meters) up the slope of Mt. Carmel, and
the third tier, the Carmel district, is located on
the top of the mountain, 540-750 ft (180 to 250
meters) above the Hadar level. During the past
years, as the more level areas of the tiers have
developed, building has extended to the steeper
slopes, gradually infilling within the areas between
the tiers, though much open space still separates
them today. Construction has adapted to the topography; terraced housing and winding streets typical-
ly climb the mountain. Because of the separation
between the tiers, each has developed its own central business district (CBD) and urban structure.
(Figure 6.1)
     The rapidly developing industries east of the
harbour, more developed than those in Tel Aviv in
the 1920s and 1930s offered work opportunities for
the arriving Jewish immigrants. Many settled in the
original city area, and working class housing quickly surrounded the up-slope side of the harbour-level
CBD. New housing was later initiated to either side
of the harbour area, including the construction of
Bat Gallim, Neve Sha'anan and other residential
zones.
     Already before World War I, Jews began to ac-
quire land on the Carmel slope. In 1920, Hadar Ha-

Figure 6.1: The Central Business Districts of Haifa

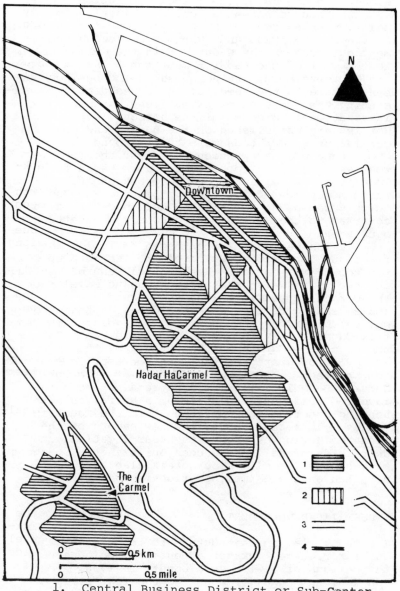

1. Central Business District or Sub-Center.
2. Transition Zone between Centers. 3. Road
4. Railway Line.

Carmel was founded on the broad level step above the
harbour area. A site was determined for the Tech-
nion(4) in the Hadar tier; the institution opened in
1925 and became a central cultural institution in
Haifa, much as did the Herzliyya Gymnasium in Tel
Aviv. In the 1920s and 1930s, much Jewish settlement occurred in the Hadar and in the German Colony
to the west of the Hadar. Near the Technion, a second CBD developed, including shops and business or-
iented more to the needs of Haifa residents, complementing the focus on port services, national and
international commerce of the harbour level CBD.
Hotels were established on the Hadar, and new residential neighbourhoods were built around the new
CBD. Land prices, particularly near the Technion,
rose as development progressed. Jews began to buy
land from the Templars, who were anxious to sell to
raise money needed for their expenses. The Hadar
quickly became an established Jewish district in
contrast to the more heterogeneously populated harbour area.

Jewish settlement then began to follow the
roads and former properties of the Templars up to
the top of Mt. Carmel. Residential suburbs, including exclusive neighbourhoods, began to develop on
the Carmel, spreading along the mountain's main axis
and extending to its western ridges. A third com-
merical district, though smaller, developed in Central Carmel, serving the Carmel residents. Development of the Carmel was encouraged by the relatively level topography of the mountain top, in contrast
to the steep slopes that separated it from the
Hadar HaCarmel tier. The area remains among the
favoured residential districts in Haifa, as new
housing construction continues onto the mountain
ridges. In recent years, the new campus of the
Technion,having outgrown its Hadar location, and the
University of Haifa have been built in the southeast
part of the Carmel. Fine hotels also have been constructed on the Carmel, overlooking the bay.

INDUSTRIAL DEVELOPMENT

The industrial infrastructure to the east of the
harbour received further attention simultaneous to
the periods of Jewish settlement. In 1928, the Jewish National Fund (5) acquired the flat strip of
land adjoining the bay shore almost to Acre permit-
ing the allocation of areas to different functional
tasks. The southern sector, near the mouth of the

84

Qishon Stream, was earmarked for small, medium and large industry, as it is nearest to the city and to the port, which was then about to be built, and could be most easily linked by branch lines to the railway. The oil harbour was built there in the years before the Second World War. Between 1952 and 1956, the Qishon harbour was built to serve Israel's high-sea fishing fleet. It also contains a floating dock for ship repairs, and ship construction wharfs. Inside the industrial zone, most factories giving off obnoxious fumes (oil refineries chemicals and phospates, cement works, etc.) were placed furthest from the city to the east, where they were the last in the chain of dominant wind direction. The swamps in the Zebulun Valley had to be drained, of course, before industrial development could take place in the area. Industry in the Haifa-Acre region has continued to expand, particularly in the Acre Steel City area south of Acre, and much land is available for the future growth.

THE QUERAYOT (6)

North of Haifa's industrial zone, a series of
Querayot - small residential urban communities -
were established in the 1930s, including Quiryat
Hayyim, Quiryat Motzkin, Quiryat Bialik and Quiryat
Yam, among others. They were originally comprised
mainly of small single family homes, nearest to
house industrial workers. In later years, the housing density increased, as many of the small houses
were replaced by apartment buildings and residents
found employment in Haifa proper and Querayot as
well. These Querayot have steadily developed distinctive status from the City of Haifa, though some
remain within the municipal boundary.

SOCIALIST LEADERSHIP

The organization of the land strip along the bay,
including the industrial zone, was perhaps the first
comprehensive planning step to be taken in Haifa's
development. Throughout most of the city's growth,
until recent times, planning has remained on a loc-
alized scale. Haifa is the only town in Israel for
which its leadership maintained an adherence to
Zionist pioneering and socialist ideals - in the
context of an urban framework. They attempted to
make Haifa a semi-kibbutz (7), semi-town, by focus-

ing on neighbourhood units. Shopping and cultural
facilities, Histadrut (8) branches and labour com-
mittees were all established on a neighbourhood
basis; each neighbourhood had its political committee responsible for directing local functions. Even
the school system was for many years run by the
Socialist Movement. The institutional similarity of
the neighbourhoods, primarily in the Hadar HaCarmel
and Querayot, to the kibbutzim was quite apparent;
for example, the role of residents in promoting and
participating in cultural activities parallels that
of the kibbutz members.This organization was a sig-
nigicant factor in encouraging the decentralized
structure of the city, rather than focusing on a
single CBD. Support for such a political organization was clearly based on the labour element in
the population, engaged in harbour and industrial
jobs. Even with a changing population, with a higher proportion of professional and business people
today than in the past, Haifa maintains a reputation
as the red city. The labour influence of today may
be considered somewhat artificial, as the municipal
boundaries include some of the labour-oriented
Querayot, such as Quiryat Hayyim which are struct-
urely, locationally, and in some ways, socially
apart from Haifa proper, in contrast to neighbourhoods such as those on the Carmel.

THE OUTLYING SUBURBS AND CONURBATION

In the past couple of decades, suburban development
has established the Haifa region as a conurbation,
much like the Tel Aviv conurbation though on a
smaller scale. The area of the conurbation is approximately 16,800 hectars in contrast to the 5,100
hectars within the Haifa municipal coundaries. The
conurbation extends along the coast from Mt. Carmel
to Acre, includes the Zebulun Valley and reaches
into the Alonim hills in the northeast and to the
southern side of Mt. Carmel. The development of new
communities and urbanization of rural settlements
has enlarged the population within Haifa's sphere,
many of whom commute to Haifa's employment districts.
Beyond central Haifa, both an inner and outer ring
of settlements can be distinguished. The Querayot
along the Haifa Bay, Quiryat Ata and the other eastern suburbs and the Carmel Coast region south of
Haifa, including Tirat Karmel, comprise the inner
ring. The outer ring includes settlements such as
Quiryat Tivon in the Tivon Hills.These rings are not

continuous as elements of the uneven topography such as Mt. Carmel break up the pattern; agricultural areas are also interspersed within the conurbation, particularly in the east and along the Carmel coast. Whereas additional development possibilities in the central core of Haifa are limited, only the Querayot and the Carmel residential areas have growth potential, without having to disrupt and redevelop existing urban districts, future expansion is expected to occur in the outer areas of the conurbation, particularly due to the favourability of such factors as development cost, the quality of the suburban environment, and commuting access to the central core.

POPULATION DISTRIBUTION

The population of the Haifa conurbation exceeds 300,000 inhabitants, with approximately 225,000 residing within the municipal boundaries and 100,000 in the surrounding rings. The central lower tier of Haifa contains about 25% of the municipal population, an equal number are residents of those Querayot which are part of the municipality, and another quarter of the population resides in the eastern flanks of the town along the sides of the Giborim Wadi. The Western section of Haifa, including the Carmel, comprise about 10% of the population and the remainder live in Hadar HaCarmel.
    Haifa has, however, lagged behind Tel Aviv in population growth, as shown in Table 6.2

Table 6.2: Increase of Haifa's Population Against the Population of Tel Aviv

Year	Haifa	Tel Aviv
1948	98,600	248,300
1949	121,000	311,000
1950	140,000	335,000
1955	158,000	359,000
1961	183,000	386,000
1967	209,000	388,000
1974	225,000	357,700
1981	227,400	329,500

The latter's central location in the coastal plain, proximity to the major transportation means and routes, and its role as the economic and cultural center of Israel, has continually stimulated further expansion. Haifa lost most of its hinterland behind hostile borders with the founding of the State in 1948. Located to the north, apart from the coastal plain, and with government attention focused on development towns. Haifa even declined in influence during the first years of statehood. Haifa, however, remains one of Israel's major ports, though the completion of a Mediterranean port at Ashdod in 1965 has detracted from Haifa's role, and the site of important industries and institutions. Though it will likely to continue to be second in status to Tel Aviv, it is expected that Haifa's population and conurbation will steadily increase, particularly with government objectives to stimulate development in the north, especially in the Galilee, for which Haifa will be the nearest major city, identifying the city as one of Israel's primary urban centers in the future as well as today.

NOTES

1.   Y. Shattner, Haifa: A Study in the Relation of City and Coast (Israel Exploration Journal, Vol.4, 1, 1954), pp.26-46.
2.   The first wave of Jewish immigration to the Land of Israel took place between 1882-1904, during which about 25,000 came from Russia, Rumania, and Yemen. The second wave of immigration took place between 1904-1911, during which 35,000-40,000 Jews came mostly from Russia.
3.   The third wave of Jewish immigration to the Land of Israel took place between 1920-1924, during which about 32,000 Jews came from Central Europe.
4.   The Israel Institute of Technology, located on Mt. Carmel in Haifa.
5.   A Jewish and Zionist organization founded by Prof. Z.H. Shapiro in 1901 with the aim to buy land in Palestine for Jewish colonization, and to reclaim land for potential agricultural settlement.
6.   Quirya (pl.Querayot) is a term in Hebrew which indicates a satellite neighbourhood. The general term Querayot is directed to the urban satellites in the Haifa Bay.
7.   Semi-urbanized town within cooperative and socialist elements in it.
8.   The Federation of Labour in Israel.

Chapter Seven

OLD TOWNS

There are many old towns in Israel which today fun-
tion within an independent framework. In the past
there was a vast number of these towns in Israel but
most of them were totally destroyed, a part remained
as little villages or only as archaeological and
historical remnants, while another part still functions as an old nucleus in the CBD of new and modern towns. If we exclude from the list of existing
ancient towns the capital Jerusalem, which was discussed above, Jaffa which was included in the conurbation of Tel Aviv and the Arab towns of Judea and
Samaria and the Gaza Strip, which will be discussed
later on, only the towns of Safed, Tiberias and Acre
remain.

SAFED

Of all the ancient urban settlements which once existed in the mountainous Galilee, only Safed functions as a town today. In contrast to other towns,
there were good reasons for Safed's perpetual existence for hundreds of years and therefore Jewish
population lived there continuously throughout all
time periods.

LOCATION AND TOPOGRAPHY

Safed is located in the southeast corner of the upper Galilee and is the second oldest mountainous
Jewish town after Jerusalem. The town is located
2,500 ft. (834 meters) above sea level and its surrounding mountains are even higher: Mt. Biriya in
the north 5,865 ft (1,955 meters) and Mt. Kena'an
in the east 5,808 ft. (1,936 meters). The hills on

which Safed was built are bordered by two Wadis.
Wadi Akbarah and Wadi Biriya which create steep
flanks. Actually the town extends on one prominent
hill which is the location of the main developed
area, and on Mt. Kena'an to the east which is connected to the former hill by a narrow saddle 2,300
ft. (766 meters) high. This saddle is the gateway
to the town and from it roads branch out to all
parts of Safed itself, and even to the towns of Tiberias and Acre. Safed, on its narrow hill is about
1.8 miles (3 kms.) long and not more than 3,900 ft.
(1,300 wide, one of the smallest towns in its area
in the country. Her highest point, 2,500 ft. (834
meters) is at the Crusaders' Castle in the north.

The towns's topography is highly dissected with
steep slopes of a 20% to 40% gradient which does not
permit building to be done on flat land tracts. Mt.
Kena'an on the other side, has level slopes of not
more than a 10% gradient which facilitate construction. The hill of Safed contains an area of 315
hectar of which only a third of that area is suitable for building purposes, while two-thirds of Mt.
Kena'an's 600 hectar area are appropriate for construction. (Figure 7.1)

Safed has a pleasant climate, especially in the
summers which attracts people to come for recreation
purposes. In the winter its climate is quite severe.
The temperatures of Mt. Kena'an for instance are be-
tween 4°C to 9.8°C (39.2°F to 50°F) as contrasted to
June's temperatures which are between 18.4°C and
28.9°C (65° to 84° F).

THE HISTORY OF THE TOWN

Safed is known as one of the Four Countries, those
towns holy to the Jews throughout many years. The
town became a place of inspiration and attraction
for Jews all over the world and many of them came to
settle there together with the wise and learned men
of the Kabbala (1). The historical and cultural
value of Safed is quite significant for the Jews in
the Land of Israel and the diaspora.

Until the Crusaders' period Safed was a very
small village. The Crusaders chose to settle there
and make it a center in the Galilee due to its proximity to the Acre - Damascus road and therefore they
built a large castle there which guarded this axis.
This fortress, constructed on an acre of approximately 40 hectar, was the largest one ever built in
Palestine and in it 2,000 soldiers were permanently

90

Figure 7.1: Safed-Main Land Uses

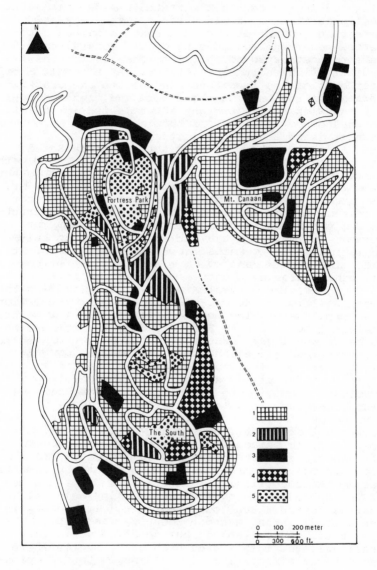

1. Residential Area   2. Commercial Zone
3. Institutions and Hotels
4. Industrial Zone   5. Public Open Space

encamped. In the 14th century, Safed was taken over by the Mamelukes who made it the capital of the Galilee and in the town concentrated a wide range of Muslim activities, administration, security and culture. During the Ottoman conquest relations with Europe were renewed and most of the coastal towns were reconstructed so that Acre then became the capital of the northern district. As a result Safed lost much of its importance and became the center of a small region. On the other hand, renewed relations with Europe brought about Jewish immigration to the country and many of them settled in Safed and rebuilt it as a Jewish spiritual center.

As stated above, Jewish settlement in Safed existed continuously throughout generations. During the Mameluke regime they were expelled from agriculture which brought an overconcentration of Jews in the town. The town's growth is also connected to the expulsion of the Jews from Spain which happened during the Mameluke period. Expecially during the Ottoman regime, from the 16th century onwards, Jews could immigrate to Palestine without difficulties. Thus, immigrants came to Safed from Turkey and from all other European countries that had expelled them. During that time Jerusalem was not in a strong economic position to absorb these Jews and its security conditions were quite poor, so Jewish immigrants preferred to settle in Safed. There they developed commerce and light industry, increased the towns' economic importance, and made it a center for weaving and dyeing. This occupational branch was quite convenient for the Jews because of the town's proportional proximity to the harbour of Acre and Sidon, and due to the nearby water sources which were needed for the operation of this industry. As is typical of mountainous towns which lack natural resources, this industry in Safed was based on specific skills and enterprise not connected to the local resources as the needed wool was imported from the Balkan countries.

In the middle of the 16th century Safed flourished as the spiritual center of the Jewish people. By the end of that century security was poor, the town's economy collapsed because of competition from European countries such as France and England, and even spiritual activity in Safed began to decline. The town suffered from natural disasters in the 17th Century and only in the 18th Century was immigration renewed when Jews from Central Europe came to Safed and developed an Ashkenazic (2) settlement there beside the previous existing Sephardic (3) settle-

ment. Immigration of Hassidim (4) from Europe
strengthened the town's numbers and quality of life,
but again natural disasters, diseases and plagues
continuously diminished Safed's achievements. At the
beginning of the 19th Century the town numbered 5,000
inhabitants and in 1839 after an earthquake and other
disturbances only 1,357 Jews were left.
   Since the beginning of the present century many
changes have occured in Safed: the Arab population
greatly increased thereby out numbering the Jews,
the Jewish population gradually decreased, and the
town lost its importance in Palestine. In 1922 Safed
numbered 8,760 inhabitants of which only 2,986 were
Jews, in 1931 - 9,440 inhabitants including 2,547
Jews, by the beginning of the 1940s only 2,114 Jews
lived there out of a population of 11,980. The rate
of Jews in the population, therefore, decreased from
34% to 17% in a time span of 20 years and with the
establishment of the State all the Arabs left Safed,
and only 1,600 Jews remained.

REGIONAL POSITION

Safed lost its regional position even during the time
of the British Mandate due to its diminishing zone
of influence which at one point, extended throughout
the Galilee into southern Lebanon. The international
border alignment between the Land of Israel and
Lebanon and the change which happened in the Arab
economy making it more autarchic diminished the relationship between the Arab villages and Safed. The
town was even more removed from the coastal plain
where vast economic activity was developing. Despite
the growth of the coastal plain's zones of influence,
Safed was still too distant from them and due to the
underdeveloped surroundings with difficult axes to
the town it faltered.
   Proportionately speaking, Safed was even remote from other Jewish settlements in the country
and security conditions for its inhabitants were
poor. The type of Jews that had settled in Safed
and their way of life was strange and unacceptable
to the immigrants who came to the Land of Israel
during the Mandate Period, so there was a separation
between the inhabitants of Safed and all the other
Jews of the country. Settlement development in the
Land of Israel can be distinguished by two main directions - on one side urban nodality as in the case
of Tel Aviv, Jerusalem and Haifa, and on the other
side vast agricultural development as in Kibbutzim,

etc. Safed did not fit into one of these directions or the other, and therefore was not part of any urban hierarchy in the entire settlement layout of the country.

Today, Safed has the status as the capital of a sub-district. The town provides a concentration of services for the Hula Valley and the upper eastern Galilee. Being located on the Acre-Rosh Pinna road and having a connection with Tel Aviv via domestic airlines gives the town some advantage, but overall it does not gain very much for these relationships so that its main economic functions still remain in the areas of tourism, recreation, education and health.

BUILDING

In the old part of Safed, which is the Old City, most of the houses are from the Ottoman period and were built 50 to 100 years ago. In the last ten years new building and reconstruction has taken place. Construction on the hill of Safed is concentrated along two main streets. Jerusalem Street is the CBD where most of the business and commerce is found. The streets in the ancient quarter are very narrow and winding without sidewalks. The street system itself was laid-out on mild slopes. In Safed few antiquities remain as an earthquake in 1837 totally destroyed the town which was later rebuilt. The old town today is a historical and architectural ensemble. Safed has special prominent features in the midst of its overall landscape as low storey, low density houses above which stands the Crusader's fortress and the forest surrounding it which can be seen in all directions.

POPULATION

Safed numbered 2,300 the year of the establishment of the State and the population grew as follows: (Table 7.1)

Table 7.1:   Increase of Population in Safed 1948-
1981

Year	Population
1948	2,317
1949	4,046
1951	7,000
1953	7,900
1955	8,500
1957	9,000
1959	10,300
1961	10,000
1967	13,000
1974	14,200
1981	16,500

If 35 years after the establishment of the State
and with the absorption of new immigrants the popu-
latin of Safed reached only 16,500 inhabitants, the
town's growth rate has not been very impressive and
its place in the urban hierarchy has been reduced.
A hundred years ago the town was in the 3rd or 4th
place of the hierarchy, in 1931 the 9th, in 1944 the
12th, in 1958 the 24th, and in 1981 the 26th position of the hierarchy. This decrease in the urban
hierarchy on the background of rapid urbanization
in Israel demonstrates a continuous population
withdrawal from the town. This phenomenon can be
viewed as part of an overall process in the decrease
of the population in mountainous towns since the beginning of the century, until the establishment of
the State and even sometime afterwards. Safed was
unable to strengthen its regional position on the
agricultural hinterland of the Moshavim and small
Kibbutzim. The conpetition of urban elements from
Tiberias and Qiryat Shemona hindered its economic
growth. It appears that mountainous towns which are
remote from the economic activity in the center of
the country lack dynamic development and attraction
power, and therefore are unable to compete with the
high urbanization in the coastal plain.
        Obviously, it can be said that Safed's site
is not suitable for a town due to its difficult physical conditions and limited area for housing. Services are costly to provide and living there in the

winter is unpleasant. All of these factors could be overcome if Safed had something outstanding attractiveness which would justify urbanization efforts. Safed's continuous existence is almost a national and historical order. The town is a source of spiritual inspiration along with being a place that people enjoy visiting. Therefore, it should be planned and developed on a physical and spiritual style, suitable for a town like Safed with cultural and recreational functions.

TIBERIAS

Like Safed, Tiberias is also known as one of the Four Countries together with Jerusalem and Hebron. Tiberias is characterized as being a historical town in the eastern part of the Land of Israel between mountain and sea. Its past is full of events and changes on the background of wars, destruction, and along with this, a continuous effort by the Jewish population to remain in this town.

THE GEOGRAPHICAL SITE OF THE TOWN

Tiberias is located on the western coast of Lake Kinneret halfway between the Jordan River's outlet to the Lake in the south and inlet from the north. Its location on the shoreline of Lake Kinneret was due to the natural attractiveness of this area to the people who settled there in the past. The surroundings of the sea were quite convenient for settlement as the climate is mild, an abundance of water exists and the lake contains a large amount of fish. In ancient times the Lake's coast was used as a transit area between the Jordan Valley in the south to the northern regions of the Land Of Israel and even the Via Maris past by there. It's no wonder that remnants of early man were discovered at Tel Obadiya and in the caves of Wadi Amood near the Kinneret. Many tels as Bet Yerah, Tel Raqat and Tel Kinarot demonstrate that dense settlement existed here in the past.

In the area surrounding Lake Kinneret intensive life existed in the past, especially during the Roman and Byzantine periods, due to an understanding of how to preserve fish by salting them with minerals from the Dead Sea, and because of their ability to grow vineyards on Basaltic soils. During those times many Jews lived in that area, a fact which brought Jesus to that region for his activities.

Most of the town of Tiberias is situated along the coast of an inner lake and on a main road which makes a semi-circle around the Kinneret from the west. The town is located on difficult topography and on the flanks of the northern Poriya Highlands. The topographical restrictions in the north, the antiquities of Hamat in the south and Raqat in the north prevented the town's sprawl along the coastline of the Kinneret. Therefore, construction had to be developed to suit the terraces of the basaltic slopes where the town was already located. Therefore, Tiberias of today is a town built-up on three different topographical tiers, similar to the town of Haifa. The downtown is located on the tier along the coast, the second one 0-390 ft. (130 meters), contains neighbourhood units built during the British Mandate, for instance Qiryat Shemuel, while the third tier, which is on flat, high topography at the elevation of 240-750 ft. (80-250 meters), is where upper Tiberias was developed after the establishment of the State. (Figure 7.2)

HISTORY

Tiberias, as stated above, is one of the most ancient towns in the Land of Israel. Its beginnings were as a Hellenistic town during the time of Herodotus Antipas 14 AD, not far from the ancient town of today and was named after Caesar Tiberius. The town was further developed due to political decisions to build a capital in the eastern Galilee across from the towns of Arbel and Migdal which were in the hands of the Kanaaim (5). A main road between Egypt and Syria helped to support the town which dominated the road to Jacob's Daughter's Bridge, Valley of Gennosar, Bet Yerah, and the road to the valleys in the south. The soil in the town's surroundings was not rich and no vast agricultural hinterland existed which could maintain Tiberias economically. The town was artifically populated, as the people who lived there were subsidized by not having to pay taxes, by receiving already built houses, and those who were wealthier, even received parcels of land. The hot springs used for medicinal purposes along with the abundance of fish in the lake added to the town's attractiveness. In the southern part of the town the Romans left a necropolis and therefore the Jews arriving afterwards built their town only towards

Figure 7.2: Tiberias - Main Land Uses

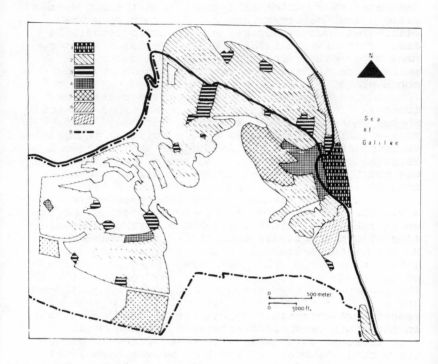

1. The Old City   2. Residential Area
3. Institutions   4. Commercial Zone
5. Industrial Zone   6. Recreation Area
7. Cemetery   8. Town Planning
   Boundary

the northeast and along both sides of the present
day Tiberias - Nazareth main road. After several
purifications were done by Simon Bar Yochai (6),
Jews were even permitted to settle in the southern
site. Tiberias became the burial center for Jews
all over the world after the destruction of Jerusalem. Coffins were brought there from Babylonia and
many other countries. Being a center for such a
purpose limited the amount of urban sprawl which
could occur.

In the second century Tiberias became a very
important Jewish center and the headquarters of the
Sanhedrian (7). In that town the Mishna (8) was
signed and it is also possibly the site of the gra-
ves of Rabbi Aqivah, Rabbi Yochanan Ben Zakai, and
Rabbi Meir Ba'al Ha Nes. For many years Tiberias
was the spiritual center for Jews both within the
country and those in the Diaspora.

During the Moslem rule, Lake Kinneret became
a winter residence for the kaliphs of Omaya. Later
on in the 12th Century the eastern part of the Galilee was the battlefield of the Crusaders and the
Moslems. The Crusaders erected a fortified town in
Tiberias, north of the Roman town which was destroyed in the famous battle of Qarney Hittim in 1187.
The remnants of the Crusader's town are actually the
known ancient town of Tiberias today. The town extends over 142 hectars as compared to the Roman town
in the south which once stretched 800 hectors.

During the Ottoman period, in 1560, an effort
was made to reconstruct the town and to base its
economy on the silk industry. As one of the holy
towns in the country, Tiberias attracted Jews. The
present town was built by Daher El Amar in 1740 who
was the governor of Acre. He built walls and towers
but in 1837, the town, along with Safed, suffered
from an earthquake and floods.

Throughout most time periods, life in Tiberias
was concentrated in the old town which was settled
by Arabs. In 1912, the first of the town's Jews
moved outside its walls, and only after World War I,
with the immigration of Jews from Iraq, were the
first neighbourhoods of Ahvah and Mymoniya erected.
Qiryat Shemuel was built in 1920 on the second topographical level, about 240 ft. (80 meters) above sea
level. This neighbourhood brought a change in the
trend of urban development in the town because from
its inception onwards a new Tiberias arose.

THE TOWN AFTER 1948

Until 1947 the town numbered about 11,300 inhabitants, half of which were Arabs. Most of them left
after the War of Independence and in their place,
in the downtown area, new immigrants arrived but,
due to a housing shortage it was difficult to settle
all of them. Most of the downtown area functioned
as a CBD which was destroyed during the war. Afterwards, business developed along the main street -
Nazareth Street which bypasses the old town from the
west. The building of new neighbourhoods was generated by the absorption of immigrants. Upper
Tiberias was built at an elevation of 1,200 ft. (400
meters) above Lake Kinneret's sea level, and despite
the town's topographical difficulties the downtown
area still remains the CBD.

The population growth of Tiberias has not been
very impressive (Table 7.2):

Table 7.2: The Population Growth of Tiberias 1948-
1981

Year	Population
1948	5,555
1950	12,000
1952	16,200
1954	16,500
1956	17,500
1958	19,800
1960	20,700
1962	22,300
1967	23,500
1974	25,200
1981	29,000

Most of the town's inhabitants are either employed
in the factories of the Kibbutzim of the Beit She'an
Valley or in tourism and recreation. Lake Kinneret
lures those interested in maritime sports, while the
town itself is a very important winter resort in the
country. Pilgrims to the town take place all the
year round. Tiberias has practically no industry due
to its geographical conditions and its distance from

the center of the country which usually makes investment unfeasible.

Tiberias is a prime example of the adaption of
modern construction and people to a historic location which in the past was of significant importance.
Today, this means that construction costs on the different topographical levels are high, as are the
costs of administering a town which has no continuous housing build-up, where transportation is on
steep slopes, and that has much open space left that
way because of the lack of economic resources which
could attract more people's to the town and supply
them with work. The town's main function, as a recreation center appears to be the most it can attain,
but it is well known that such towns can never become large ones.

ACRE

Of all the towns in the Land of Israel, Acre is the
most extraordinary due to the fact that after going
through so many historical changes, it still has remained a town which is inhabited by both Jews and
Arabs. The percentage of Arabs as contrasted to
Jews has always been very high and today is 24%. In
the past, Acre was the least Jewish of all towns in
the Land of Israel, and even though Jews lived in it
throughout many periods, they did not leave any sort
of influential mark on the town. Acre was always
under outside influences, by the Europeans or Muslims and the rises and declines of the town Acre, a
part of the history of the people who lived on the
eastern front of the Mediterranean.

THE TOWN'S GEOGRAPHICAL BACKGROUND

Acre is located on the northern corner of Haifa Bay
on a small peninsula which jets out into the sea.
This peninsula creates a small bay where docking is
possible in the southeast part. The town itself lies
halfway between the Lebanese border in the north and
Haifa in the south and is centrally located in regards to the Acre Valley and the Western Galilee.
Acre's advantageous location between the sea on one
side, the valleys on the other, the intensively cultivated coastal plain in the north, and the wide
Zebulun Valley in the south gives the town some
regional importance. Because of its location between
different geographical regions and outside of the

swamp area which once existed in this region, many transportation routes ran through Acre making it the capital of the northern Land of Israel. (Figure 7.3)

Today Acre's municipal boundaries are very long and narrow. The northern part of the town borders the agricultural lands of Bustan HaGalil, the southern part with the industrial zone of the Quera yot, and in the east with the agricultural lands of the nearby Kibbutzim. The town's municipal area stretches over 1,056 hectars. The main highway Haifa - Nahariyya along with the railway divides the town into two parts. In the western part is the old city and the sections built during the British Mandate period and in the eastern section are the new housing developments which were established in the 1950s.

The distribution of the population which presently numbers about 39,100 inhabitants is in three sections of the town. One third, including the Arab population lives in the old city, one third in the northern neighbourhoods outside of the walls and one third in the eastern neighbourhoods.

THE HISTORY OF THE TOWN

Acre is one of the most ancient towns in the eastern part of the Mediterranean. In the time of the Canaanites and the Phoenicians a harbour was located there and the town was also a station for caravans travelling to the Galilee, Jordan and Damascus. The ancient city of Acre was built on a tel one mile inland, and not where the old city is presently located. The inhabitants were employed in the glass industry using the clear sands found along the bay and also in colour making which was accomplished by utilizing the snails found in the brackish waters of the bay. Afterwards, they were engaged in dye industry which developed only in the areas with plenty of water. It was during the Hellenistic Period that Acre moved to its present location using the sandstone ridge of the peninsula to provide secure surroundings. From there the town could defend itself from a sea attack which was a much greater threat than an inland attack.

Acre functioned as an important harbour during the Roman and Byzantine times, but no archaeological remains have been found from these periods. During the Muslim rule from the 7th Century until the 11th there was an economic decline, but Acre's status increased during the time of the Crusaders. During

Figure 7.3: Acre - Changes in Main Land Uses

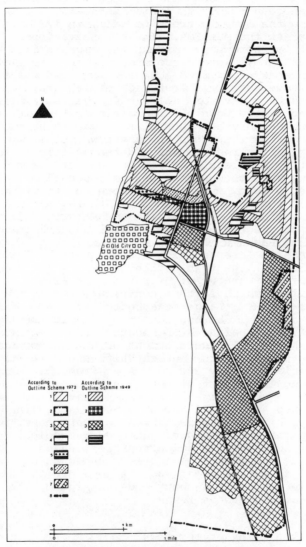

1. Residential Area   2. Commercial Zone
3. Industrial Zone   4. Institutions
5. Commercial Zone Changed into Institutions
6. Institutions Changed into Residential Area
7. cancelled Industrial Area
8. Town Planning Boundary 1972

the time of the Crusaders. During that period, the
town was used as a gateway for the people of Europe
and as a main harbour which connected southern
European countries with India in the Far East. Acre
was also the last fortress to fall, in 1291, in the
war against the Muslims. In the excavations of the
Old City of Acre many impressive remnants from the
Crusader's town were discovered. After the Crusaders were expelled from Acre and the town was under
Muslim rule again, it lost much of its status and
remained this way for the next 450 years. The rebuilding of the town started again in the middle of
the 18th Century by Daher el Amar and Pasha el Gizar.
They had a wall surrounding the town, constructed
along with fortresses, which defended Acre from an
attempt by Napoleon's armies to conquer it in 1799.
The construction was done on the foundations of the
Crusader's town. Large Khans were built making it
possible for merchants to remain there, and so
Acre's status as a commercial center grew. In the
center of the town a large minaret was built in
honour of Pasha el Gizar. With the last of Ottoman
dominance in Acre and with its conquest by Ibrahim
Pasha in 1832 the town declined again. The construction of the harbour of Beirut by the French created
competition which further contributed to Acre's
loss of status. Large steamboats could not dock in
the town's small harbour and they had to use the
facilities of Haifa which became Acre's competitor
in the south. The development of a transportation
line by the Templars between Haifa and Nazareth and
to Tiberias totally excluded Acre from this network
in the northern part of the country.

Until the beginning of this century Acre still
functioned as a small harbour, but has declined ever
since. This process is typical of many other Middle
Eastern and ancient towns which were unable to take
on additional economical activities, which did not
modernize and therefore barely changed at all. This
lack of change at least made it possible to build
new towns or new neighbourhoods outside of the ancient parts of these towns.

THE CONSTRUCTION OF THE TOWN

The first construction begun outside of the walls
and took place during the Ottoman Period. In 1909,
the German engineer Schumacher prepared a plan ac-
coring to which new houses would be built outside of
the town in order to create place for the additional

population. His plan was based on a gridiron system and therefore construction of housing was done in long and narrow rows.

During the British Mandate very little construction occured in Acre and the little that was built was according to this system. The rapid growth of Haifa and the British interest in that town interfered with Acre's development. The Jewish population living there eventually moved to Haifa and Acre's harbour filled up with sand thus making it suitable for fishing purposes only. The old city changed very little and Acre functioned no more than as a market town for the Arabs of the Western Galilee who came to the town to sell their goods.

The British assisted in Acre's development by planning an industrial area north of the Na'aman River. They also designed a main road to the east of the town, but nothing was executed from either of these plans. During the Mandate Period, Haifa sprawled to the north while developing industrial sections and labour neighbourhoods in the Bay Area. Jewish settlement developed on the lands of the Zebulun Valley after the draining of the swamps and soil reclamation had taken place. The new settlements of the Western Galilee surrounded Acre with their agricultural lands, so the town was enclosed from all sides preventing the possibility for further enlargement.

THE TOWN AFTER 1948

Acre was one of the first towns settled by new immigrants after the establishment of the State, primarily because many abandoned houses were there and the State had a political interest in resettling the town with a Jewish population. Due to population pressures and lack of resources for modern construction, the abandoned properties were immediately inhabited by new immigrants and no new housing was constructed.

From the point of view of population, a tremendous change took place in Acre since 1948. From 13,000 inhabitants during the Mandate Period, only 8,000 were left after 1948. With this decline in population, planners had an opportunity to fundamentally change and replan the town, but the Jews continued to build on the setting of the old framework and lived in the housing from the old urban system. With the exception of the old city and neighbourhoods built during the Mandate, only two neighbour-

hoods were added to Acre - one in the north and the
other in the east. The new neighbourhoods were
built 2 miles (2-3 kms) from the old city where
public open space separated the ancient and new
towns. Because the houses that were built were of
poor quality they did little to enhance the town's
beauty.

Today 39,100 people live in Acre. Comparitively speaking, this is not a very impressive increase
to its more than 35 years of existence as a Jewish
town. Because the Arab population returned to Acre
throughout the years, Jews are reluctant to live
there as communal sharing exists between the two
groups in administrative, residential, educational
and municipal services, etc. Even though new housing for immigrants were built, a new industrial area
was planned in the south to be serviced by expansive
roads, and a hotel zone was established to popular-
ize Acre, the town has not been greatly affected.
In the national and regional planning system, Acre
is listed only as a medium-sized town, and will remain in a lower position in the hierarchy of towns
in Israel. Today the town functions mainly as a
tourist attraction and its Arab inhabitants are
mostly employed in commerce, services and fishing,
while the Jewish inhabitants find most of their
employment in the industrial zone of Haifa.

Acre did not attain comprehensive urban development because of the following reasons:

1. From the beginning it was never received
   as a large town, nor as the capital of
   the district, but only as a small capital of a sub-district.
2. No alterations were done in the town
   with the large population wave that
   came in the 1950s so the opportunity for
   change in the infrastructure was lost as
   was the chance to make adjustments to
   the Ottoman and British urban systems
   and to fill up the town's squares with
   housing.
3. Until the present, none of the agricultural land in the town's periphery has
   been for other land uses which would
   enable Acre to enlarge its built up area.
4. Most of the new population in the town
   was located in housing of poor quality
   in the eastern part of the town without
   modernization in urban life.
5. Until today, no favourable solutions

have been found to the common problems
which have arisen for both the Jews and
Arabs in their urban life in Acre.
These factors are only part of the problems facing Acre today on the background
of the many changes which have occurred
throughout its historical periods.

NOTES

1.   'Kabbala' is a stream in Jewish mysticism which originated in the 11th and 12th Centuries
in southern France and Spain. It is also called
'The Secret Wisdom'. Its main fundamentals are: the
explanation of interrelationship between God and the
world, the creation of the world, and the finding of
ways to achieve perfection in morality and spiritual
life. Safed was during hundreds of years the center
of the Kabbalists.
2.   'Ashkenaz' is a Hebrew term for Germany
of the Middle Ages. 'Ashkenazim' are the Jews or
their descendants who lived there or in other European countries during centuries.
3.   'Sephardim' (pl.) is a Hebrew term for
the Jews who lived in Spain in the Middle Ages, or
for their descendants who dispersed all over other
countries through the inquisition.
4.   'Hassid' (pl. Hassidim) is a Hebrew term
which means: follower or devotee. During the period
of the Second Temple Hassidim were a sect of pious
Jews. From the 18th Century it became a sect founded by Rabbi Israel Ba'al Shem Tov. It is a stream
in Judaism, originated in Europe, which preaches for
pure of heart, devoutness to God, moral behaviour
and fulfillment of precepts.
5.   'Kannaim' - a Jewish political party in
Second Temple times, which called for non-compliance
with the Roman demand for a census.
6.   One of the greatest Jewish authorities
after the destruction of the Second Temple. He re-
volted against the Roman decrees.
7.   'Sanhedrin' was an assembly of 71 or-
dained scholars, which was both supreme court and
legislative in the 4th Century.
8.   'Mishna' is a collection or oral laws
compiled by Rabbi Juda Ha-Nasi, which forms the
basis of the Talmud.

Chapter Eight

MOSHAVAH - TOWNS

In 1981 there were 37 settlements in Israel that had
achieved town status, but were quite different from
other towns because of their settlement history,
number of inhabitants and municipal area. Most of
these towns gained their municipal urban status only
after the establishment of the State. It appears
that the veteran agricultural Moshavot (1), which
had more favourable urban conditions in comparison
to other forms of agricultural settlements, and
which make up more than one third of the towns in
Israel, are not the largest towns in the country.
Veteran towns such as Petah Tiqva, Rishon LeZion,
Rehovot, Hadera and Kefar Sava are considered to be
small and medium-sized towns in the country.
     An analysis of the Moshavot according to geo-
graphical regions shows that those which were established in the Galilee and in remote valleys far from
the country's center such as Yesud Hamalah and Rosh
Pinna, or those found along the Carmel coast or in
the southern plain as Zikhron Ya'aqov or Nes Ziyyona
retained their agricultural character and did not
urbanize. In contrast, are the Moshavot of the
coastal plain whose special development promoted
urbanization enabling them to become towns.
     Today in Israel there are 13 Moshavah - Towns
(2) which are - Petah Tiqva, Rishon LeZion, Rehovot,
Hadera, Kefar Sava, Ramat Gan, Bene Beraq, Bat Yam,
Givatayim, Netanya, Holon, Herzliyya and Nahariyya.
Five of them, Holon, Bat Yam, Ramat Gan, Bene
Beraq and Givatayim became towns within the framework of the Tel Aviv conurbation and were previously
discussed. (Figure 8.1) Here we shall focus on the
urban development of the Moshavah - towns in order
to gain an understanding of their special characteristics and their future development as towns. The
following questions will be discussed: What were

Figure 8.1: Distribution of 'Moshavot'

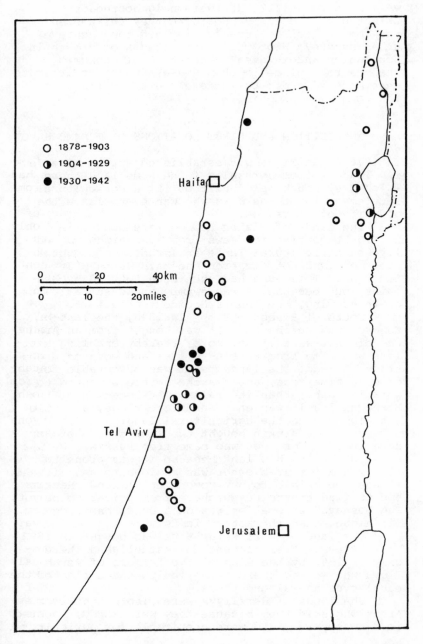

the ideas behind the Moshavot locations which later
became towns? How many people founded them? How
was the core built? How were neighbourhoods dis-
tributed around them? How were they influenced by
the immigration to Israel? Why did they achieve
urban status? What were their stages of growth in
population and in area? What type of economic
changes took place in them and what sort of attempts
were made in order to improve the urban features of
the towns via planning?

LAND ACQUISITION AND FIRST LOCATIONS OF THE MOSHAVOT

In 1878 Petah Tiqva was established after three Jewish leaders from Jerusalem found some land there
which they bought and built on it an agricultural
settlement for those Jews who wanted to leave the
old city of Jerusalem.

     The lands of Rishon LeZion were bought in 1881
by Z.D. Levontine for Jews from Russia who wanted to
live on agricultural lands in Israel. He bought this
piece of land not far from the main Jaffa - Jerusalem road. This land had once been settled by Bedouins, but because it was swampy and unsuitable for
grain growing, the owners decided to sell it.

     South of Rishon LeZion, in 1890, the land of
Rehovot was purchased. It was bought from an Arab
who did not want it any more, thereby enabling settlers who came from Russia to live and work on a good
tract of land. The land itself was favourable for
growing vineyards, an area the settlers wanted to
work in rather than in grains. The location of the
Moshavah itself was on a sandstone ridge, a little
bit higher than the agricultural land.

     Yehoshua Hankin bought the land tracts of Ha-
dera in 1891 for Jews who came from Russia. He was
able to obtain this land because it was prone to
floods and its Arab owner was anxious to sell it. As
it was impossible to buy governmental land, Hankin
had to find tracts to purchase from private owners.
The Moshavah's location was on a sandstone ridge, a
bit higher than the actual lands.

     The land area of Kefar Sava was bought in 1892
by Y. Pines. A settlement was established there
only in 1903 by the sons of the farmers of Petah
Tiqva who worked there in agriculture and planted
eucalyptus and almond trees.

     The lands of Herzliyya were also bought from
Arabs who sold them because they were sandy, located
in a swamp area, and were unsuitable for agriculture.

110

As the Jews desired to settle in the middle of the coastal plain, buying land in this area was of great importance to them. From the examples mentioned above, it can be assumed that the locations of the first Moshavot were not selected for any particular reason, rather in most cases land was purchased from owners who were anxious to sell it. For the most part, this land was of poor quality, flat and undrained. Thus, settlement location was the result of finding available land for sale and perhaps to local security factors, but was not due to any type of regional planning perspective.

It is surprising then that the urban-minded immigrants who came from European countries did not decide to build a town on this land which was unsuitable for agriculture, rather than eagerly work it according to their idea of conquest of the soil.

LAND AREAS AND NUMBER OF FIRST SETTLERS

The tracts of land bought for the first Moshavot were not so small: Petah Tiqva had 337 hectars and in 1879 only 12 people lived there. In 1882 the population reached 66. Rishon LeZion contained 334 hectars and in 1882 approximately 100 settlers lived there. In Rehovot more than 1,000 hectars were purchased on which only 17 families settled. After a year the number of farmers reached 77, and 200 labourers from the surrounding areas were employed to work on this land.

In Hadera, about 3,000 hectars were bought, but only a small part of this land was put into use. In 1891 about 50 settlers lived there. Seven hundred hectars in Kefar Sava were purchased and only in 1912, after many years of desolation, 13 houses were built there.

As stated previously, the amount of land purchased was quite large reaching over 3,000 hectars. This land was reclaimed for agricultural settlements by Jewish pioneers. In all of these cases there were trial and error attempts during the creation of these agricultural settlements on an incidental background due to the ideology and eagerness of the settlers who did not always bring about desirable settlement development.

THE CBD OF THE MOSHAVAH -TOWNS

The first center of Petah Tiqva contained only a

few houses established on an area which today is called Founder's Square. Each dwelling unit included a central building and an inner yard surrounded by a wall. Brick and sandstone were used for building materials due to the lack of natural stone. Houses were even constructed from wood. Due to the horizontal distribution of housing, a lot of space was taken up. The main investments were in agriculture and therefore the function of the CBD in the Moshavah was primarily agriculture.

The first center of Rishon LeZion was situated on what today is known as Synagogue Hill and along Rothschild Street which descends in a westward direction perpendicular to the main road. Near the synagogue, a kindergarden, cultural center and school were erected. Initially, the people had a communal life style but later private parcels of land were developed. The sprawl of the center towards the perpendicular roads to Rothschild Street was the result of the settler's ties to their vineyards and distilleries and was not a part of an overall master plan.

Rehovot's first center was built in the form of a few small farms very close together which mainly included houses, a synagogue, and a few other public buildings, but no commerce. Land parcelation was in the form of squares which faced two main streets where most of the one-storey houses were built.

The first center of Hadera was in the Khan, on which today stands the main synagogue on higher topography thus providing secure conditions for the rest of the town. The first wooden houses were built in 1896, 35 additional houses were erected towards the west. The streets were in a gridiron layout and the houses and yards were erected on both sides of the streets. The center's main function was agriculture.

In Kefar Sava the first center was also a Khan, which provided shelter for the farmers of Petah Tiqva who worked there. The first houses were also built along the one or two streets which existed there.

It can be assumed that the centers of the first Moshavot were located according to local land and agricultural conditions. Security problems enforced the need to cluster housing and this arrangement was for functional community purposes and for basis of the outside agricultural work. The sprawl of the center in the Moshavot was very slow and was always according to a gridiron system or in parallel directions, similar to the sprawl of a typical

112

European village. On the main street of the Moshavah, the first building was located along with a few institutions nearby and these became, after many years the CBD of the Moshavah - Towns. It's sprawl which was mostly linear did not advance great distances and widened only into a few neighbouring streets. In none of the cases did the CBD develop proportionately to the growth of the Moshavah itself, so that the functions of marketing, business, communication, and services did not expand very much. Also, the CBD did not expand vertically, and even today empty lots can be found in the CBD's zone. In most of the Moshavot real development took place later on by semi-urban settlers such as merchants and craftsmen rather than by the farmers. The fact that the CBDs were located on private land made expansion of them quite difficult and that is one of the main reasons why urban development was so slow.

In urban development, the gridiron system is very old and characterizes ancient towns. In most settlements this system encourages concentration of buildings and economic functions, but in the case of the Moshavot most of the land parcels remained for agricultural use thus preventing the crystallization of an urban CBD. Later on a CBD area with an agricultural character had to compete with the needs of a Moshavah which became a town.

THE NEIGHBOURHOODS AROUND THE MOSHAVAH - TOWNS

Between 1909 and 1937 an important change took place in Petah Tiqva as a result of the construction of agricultural neighbourhoods outside of the old CBD. These neighbourhoods were built at a distance from the center and their main function was to supply labourers for the new farmers and their fields. The center of the Moshavah was surrounded by an unplanned ring of satellites whose inhabitants worked in citrus. En Gannim was the first neighbourhood established in Petah Tiqva after which Mahane Yehuda, Givàt Hashelosha, Gat Rimon, Kefar Gannim, Kefar Avraham, Kefar Sirkin and other neighbourhoods were founded. Between 1938-1948 the neighbourhoods that were constructed were better planned and were located mainly on the empty lands which remained between the CBD and the previously built neighbourhoods. Most units were erected for the labourers who settled in the Moshavah and villas were even built for the veterans. Each settlement period created in the Moshavah a new ring of neighbourhoods more remote from the center.

Nahlat Yehuda, established in 1912, was the first neighbourhood of Rishon LeZion. In the 1920s other neighbourhoods were built at various distances from the center and without coordination between them. Some neighbourhoods were constructed on private lands by the owners and were located closer to the center, while the neighbourhoods for the new immigrants who came later were erected on public land further from the center. Rishon LeZion was surrounded by 10 neighbourhoods until 1948 and after that by an additional 14 housing projects.

The first neighbourhood in Rehovot was Sha'arayim established with the Yemenite immigration of 1912. Between 1920 and 1940 two additional neighbourhoods were founded, one for Yemenites and one for ex-German Jews. Six more neighbourhoods and housing projects are similar to those of Petah Tiqva and Rehovot.

In 1912, a Yeminite neighbourhood was established in Hadera inhabited by citrus labourers. Many others were established later on and all were agricultural in nature, had ties with the old center, but almost no relationship with the other neighbourhoods. After 1948, several new neighbourhoods were created in the western and eastern parts of Hadera on abandoned land and on the periphery of the Moshavah.

It can be assumed that there was no continuous crystallization process of the center which normally occurs in a town. Due to the citrus areas in the Moshavah, the neighbourhoods were located on its outskirts, and along with this fact many of these neighbourhoods were inhabited by people from the outside rather than by those who migrated internally. This phenomenon of neighbourhood rings began in all the Moshavot before World War I, achieved its agricultural peak in the 1940s and by the 1950s had developed an urban character. Between the neighbourhoods and the center were the agricultural areas. The growth of these neighbourhoods did not effect the development of the CBD and so they expanded faster than the center of the Moshavah. Mass immigration to Israel created very densely populated neighbourhoods and absorption was primarily done by locating people in urban settings. In comparison to other urban development areas the Moshavot lacked continuity in their construction and development. Growth took place in concentric rings because of the citrus in the center, the public land in the periphery, and the need to rapidly populate the Moshavot with new immigrants.

THE INFLUENCE OF AGRICULTURE ON THE URBAN PROCESSES

In Petah Tiqva's first decade of existence, intensive agriculture was the dominant monoculture. Between 1889 and 1903, with the assistance of Baron
Rothschild, vineyards dominated the agriculture.
Petah Tiqva's present center was once covered by
hundreds of acres of vineyards. After the vineyard
crisis, almonds and olives took over the dominant
crops and since World War I the main agricultural
branch has been citrus. Petah Tiqva was the most
successful in citrus growing and became known as the
center of this agricultural branch throughout the
country. Even today, this type of agriculture is
still grown in parts of Petah Tiqva.
    The goal of the first settlers in Rishon LeZion
was to live from the agriculture they raised. In
this Moshavah vineyards and almonds were also grown,
but by the 1930s citrus covered nearly a quarter of
Rishon LeZion's area. Today most of agriculture
grown there is citrus. Before the addition of the
sand dunes in the west to the municipal area of the
Moshavah, almost half the area of Rishon LeZion was
covered by citrus groves. Proportional to its area,
not many citrus trees were uprooted for construction
purposes in the Moshavah. Later on, urban and industrial development occurred because of Rishon
LeZion's proximity to Tel Aviv, but the citrus
branch still exists there.
    In Rehovot, citrus brought about, among other
things, industrialization, transportation, services
and non-agricultural employment. Three quarters of
the citrus groves are privately owned and among
these owners more than half of them do not work in
agriculture. This agricultural base attracted different businesses who employed labourers. There was
a gradual transition from citrus to commerce so that
the agricultural character of the Moshavah began to
disappear. Even though industries connected with
agriculture developed there, agriculture itself is
still a central economic branch in the Moshavah.
    Even Hadera started by growing vineyards,
switched to mulberry, after an economic crisis grew
almonds and by the beginning of the present century
changed to citrus. Almost half of Hadera's land
is still used for agriculture and this Moshavah
lacks an urban character. It's housing areas are
very small and a declared aim of the Moshavah is to

retain its agricultural character. This point of
view has brought about low density, one-story houses
with a horizontal sprawl instead of one that is vertically built up so that the Moshavah stretches 5
miles (8 kms.) from east to west. Private land
ownership in Hadera is approximately 6% and most of
the housing has been erected on public land. Even
though the Moshavah is still agricultural, only 10%
of its inhabitants live on cultivated land. Approximately 20% of the urban area still has citrus
groves on it.

It appears that agriculture, the original basis
of the Moshavot, had a great influence on their construction, shape and in the prevention of the creation of a true urban system. Most of the large
Moshavot developed in the central part of the
coastal plain. The citrus branch could be developed
in the Moshavot only after the modernization of
water pumping systems which was the basis for the
expansion of this sector. Until World War II citrus dominated employment in agriculture and only
after the war, due to a crisis in this branch and
along with encouragement from the British, did a
real change in basic employment structure occur.
Even after the farmers transferred to jobs in industry or services, the citrus remained and still gives
the Moshavot an agricultural character which has
prevented urban growth. In most of the Moshavot
there is an equilibrium between agriculture, industry and services, although in a number of them such
as Petah Tiqva, Rishon LeZion, Rehovot and Herzliyya
and even in Netanya, a rapid change from agriculture
to high urbanization did take place.

THE INFLUENCE OF IMMIGRATION ON MOSHAVAH - TOWNS

Between 1949 and 1951 Petah Tiqva absorbed 14,000
immigrants and between 1950 and 1980 its population
tripled while the municipalarea grew by a factor of
seven. Because of this vast immigration and populating by non-agricultural inhabitants, industry and
services developed extensively and much agriculture-
al soil was converted into residential and industrial areas.

In Rishon LeZion housing for immigrants at the
beginning of the 1950s was concentrated on abandoned land. From the middle of the 1950s onwards, housing sprawled towards the sand dunes in the west and
to a certain extent it filled in the gap between the
center of the settlement and its periphery.

116

Even in Rehovot the waves of immigration between 1948 and 1952 necessitated that housing be
built in the western, southern and northern parts of
the Moshavah. Housing was further expanded when
more immigrants arrived between 1956 and 1957. The
immigrant housing sprawled all over the Moshavah and
also partially on private land.

Immigrants who arrived in Hadera after the establishment of the State were initially housed in
abandoned military camps and were employed in citrus
work and industry. Later on, housing for the immigrants was constructed on the outskirts of the
Moshavah in Givat Olga to the west and Bet Eliezer
to the east as cheaper land was available there enabling low-cost housing to be built.

As seen, the main growth of the Moshavot was
due to the influx of immigrants and the vast amount
of housing that was built for them. The transition
from employment in agriculture to industry and from
rural living to a state of semi-urbanization occured
more rapidly during the past 20 years than it had
for tens of years previously. Other observations on
effects of the absorption of immigrants by means of
housing projects shows that these projects did not
contribute much to the crystallization of the Moshavah. Rather, they caused a construction sprawl and
an increase in distances so that in the center of
the Moshavah there was a change in the use of agricultural land. In addition, most of the neighbourhoods built did not usually improve the standards of
living and urban character of the Moshavah, nor did
they integrate with the ancient parts or the CBD.
Later on measures were taken to improve the level of
construction and urban character, especially in the
veteran Moshavot close to Tel Aviv.

Urbanization in the Moshavot was caused by the
influx of outsiders, rather than inner population
growth. It occured with the rapid, unexpected
events of mass immigration and its influence was
much greater than the slow development sprawl which
had previously taken place.

THE REASONS FOR DESIGNATING THE MOSHAVOT AS TOWNS

The first Moshavah to achieve municipal status was
Petah Tiqva. In 1934 the British suggested that
Petah Tiqva be granted this status. At that time,
not all of the inhabitants were eager to achieve
this classification as it meant higher taxation for
them. Today, the sentiment is the exact opposite

as intensive housing raises the value of agricultural land. In 1937, urban status was finally granted to Petah Tiqva on an area of only 250 hectars out of 2,300 hectars, when the population numbered 11,000 inhabitants.

Rishon LeZion became a town only in 1950 because of its inhabitants desire to achieve this status. They felt that the Moshavah was gradually changing from its agricultural background to industry and services and saw that many of the non-agricultural immigrants were employed in other economic jobs so when the Moshavah numbered 18,000 residents, it was declared a town.

One month after Rishon LeZion, Rehovot achieved the same status. As more people began to work in non-agricultural jobs and as Rehovot became an administrative and marketing center for agricultural products, the demand for a change in status arose. With this change, the inhabitants felt that investors and industrialists would be attracted to Rehovot and that the president's residence also justified such a status alteration. This request was brought up at the time of Rehovot's 60th anniversary and the change of status took place when the population numbered 17,000.

In 1952, Hadera became a town with a population of 21,000 inhabitants. They too were convinced that a status change would promote growth. In addition they desired to be a town for reasons of prestige and in order to solve budgetary problems.

In all the above cases, the achievement of the status of a town was not the direct result of settlement growth. The Moshavot did not fit into the accepted town criteria which stipulates that at least two-thirds of the population be employed in non-agricultural work and that the settlement must include no less than 25,000 inhabitants. The Moshavot were unable to fulfill these requirements.

THE GROWTH OF THE AREA OF THE MOSHAVAH - TOWNS AND THEIR POPULATION

The Moshavah - Towns have large municipal areas. Petah Tiqva contains 3,500 hectars, Rishon LeZion 4,450 hectars, Rehovot 2,278 hectars and Hadera 5,100 hectars. Kefar Sava, Herzliyya, Nahariyya have an area between 1,000 and 2,800 hectars. These areas, proportionately speaking, are quite large in comparison to those in other towns. It should be remembered that Jerusalem, prior to the Six Day War was only the size of 3,750 hectars which is almost the area of Petah Tiqva today. A comparison of the Moshavot to other towns shows that Hadera's size is equal to that of the municipal area of Tel Aviv, Rehovot is larger than Holon, Rishon LeZion is just a bit smaller than Beer Sheva and only 800 hectars less than Haifa in size. It is obvious that the size of these areas takes into account agricultural land which was included in the municipal areas of the Moshavot when they became towns.

The population growth during selected years in eight Moshavot is shown in Table 8.1.

From the above table it can be concluded that:

1. Until the beginning of this century the Moshavot's growth was very slow and each one did not have a population of more than 100 people.

2. After 40 years of existence the Moshavot of Petah Tiqva, Rehovot and Hadera had no more than 2,000 to 3,000 inhabitants each.

3. Petah Tiqva grew faster than the other Moshavot.

4. Until the establishment of the State no Moshavah had more than 12,000 inhabitants with the exception of Petah Tiqva which had 21,580 inhabitants.

5. Since the establishment of the State, until today, the population of the Moshavot grew by 4 to 5 times. Petah Tiqva has more than 100,000 inhabitants, Netanya and Rishon LeZion have almost 100,000 residents each, while the other Moshavot have populations of no more than 40,000-60,000 each.

6. In all of the cases it is difficult to understand the proportionately low increase in the number of inhabitants after almost 90 years of existence. Their agricultural background is probably the main reason for this lack of substantial increase.

The urban hierarchy of the Moshavot is shown in Table 8.2.

Table 8.1: Increase of Population in Moshavah – Towns 1882 – 1981

Year	Petah Tiqva	Rishon LeZion	Rehovot	Hadera	Kefar Sava	Herzliyya	Netanya	Nahariyya
1882	66	100	–	–	–	–	–	–
1900	818	625	300	152	–	–	–	–
1914	3,800	1,348	726	450	–	–	–	–
1921	3,373	1,500	1,400	684	–	–	–	–
1931	8,500	2,400	3,000	2,100	1,500	1,217	–	–
1948	21,850	11,638	12,522	8,343	12,000	5,300	11,589	1,722
1956	46,000	22,300	29,500	23,500	16,500	22,000	35,000	10,000
1961	54,000	27,887	29,000	25,638	17,860	30,000	41,260	14,574
1970	83,200	46,500	36,000	30,700	24,400	40,000	63,000	22,000
1972	92,400	51,900	39,200	31,900	26,500	41,200	70,700	24,000
1974	103,000	63,400	46,400	34,800	30,500	45,700	79,500	27,000
1981	127,700	95,500	67,100	39,000	41,200	60,700	99,800	28,000

Table 8.2: Location of the Moshavah – Towns in the Urban Hierarchy

Year	Petah Tiqva	Rishon LeZion	Rehovot	Hadera	Kefar Sava	Herzliyya	Natanya	Nahariyya
1950	4	9	8	11	14	15	6	34
1952	5	11	8	9	15	14	6	30
1956	5	13	9	11	22	14	6	30
1961	5	13	12	15	22	16	9	24
1966	6	12	15	18	24	14	10	23
1970	7	11	16	20	23	14	10	26
1974	7	11	17	20	23	16	10	24
1981	6	8	10	20	17	12	7	25

From the table it can be assumed that:

1. There has been a continuous decrease in the Moshavah – Town's position in the urban hierarchy of Israel due to the rapid growth of the large towns.

2. The decrease in Petah Tiqva's, Rishon LeZion's and Kefar Sava's rank is slow, but in Hadera it is high. Netanya's positions has remained stable.

3. Rishon LeZion's decrease was quite high until 1961 but because of its large housing projects south of Tel Aviv this Moshavah moved up in the urban hierarchy.

4. Because Hadera and Rehovot are located to the north and south of Tel Aviv, their positions in the urban hierarchy are quite low. They rank at the 20th

121

and 10th levels, respectively.

It can be seen that the location of the veteran Moshavot in the urban hierarchy in Israel is still low despite the inertia received from the waves of immigration and that these towns did not achieve the growth in population that newer towns like Ashdod or Beer Sheva did. Undoubtedly, their agricultural backgrounds functioned as a buffer against the urban processes.

LAND OWNERSHIP

In Petah Tiqva 2,300 hectares (67%) of the land belongs to private owners while the rest is in the hands of the Land Administration, the Jewish National Fund, and the Municipality. Many plots of land are privately owned in eastern Rishon LeZion and even in the western parts 400 hectares out of 2,100 hectares are in private hands. In the older section of Rehovot most of the land is privately owned and only those plots added onto the Moshavah after the establishment of the State are in public hands. There is a small number of private owners who have hold of land in the center of the Moshavah which disrupts the crystallization of housing and construction there. Sixty-seven percent of the land in Hadera is privately owned and the rest is controlled by the Land Administration and the Municipality. The land ownership situation is similar in all the other Moshavot.

Rapid development could not be undertaken in the Moshavot due to the speculative conditions of the private land. Therefore, housing for immigrants was located on the periphery and on public land. The private land was primarily agricultural and as a result the Moshavot became important factors which influenced change in the future use of agricultural land.

CHANGES IN THE FUNCTIONS OF MOSHAVAH - TOWNS

Industry came to Petah Tiqva only at the end of the 1930s and expanded during World War II, after agriculture had been the dominant function of the Moshavah for close to 60 years. During that time, Petah Tiqva was also an important transportation hub and a marketing core for citrus in the country, and was therefore developed as a national transpor-

tation center. Today it has a high percentage of
employees in industry, which is above the national
average. In 1971, 45% of Petah Tiqva's labour
force was employed in industry, 46% in services and
only 4% in agriculture.

Employment in agriculture was dominant throughout the years in Rishon LeZion. For instance, in
1927, the rate of those employed in agriculture was
38%, but by 1948 it had decreased to 13%. Even today there is a continuous decrease in the percentage of employment in agriculture due to Rishon Le-
Zion's proximity to Tel Aviv along with the industrial processes that took place there.

From its beginning as a settlement, Rehovot's
main function was also agriculture and during 40
years of its existence most of its inhabitants were
employed in this branch. Later, the transportation
and export of agriculture along with a packing plant
became the main economic activities in Rehovot. For
many years there after Rehovot was a service center
for the surrounding settlements and a core for
health services, commerce and economy and was even
the capital of a sub-district. Governmental functions in administration and services were added. The
immigration of many educated people from Europe
helped to bring about the establishment of a center
for science and research, the Weizmann Institute
and an Institute of Science and Agricultural Research so that by 1961 more than 60% of Rehovot's
population were employed in the services.

Until 1950, Hadera functioned mainly as an agricultural settlement. Later on the percentage
employed in agriculture decreased to 20%, by 1961
to 14% and today to approximately 12% in contrast
to 48% who are occupied in services. Industry
moved to Hadera primarily because of the erection
of two large factories - a paper mill and a tire
factory. Hadera also took on some sub-district
governmental services.

It can be seen that all of the veteran Moshavot gradually changed their functions from agriculture to industry so that today, in all of them,
industry forms the economic base which continues
to gain in importance. The reasons for this
transfer to industry are World War II, the presence
of external factors, the capitalists among the inhabitants of the Moshavot who established and built
projects, and the presence of professional and en-
terprising people in the population.

This gradual switch from agriculture to industry and services is quite accepted and is viewed as

a positive development towards urbanization. But
in these Moshavot, this phenomenon occurred late
and under the pressure of mass immigrant development was not organic.

NEW TRENDS IN THE URBAN PLANNING OF MOSHAVAH -
TOWNS

The trend expressed in the outline schemes of the
Moshavah - Towns show changes in the CBD, in the
residential areas, an increase in residential densities and the preservation of public open spaces.
     For example, the CBD of Petah Tiqva will
sprawl towards the southwest following the population's center of gravity. The northeast section
is designated for different industries, while the
eastern suburbs of the Moshavah will be more densely built up as residential areas, and in the south-
west the agricultural areas will also become residential. An extensive amount of industry is planned for the western and northern sections of Petah
Tiqva.
     In Rishon LeZion, the plan is to transfer the
gravitational center of the Moshavah towards the
sand dunes in the west. In the future, two urban
blocks will be established there along both sides
of the main road Bet Dagan - Rehovot. In the area
of the western sand dunes even new recreation and
industrial zones are planned. The plan envisions a
population of 150,000 by 1992 with almost half of
them living along the western sand dunes.
     Rehovot's outline plan anticipates a future
population of 100,000 people, with industrial areas
in the north, south and west. New bypass roads
have been planned in order to alleviate the traffic
pressure on the main roads, while enabling better
connections between all parts of the town. The
focus is on the development of the town towards the
west between the new center and the old CBD.
     In the outline plan for Hadera, there are two
conceptions for the future. One is to rebuild the
ancient center making it more dense with a gradual
sprawl towards the periphery in spite of the private land located in the center. The second idea
is to develop the town in the direction towards the
coast with an axis, densely built along a road which
will connect old Hadera with the western part of
Hadera and with the coast. The aim of this scheme
is to encourage westward development.
     At present the Moshavah - Towns are looking for

methods to improve their historical development by means of these outline plans. Most do not have the possibility to achieve internal crystallization with the exception of Hadera where urbanization is still relatively low. Their main plan is to adjust to existing conditions and to have few changes in the physical structure.

In summary, it could be stated that most of the Moshavah - Towns did not really become towns because of several reasons:

1. From the beginning their location was never a part of a national regional system. Moshavot were founded for agricultural purposes and even with an anti-urban ideology. Typical of the urban immigrants who arrived in Israel was their desire to settle in a Moshavah because of social and agricultural ideology.

2. There was an imbalance between the small number of settlers who arrived and their ability to effectively exploit the vast amount of land they had received.

3. The Moshavah location was incidental as a result of a limited amount of available land on one hand, and because of the activities of professional middlemen on the other.

4. The center of the Moshavah was built according to an agricultural gridiron system like that of a European village. Many of these villages in Europe also did not become towns.

5. As agricultural land surrounded the CBD there was no integration between the older and newer parts of the Moshavah and as a result the urban growth of the CBD was not effected by the growth of the Moshavah's area and its population.

6. Due to the basic agricultural structure, neighbourhoods and suburbs were pushed to the periphery in remote rings which prevented urban crystallization and disconnected residential areas from the Moshavah. Rather than being a town the Moshavah became a mosaic of neighbourhoods lacking social ties.

7. Urban development in the Moshavah happened as a result of immigrant pressure rather than due to planning. Other

factors encouraged this process outside of internal economic ones. Urbanization was the outgrowth of immigration waves.

8. For the most part, the town classification delegated to the Moshavah was not due to an urban need, and according to accepted criteria in urban geography the Moshavah should not have been accorded this status. Most Moshavot earned this status early in their history and it is doubtful whether this achievement was even necessary. Through this designation of town status the Moshavah tried to solve budgetary problems.

9. It is no wonder that the rank of the Moshavah - Towns in the urban hierarchy is very low. In comparison to the amount of time they have existed, towns previously established outnumber them in population as do towns that were established after 1948.

10. It is very difficult to urbanize on private lands when entrepreneurs are unable to construct large projects on them. Ownership of private land in the Moshavah prevented continuous urban development. The Moshavah had no other alternative than to remain agricultural in nature and to wait for other changes in their region. This process of urbanization began in the 1960s.

11. The Moshavah gradually switched to industry even though this is the key to urbanization, in this case it did not succeed because industrialization was not intensive enough and it thus slowed down the processes or urbanization.

12. Improvements by means of outline plans are no more than patchwork attempts which will not succeed in correcting the Moshavah's problems.

The real facts of the Moshavot are that private ownership of land, the unwillingness to convert citrus groves into areas for building and their distance from national urban activities in the country, prevented rapid urbanization from taking place in them.

NOTES

1.   'Moshavah'(p. Moshavot) is the Hebrew term for a village of the regular European type, with land, building, farming installations, all privately owned.

2.   A term for a medium-sized town which grew out from a settlement which was once a village or 'Moshavah'.

Chapter Nine

BEER SHEVA: A TOWN ON THE FRINGE OF THE DESERT

Beer Sheva is a typical desert town in Israel located on the border of the Negev in the semi-arid area of the Beer Sheva valley. Town existence and a desert are two phenomena which are in direct contrast with each other. In order for a town to exist certain conditions are needed such as: water, transportation routes, agricultural hinterland, security and economic potential. These conditions do not exist in the desert, nor even in the semi-arid areas. The desert is where nomads and shepherd tribes are located rather than towns and urban inhabitants.

History shows that throughout many generations there has been a conflict between inhabitants of the desolate areas and those who live in cultivated zones. Quite often, during periods of drought, the desert tribes from the semi-arid areas would invade the cultivated zones while the inhabitants of these zones would fortify their villages and defend themselves from the invaders. Very few cases exist where inhabitants of the cultivated areas went into the desert in order to create new settlements. In the last decades, the phenomenon of urban growth on the desert fringe has been witnessed, and even in Israel this has been manifested through the creation of towns like Beer Sheva, Elat and smaller settlements such as Dimona, Yeruham and other places.

THE BACKGROUND OF THE TOWN'S LOCATION

Before Beer Sheva was built only a few wells and a hostel for passing caravans existed in that area. Pumping wheels which lifted up pails of water were constructed on a few of these wells and were operated by the circular movement of animals walking next to them. The importance of this location was its func-

128

tion as a source of water in the desert.

The Ottoman administration in the Land of Israel yearned to govern the Bedouins in the Negev, but were unsuccessful as Bedouin opposition was quite strong. Among the Bedouin tribes were inner conflicts together with frequent bloodshed. When war between the Bedouins was quite intense, the Turks decided to break the connection between the northern Negev and Gaza Strip in order to establish a separate district for the Bedouins where they could be watched and also where a townlet could be built which would function as an administrative center for the entire region. Their objective was to have the Bedouins switch from nomadism to agriculture through Turkish administration from this townlet. They also wanted to prevent the Bedouins from wandering towards the coastal plain and the Judean lowlands and to gradually make them a sedentary people. The Turks even wanted to receive taxes from the desert inhabitants who were never under any type of administration and thus never paid taxes. There was also some political importance attached to administering the Bedouins as the Turks were interested in strengthening their forces close to the borderline between Palestine and the Sinai Peninsula in order to prevent any danger of possible invasion or conquest from the Egyptian side.

LOCATION OF THE TOWN

Beer Sheva was planned in the year 1900 according to a system of town design which was viewed as being modern especially in contrast to Arab towns which lacked any type of organized development. Two architects, a Swiss and a German who worked for the Turkish government planned the town. Today, as one tries to understand the reasons the Turks chose the particular location of Beer Sheva one realizes that it is due to the topographical, hydrographical and transportation advantages of that area. The town is situated at the entrance to a wide valley drained by the tributaries of Wadi Beer Sheva. The height of the location is 810 ft. (270 meters) above sea level. To the north are the southern ridges of Mt. Hebron and in the south are the northern hills of the Negev. Climatically, the area is on the borderline expressed by the isohyet of 8 inches (200 mms.). In addition, at the beginning of this century sweet-water wells were discovered. This water source added to the attractiveness of the area so that the Bedouins

naturally brought their flocks to water there which
eventually brought about the establishment of Beer
Sheva. The town's location on loess soil which is
good for agriculture and for grazing, also promoted
the chances of the Bedouins settling into a sedentary, agricultural way of life. Another advantage
of this area was its location as a junction along
the natural routes. At that time the caravans in
the Negev went along the wadi routes and because
these wadis drained into Wadi Beer Sheva which goes
through the valley, the town was situated on the
natural junction of the tributaries where the caravans came together. The town was established north
of the wadi in order to have convenient transportation lines with the center of the Ottoman administration in the northern part of the country and to
defend itself with the broad riverbed of Wadi Beer
Sheva from any danger which could threaten from the
south. The town's location was also influenced by
the borderline between the tribes: Azzazmeh, Tiyaha
and Terabin. In order to take a minimal amount of
land from these tribes which had continuous conflicts amongst themselves, it was necessary to find
a site which would cause the least amount of dis-
ruption. From what was stated above, it is apparent
that the reasons for Beer Sheva's establishment on
the background and geographical knowledge of 80
years ago were quite reasonable.

It is doubtful though that these considerations taken before establishing this town would be
acceptable today. Its location in the center of a
valley with loess soil creates sandstorms in the
Negev making life in the town difficult. Situating
Beer Sheva on one of the hills in the eastern part
of the valley at an elevation of 900-1,200 ft. (300-
400 meters) above sea level would have been a great
improvement. Location on a higher topography would
lower the average hot temperatures experienced in
the town during the summer. The area where the town
was built is on loess soil which can be productive
with the proper amount of water. It is doubtful
if today a town would be established on a site with
such a high agricultural potential. These factors
which existed in the past such as wadi routes,
wells, borderlines between tribal lands, etc., are
not as important today because with technology water
can be transferred from long distances, roads can be
paved on difficult topography, and a town's infrastructure can be arranged under any type of physical
situation.

TOWN PLANNING

The basic concept behind Beer Sheva's planning was
to build the town according to the classic European
model of the gridiron system, one north of Wadi
Beer Sheva and one west of Tel Beer Sheva on a flat
plain. This arrangement afforded a view of the
desert from every street across section which was
perpendicular to another. The town was divided into
squares of 180x180 ft. (60 by 60 meters) which were
aligned and parallel to the streets. It was decided
that the main road would be an axis running from the
southeast to the northwest which is HaAtzmaoot (Independence) Street of today that divides the town
into two equal parts. The streets were planned with
a width of only 3-6 ft. (1½ - 2 meters) while the
main street was much broader and along it centers
were built for the municipality, administration,
police together with a minaret and a courtyard (1).
  Light stone, taken from the nearby hilly area
from old stones which were the remnants from the
surroundings, was used to build houses in Beer Sheva.
Some of the houses were also built from grey sandy
bricks which were used in the building of Arab
villages. Most of the houses were one-story with a
large yard surrounding them which was the result of
the quadrant parcelation previously decided upon.
Bedouins willing to settle in the town received 1/4
acre of land without payment. Despite this offer
few people settled in the town so it remained small
and did not expand into other large areas. (Figure
9.1)
  As Beer Sheva was once based on the well system and there was a need to distribute this water to
the houses, the concentration of residential quarters made water distribution in the town easier. The
concentration of buildings in Beer Sheva created
shade on the streets, an important factor for living
in a desert town. The gridiron system facilitated
security in the town from the outside, because from
every point along the parallel streets one could see
towards the desert.
  The town's gridiron system was constructed in
a northwest-southeast direction facing towards the
main roads from Gaza, Hebron and the Negev (2).
This was also convenient from a climatic perspective
as the town was opened towards the winds from the
sea which came in from the northeast. The breezes
cleaned the streets from dust and sandstorms. One
of the system's deficiencies is that it did not account for the local topography. This topography

Figure 9.1: Beer Sheva - Land Uses

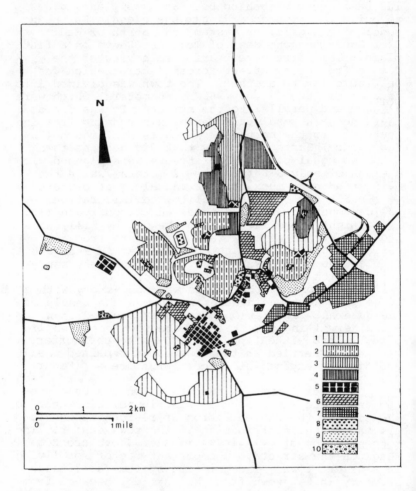

1. Low Density 2. Low to Mid-Density
3. Mid to High Density 4. High Density
5. Commercial Zone 6. Institutions
7. Industrial Zone 8. Intensive Public Open
   Space 9. Extensive Public Open Space
10. Cemetery

does not allow for the creation of an overall gridiron system so that difficulties occurred in the
water supply and sewage networks. Even the materials used to build houses were not suitable for the
desert climate and within a short time period the
facades of many homes began to crumble.

URBAN PROCESSES IN THE PAST

Until the outbreak of World War I, Beer Sheva functioned as the center of the Turkish government in the
Negev in order to control the Bedouins, to supervise
their commerce, and as a market center for Bedouins
who came from all parts of the Negev to meet with
merchants from Gaza and Hebron. Despite these activities the Turkish authorities were unsuccessful in
encouraging the growth of Beer Sheva's population
and during most time periods it remained a village
where houses were uninhabited or were used as storage places for grain by the Bedouins.
       With the outbreak of the war Beer Sheva gain-
ed importance because of its geographical location
in the northern Negev and its strategic position in
the arrangement between the Turks and the British
who then ruled Egypt and the Suez Canal in the south.
Beer Sheva became a base for the Turkish military
operations in the Sinai by command of Gamal Pasha,
Turkish Commander-in-Chief in Palestine in order to
prevent a British invasion there. A printing press
was erected in Beer Sheva for the publication of
newspapers for the army, roads were constructed between the town and Hebron and also from Beer Sheva
to Nizana and towards the central Sinai. Water
pipelines were laid in the desert to points of
strategic importance, bridges and other installations were erected causing an increase in the population of the town.
       The British conquest of Beer Sheva in 1917 put
a halt to the first indications of urbanization
which were distinguishable by the era of the Turkish rule. Many installations, electricity lines,
the printing house and the railway lines were completely destroyed. The British supplied the towns
with all of its needed services but did not initiate
any type of urban development. Only at the beginning of the 1940s, following the movements of the
British army during the Second World War, attempts
were made to revitalize Beer Sheva, but they did not
last very long because with the outbursts of the War
of Independence the town became desolate again.

POPULATION

Since the establishment of Beer Sheva until 1948, the population numbered no more than 6,000 to 7,000 inhabitants. The population was categorized into three main groups: merchants who came from Gaza, people from Hebron and Bedouins who settled in the town. The rate of population growth was very slow. In 1903 there were 300 inhabitants in the town, and on the eve of World War I, 800 people lived there. During the war, due to compulsary labour used in building the town and its infrastructure, the population grew to 1,000. In the census of 1922 Beer Sheva numbered 2,356 inhabitants, and 2,959 residents in 1931. The population did not directly contribute to the development of the town because most of the inhabitants were not of urban origin and those who settled there remained in Beer Sheva only for short periods. In 1946, there were only 6,450 inhabitants in Beer Sheva despite the British presence there.

The number of Jews living in Beer Sheva remained low throughout all periods. In the 1922 census they numbered 98 and were employed in building and construction. With the outbreak of the Jewish-Arab conflicts of 1929 most of them left and until the establishment of the State, Jews did not live there.

NEW APPROACHES IN THE PLANNING AND CONSTRUCTION OF BEER SHEVA

At the time of the establishment of the State, Beer Sheva was vast in size and the town's small one-story houses were dispersed on a small area of approximately 125 acres. Repopulating the town took place within the framework of immigration absorption which at its first stage entailed inhabiting the abundant number of houses which were available. Due to the absence of an outline scheme and neighbourhood plans, the immigrants occupied the empty houses and remained in them. In the beginning of the 1950s business services and administration grew in Beer Sheva. After establishment of the State, development of the Negev was given high priority and this impetus generated much human and vehicle traffic passing through the town which caused services to flourish. As a result, the CBD of the ancient part of the town crystallized. In a relatively small area of about 7 hectars which are located in the old

134

Turkish and Mandatory part of town, more than a half of the businesses of Beer Sheva are concentrated.

In the middle of the 1960s, the planning of Beer Sheva began in an area of 1,300 hectares for a population of 70,000. It was decided at that time to enlarge the town towards the north, northwest and northeast, with the aim of building new and modern neighbourhoods and to desert the old center north of the old town which meanwhile had become the CBD of Beer Sheva. Five neighbourhoods were planned and built along an axis of favourable topography. These neighbourhoods were built as self-contained units according to the principle of secondary CBDs in each one with a system of encircling roads. The original idea of adding gardens and public open spaces in these neighbourhoods was not undertaken due to the lack of water and the fact that public open spaces are unsuitable in a town with an arid climate.

Beer Sheva has always had favourable conditions for town planning. Geographically, it is located on a site which is appropriate as the capital of the Negev and as the capital of a district. The surrounding area is sparsely populated and broad lowlands surround the town, but despite all of its geographical advantages from the beginning a clear concept of Beer Sheva's future urban dimensions was never planned. Many experiments were done in absorbing immigrants and finding the appropriate model for its neighbourhoods and the design of the local CBDs, so that in many respects Beer Sheva has been little more than a large laboratory for housing and building in Israel.

In the meantime, the population of the town grew. Since the establishment of the State until 1981 the expansion is as follows: (Table 9.1)

Table 9.1: Population in Beer Sheva 1950-1981

Year	Population
1950	8,300
1955	20,500
1961	46,400
1967	69,500
1974	93,400
1981	111,200

According to this rate of increase the town should be planned for a population of 250 thousand by the year 2000. In revised plans from the late 1960s, a trial experiment was made to stop urban renewal from expanding northwards and to develop construction towards the west. Opposite the ancient CBD of Beer Sheva a new CBD was planned. The many investments made in the new area along with the sprawl of the ancient CBD towards the new area gives rise to the hope that the two sections will unite in the future. The new CBD is located northeast of the ancient one, a site which is suitable for handling the transport of large loads of goods to Gaza, Hebron, Sedom and even to the northern part of the country. The planners' goal was to transfer commercial activity to a more central location where most of the population was found. But, despite the town's growth and the distribution of population throughout it, most of the commercial activity still remained in the old town even with the accessibility difficulties to this area. This action of the old CBD today stretches over 11 hectars which makes up less than 0.5% of the municipal area of the town. An analysis of the urban development of Beer Sheva shows that the timing of this new location was 12 years too late in coming and was begun when the old CBD reached its height in centrality and power. As long as the possibility exists of converting houses from residential to commercial use in the old CBD, it will not sprawl into the new area.

The town today extends on a vast amount of land in which many areas are barren. With the conditions of Beer Sheva long distances for pedestrians is quite strenuous in areas that are not built up. The new planning of Beer Sheva is based on the design of the town as an oasis bringing about the development of small areas which are well defined in their surrounding landscape and it is therefore proposed to fill in all the open spaces with buildings.

The CBD with its latest planning, strives to be the geographical center of the town as much as possible. The rapid development of Beer Sheva created a situation in which the enlarged CBD is located in the south, more than half of the population lives in the north, while low density neighbourhoods surround the town center. The new planning therefore attempts to improve the contour of the town by the addition of urban expanses of residential areas towards the west and northwest.

The town was planned by the principle of land

use arrangement according to the road network. This network therefore, has a great impact on the distribution of the different areas in the town and their uses. The new planning created a crisscross network of main roads in the northwest-southeast direction and in the southwest-northeast direction. This network is surrounded by an inner and outer circular road which closes off the entire urban area. The central meeting point of the main roads is the new CBD, an aspect which may improve accessity to the town.

LAND USES IN THE TOWN

The land use layout in Beer Sheva shows the following distribution: the old CBD is situated in the southwestern corner of the town and is the junction of the main roads leading into Beer Sheva from the west, northwest, north and east. The railway line enters the town from its northeast corner in an area of open space thus preventing pollution in the residential sections in the east. Between the railway station and the old CBD there is a large industrial area parallel to Wadi Beer Sheva which also acts as a buffer zone against the urban sprawl towards the south. To the west and south of the original CBD, a section of poor quality and densely settled housing exists, the result of immigrant settlement in the town in the 1950s. From the CBD northwards extends the main street, President's Avenue, and to the east of it lies a concentration of public institutions, governmental buildings, the courtyard, the university and other buildings. Residential neighbourhoods of medium density are located to the west and east of this central axis. Public open space is found around the neighbourhoods in the east and west.

In summary, it could be stated that Beer Sheva demonstrates the typical developmental stages of a town located on a desert fringe. Throughout its history it was a meeting place for shepherds and nomads who found sources of water there. Beer Sheva was built for the purpose of administrating and observing the Bedouin tribes and not for goal of erecting a large town in that area. Due to the lack of an agricultural and economic hinterland, the town was always dependent upon the national and regional functions designated to it by the ruling administrations. Times of prosperity and decline were dependent upon periods of stability and instability. Thus, the town went through extreme changes due to con-

struction and development on one hand and destruction and abandonment on the other. Israel's national
interest in developing the Negev and in repopulating
Beer Sheva brought about favourable prosperous conditions. This meant that new immigrants were directed to Beer Sheva, a phenomenon which was a source of
growth in many new towns throughout the country.
When Beer Sheva overcame the initial stages of its
growth it had a population of more than 30,000-
40,000 inhabitants and had reached a point of take-
off in its development where it continued to expand
by its own inertia. At that stage Beer Sheva began
to attract many investors and increased development
occurred despite the town's arid climate and unusual
geographical location.

NOTES

1.   M. Berman, The Evolution of Beer Sheva
as an Urban Center (Annals of the American Association Geographers, 1965), pp.308-326.
2.   A Hebrew term for the southern semi-
arid region of Israel, between Beer Sheva and Elat.

Chapter Ten

THE NEW TOWNS

One of the most important phenomenon in the urbanization of Israel has been the establishment of a
large number of new towns within a short time period.
Although this basic phenomenon of new town development is well known throughout the world and many
countries such as Great Britain, Poland, Holland,
Finland, United States and Canada established towns
after World War II, in Israel this occurrence is
much more apparent because within a period of 15
years more than 30 towns were constructed in which
a few hundred thousand people inhabited.

NEW TOWNS AS A BASIS FOR IMMIGRANT ABSORPTION

If the British Mandate period can be characterized
as one where most of the urbanization took place was
in the form of preservation of and local additions
to certain towns, then Israel's period is typified
by the creation of many new towns established via a
national and comprehensive approach as a solution
for settlement problems and in order to distribute
the population - two challenges confronting the
State.
        It is difficult to say whether the government
had made the decision to establish new towns at the
time of the establishment of the State. The decision to build new towns was forced upon the settlement bodies due to the pressure of immigration and
absorption needs. Not all of the immigrants arriving
between 1948 and 1953 could be absorbed into the
agricultural sector due to land and water limitation.
It was felt that other solutions should be found and
that something should be done in the urban sector.
The establishment of new towns for the purpose of
immigrant absorption and the distribution

of the population appeared to be a reasonable solution for these problems. Once this route for immigration absorption was chosen the settlement bodies
did not forego their traditional agricultural ideology of the past and so in the planning of the
urban settlements there was an intermingling of
ideas resulting in new towns of low density with one
storey houses and yards for agricultural purposes.
This penetration of agricultural concepts in the
planning of the new towns greatly influenced their
shape from the beginning. The new towns did not
immediately become urban ideological goals. For at
least 10 to 15 years this semi-urban approach continued and no social or urban ideology developed
regarding urbanization.

NEW TOWN PLANNING APPROACHES

It was first realized that Israel was in want of
comprehensive physical planning following the needs
of rapid immigration absorption. During the Mandate
period no comprehensive scheme of town planning was
developed. Planning, as it existed was concentrated
in the establishment towns only, in the detailed
outline of neighbourhoods, or in certain sectors of
towns and usually for security purposes for the
British army and government rather than for con-
structive developmental reasons. With the establishment of the State the settlement bodies had no
national plan nor principle concepts in the field of
urbanization. During the British Mandate experience
was accumulated mainly in the establishment of agricultural settlements but no one had been involved in
the development of new towns.
     The planners of the 1950s did not develop
original concepts of their own because of their lack
of experience. Rather, they attempted to apply planning models that were widely accepted in other countries. One well liked model of urban spatial distribution was the hierarchy pattern based on the
establishment of agricultural settlements which had
a direct relationship with small or medium-sized
urban centers and those - were in contact with larger centers, townlets or towns and those - had connections to a private town which was at the top of
the settlement pyramid. This model of settlement
distribution can be found especially in countries
with a long history of settlement development such
ás Holland, France, Belgium and Southern Germany.
The fundamental approach to the new towns was not

very revolutionary, rather it was very conservative and was taken from European models. What was revolutionary was the unexpected growth of the new towns in contrast to the past populating and settlement systems in Israel. During the Mandate period in Palestine urban development was nodal and typified by the growth of the three large towns - Tel Aviv, Jerusalem and Haifa. Due to 50 years of extensive pioneering there were many agricultural settlements such as <u>Kibbutzim</u> and <u>Moshavim</u>. No recognizable development was found in the middle stage of the hierarchy model so that the establishment of medium-sized towns in Israel became the intermediary between the large towns and the small agricultural settlements. (1)

The first purpose of the physical planning was to complete the missing links in the former settlement layout via the establishment of medium-sized development towns which would be used as service centers by their agricultural surroundings. The settlement bodies had three options: to develop existing agricultural settlements into urban centers, to enlarge the established small towns, or to create new medium-sized towns. The first possibility was dismissed because of ideological and practical reasons which did enable the conversion of agricultural settlements into urban ones. The second option was only practically executed because there were not enough small towns to be enlarged. Thus, what remained was the third possibility of establishing new medium-sized towns.

The new settlement hierarchy was built in five levels, beginning with the village at the lowest level until the large town at the top in order to change the nodality which had enrooted itself during the urban system of the Mandate period. This hierarchy presented the following types of settlement:

Type A - Villages with 500 inhabitants
Type B - Village centers with 2,000 inhabitants each.
Type C - Semi-urban centers with 6,000 - 12,000 inhabitants each.
Type D - 40,000 - 60,000 inhabitants each.
Type E - Large towns with 100,000 inhabitants or more.

The village center (Type B) was to supply services to 3 - 5 villages around it, and shops, stores, garages, etc. would be located in it. The semi-urban center was to provide services to 30 villages

within a radius of 6 miles (10 kms.) and the services located there would be of a higher rank, industries,factories based on local products along with
high schools and institutions. The medium-sized
towns were to have a concentration of governmental
institutions, banks, hospitals and factories. It
was envisioned that these towns would attract industries which could not find enough land in the larger
towns and that needed cheaper manpower. The large
town was to be given the status of a regional capital and was to maintain connections with the other
large towns in the country.

As mentioned interconnections links in this
system were settlement types B, C and D, so the
planners made great efforts to establish them because of their potential to absorb new immigrants.
The smaller center types of B and C gained more
from ideology because they were not significant from
an urban perspective and fitted more into the agricultural background.

Within a few years these small centers became
the weak and problematic links in the entire national urban network. The concept was to create a new
urban center but under the condition that it would
not be disconnected from agriculture. The population of such a center had to be small in size and
location in agricultural surroundings, living in
houses with plots of land which were to provide an
auxiliary source of income. The land in these yards
was designated for vegetables and daily agricultural
products and supplemented the inhabitant's income
during seasons when no outside work in agriculture
could be found. These centers were later criticized
as being too small to develop an urban lifestyle in
them.

Perhaps the real reason behind the construction of small centers was that the planners had to
gradually change their settlement ideology and to
transfer it into the type of town planning forced
upon them by the existing realities. The small urban center, comparitively speaking, was inferior to
the developed village or to the kibbutz.

THE EXECUTION OF THE PLANNING OF THE NEW TOWNS

The new towns and the different small semi-urban
centers had to be integrated into veteran regions
with established social and economical bases. The
regions where the new towns and centers were located
had been settled for many years by the kibbutzim and

moshavim. The new towns could only supply low level
services to the veteran settlements which from the
beginning were not sympathetic towards nor attracted
to these centers. Initially the Kibbutzim refused
to employ town inhabitants because of their rejection of the principle of hired labour. The absence
of an interrelationship between the immigrant towns
and the veteran settlements prevented additional
attempts to establish new towns on one hand, while
also discouraging the improvement of services in
the already existing towns so that most of them developed slowly without impetus, and with the great
concern of solving the daily problems of their own
inhabitants.

The method of establishing small and medium-
sized development towns changed in the mid-1950s
with the alteration of trends in the agricultural
policy. During that time the settlement bodies expanded their use of mechanized farming in many of
the regions throughout the country which were settled by immigrants.

This form of intensive agriculture was based
on industrial crops such as cotton, sugar, beets,
etc. which needed to be processed close to where
they were grown so that nearby factories were erected. The processing of these branches of agriculture
took place on a regional and more comprehensive
level because of the private farmer's inability to
execute the entire process. Agricultural diversifi-
cation was the result of a saturation of vegetables,
poultry, and dairy products. The new moshavim in
the development areas were based on the new branches
of industrial crops which could only be economically
grown on large tracts of land. Prior to the establishment of the State farmers did not have vast
tracts of land needed to develop and grow these
branches, but after 1948 such development could be
executed mainly in the southern coastal plain and the
northern Negev. A new settlement system had to be
planned in order to cultivate such large areas. A
single farm could not cultivate such vast areas,
only a regional settlement system with urban and
semi-urban centers was able to take on such a challenge. A regional town was needed in this system in
order to be the center of production, storage and
export of the agricultural products.

Even in the well-established regions where a
transfer to intensive agriculture occurred, there
was a need to establish medium-sized towns. Through
their creation the planners wanted to prevent a complete dependence on the large towns for their eco-

143

nomic activities. They assumed that the regional
town would develop and prosper along with the entire
region thus becoming an integral part of it. The
regional town even supplied services not related to
agriculture to all of its surrounding settlements in
the fields of education, health, transportation, administration etc. Apparently, the development towns
did close the gap between the large towns and the
small villages so far as physical space and region
are concerned but what is troublesome today and has
not been resolved are their own internal problems of
employment, education, housing and level of services.
It should be added that the approach to the development towns was not exactly suitable for Israel's
conditions, the planning of them was often not done
within the regional context, and their physical
planning was not developed in conjunction with their
social and economic planning.

GEOGRAPHICAL DISTRIBUTION OF THE NEW TOWNS

The location of the development towns was decided
according to very general criteria, the directed
functions the town would have along with suitable
geographical conditions. From a geographical perspective the distribution of development towns was
not particularly appropriate. Many were located too
close together as Ofaqim, Sederot and Netivot, while
others were situated nearby large towns such as
Qiryat Malachi, Yehud and Mavasseret Ziyyon. In
areas like the eastern Galilee, the upper and central Galilee and the Arava (2) no development towns
were established. Town location was the result of
practical reasons, immediate needs and because of
inexpensive land. By reconstructing the location
process of development towns one sees that the first
stage involved resettlement of abandoned Arab villages such as Lod, Ramla, Bet She'an, Beer Sheva and
even Arab neighbourhoods in Acre, Jerusalem, Migdal
or Yavne. Once these areas were inhabited immigrants were directed to the agricultural sector with
the aim of absorbing them in the Kibbutzim and
veteran Moshavot, but, as mentioned before ability
to absorb tnem in this sector was very limited.
Immigrants were then guided to veteran Moshavot near
which transit camps were constructed providing them
with a place to live and seasonal employment in
citrus work.
       The transit camps were manpower resources in
which many of their inhabitants were unable to find

144

suitable employment in the Moshavah or in the immediate surroundings. Many of those in the transit camps wanted to leave them in order to move to the veteran and more stable settlements, but there were also people who preferred to stay in the camps for social reasons. The development and construction bodies gradually tried to eliminate the transit camps because of their propensity to become slums. Due to the lack of new housing only a part of the camps were eliminated, therefore many of the temporary houses became permanent dwellings for their inhabitants. Thus the basis of some development towns such as Or Aqiva, Rosh HaAyin, Yehud and others was their past use as transit camps. When the waves of additional immigration to Israel could no longer be absorbed in the transit camps, the stage of new town development began in the country. Only in the Lakhish region, a development town, Qiryat Gat, was established within the framework of comprehensive regional development so that the town and its region grew simultaneously and in a homogenic manner. In all the other locations in the country development towns were situated in regions where settlements had been previously established, for example, Qiryat Shemona in the Hula Valley, Bet Shemesh in the corridor of Jerusalem, Qiryat Malachi in the southern coastal plain, Ma'alot in the upper western Galilee, Tirat Karmel along the Carmel coast, etc. This stage of town establishment greatly assisted in the absorption of immigrants on the background of the population distribution policy and for the first time changed the original distribution in the northern and southern districts so that their rate of population increase had a favourable increase over their pre-State rates. Only at the end of the 1950s did the planners begin establishing large towns like Ashdod and Beer Sheva, and when places like Arad or Karmiel were envisioned, they were planned and built with a complete urban character. (Figure 10.1)

Upon classifying the new towns according to year and place of establishment, we find that since Statehood about 30 new settlements were founded and populated by Jews. They were given the status of a local authority or town. Town distribution according to founding date shows significant variations in the number established during each time period. The maximum number of towns founded was in 1948 when Bet She'an, Acre, Yehud, Lod, Azur, Bet Dagan, Ramla, Ashqelon and Beer Sheva were populated. Although nine were established in one year it should be

Figure 10.1: Distribution of New Towns

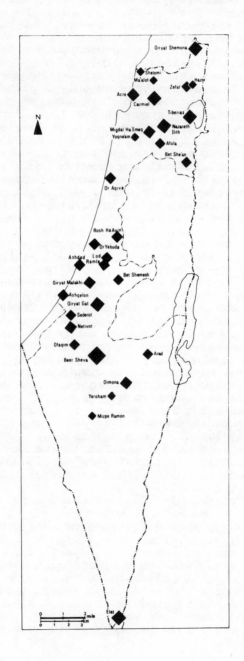

mentioned that all of these towns previously existed and had been abandoned by the Arabs during the War of Independence. Because houses were already there immigrants were directed to them and shortly occupied all of the abandoned structures.

In 1949 Tirat Karmel and Yavne, also towns with abandoned houses were populated. Since 1950 onwards, new housing has been established. In that year Qiryat Shemona, Shelomi, Yoqneam, Rosh HaAyin, Or Yehuda and Bet Shemesh were founded. All of these locations were originally transit camps which planners viewed as being suitable sites for future town development. Even in 1951 town establisment continued. Then, Rehasim, Sederot, Yeruham and Elat were founded. If Or Aqiva, Mevasseret, Ziyyon, Qiryat Malachi, and Yerham, characterized settlements on the background of transit camps, all the other places mentioned were built as new permanent towns. The time period between 1948 to 1951 is when the majority of new urban Jewish settlements were added to the map. Migdal HaEmeq was founded in 1952, Hazor in 1953, Qiryat Gat and Mitzpe Ramon in 1955, Ofaqim, and Dimona in 1956, Netivot and Upper Nazareth in 1957. Since that time new town establishment has ceased and most of the work in them is concentrated in improving their overall inner structures. This stoppage came with a decrease in the number of immigrants and those who arrived later were directed to live in existing towns. In the 1960s two additional towns were founded. Arad in 1961 and Karmiel in 1964. The first was established as a town in the locale of a natural resource in the northeast part of the Negev, while the second was created in the northern part of the Galilee for political reasons. They were different from previously established towns because their populations were selected from people living in Israel for many years and immigrants and from the beginning the town's construction was modern. Since 1964 until today no new town has been added in the country.

New town classification according to regions in the country shows that until 1950 the central district was the main location of the new towns and to a lesser extent, the northern district. As absorption initially took place in abandoned towns which were located in the coastal plain, the main population increase took place there also. For towns that were created without the basis of a former infrastructure, priority was given to the southern district, where most of the towns were built between 1951-1956. It is apparent that the first new

towns outside of the central district were located
in the northern part of the country where veteran,
Jewish populations were settled in the Western Galilee, Hula Valley, and that later on after an infrastructure had been prepared in the northern Negev
the new town development wave moved to the south.
An additional classification of towns according to
their infrastructure shows that out of 36, 24 were
completely new, 4 were mixed between old and new,
and 8 were built on abandoned Arab infrastructure.
  The influence of geography on the distribution
of the new towns was minimal. With the exception of
locations like the Gulf of Elat, the transit area
between the higher lowland and the corridor of Jerusalem, and the upper Hula Valley where new towns
were objectively needed, town location was a matter
of choice. Towns were not established on the basis
of local natural resources, and because the distance
from one place to another within the country was so
minimal with the exception of the central and southern Negev, it was not imperative to develop too many
towns. Since water and energy sources were extremely limited they were not taken into account in locating towns. Location therefore, was primarily the
result of the following factors: topography, climate and land ownership. Establishing towns in
Judea and the Negev was easily facilitated as almost
all of the land there was owned by the State.
  Since 91% of Israel's territory is in the
hands of the Land Administration (3), the decision
to establish development towns was not difficult to
make. Most of the immigrant public housing was constructed in peripheral development regions thus con-
tributing to population dispersal in towns in Israel.
From the perspective of time, towns were established
with the waves of immigration as were their geographical locations because initially they were constructed in the country's center and then shifted to
the north and later reached the south. The Negev
was opened for urban settlements only in the 1950s
after roads had been paved and new projects constructed. Once begun, development increased at an
accelerated rate from year to year so that the southern district contained 12% of the country's population. The weight of the southern district expanded
so that almost half of the immigrants were concentrated there. The advantage the Negev and the southern district had over the more populated districts
was that the growth of agriculture and urbanization
there occurred simultaneously and in conjunction
with each other. In the north, for instance, a

veteran agricultural structure existed which operated much more efficiently than the new towns. This
was not the case in the south. Agricultural settlement in the south was based on new Moshavim which
needed a strong relationship with the new towns, thus
bringing about an increase in urbanization. The new
towns promoted the populating of peripheral regions
of the country, in the northern district by 67% and
in the southern district by 83%. In the last number
of years the growth of new towns had decreased due
to lower immigration rates. The new towns have
always responded to the immigration ebb and flow.

THE POPULATION IN THE NEW TOWNS

The new towns in Israel are characterized by a cross-
section of population which has an impact on most of
the urban population in the country. The composition of the new towns was not planned in advance, but
it was well-known that it would be primarily made up
of new immigrants and not by veteran inhabitants of
the country. It was difficult to predict the immigration flow and thus the populating rate of the
towns. Population composition was therefore determined by the countries origin, the rate of immigration, and the demographic structure of the immigrants
themselves.
        It should be recalled that after 1948 immigra-
tion was a very strong demographic phenomenon which
the country was unprepared to handle. From the day
of the declaration of independence (May 15, 1948),
until the end of that year more than 100,000 immigrants arrived. In 1949, twice that amount came to
settle in Israel. The type of immigrant arriving in
1948 was quite different than the one who settled
in Israel before the establishment of the State. In
the past, most of the immigrants were young, single,
socially and economically ambitious people or pioneers with a Zionist mentality. The immigrants
who settled after 1948 came with large families, and
with a high percentage of children and elderly. They
were not Zionists at all. Prior to 1948, 17% of the
immigrants were children as contrasted to 30% after
that time. In previous immigration waves 37% were
single people while after 1948 the rate of single
individuals decreased to 19%. There were even
ethnic differences among the immigrants as 85% were
of European origin prior to 1948 and by the mid-
1950s only 5.5% came from Europe. The majority of
the immigrants came from Asian and African countries.

The weight of the veteran inhabitants originally from Europe decreased continuously and most of them remained concentrated in the large towns or in the Kibbutzim.

Although not all of the immigrants were directed to development towns, they did influence their size and character. In the 18 new towns which were established until 1951, 120,000 people lived. Between 1952-1954, four new towns were added which were inhabited by 22,000 people. Between 1958-1960, a decrease in the populating of development towns by new immigrants began. Most of the new towns expanded on their own as a result of natural increase and internal migration expressed physically by the construction of additional housing. Today, the rate of the new immigrants in the urban population of Israel is about 20%.

It can be stated that all of the development towns increased in population size and that not one was abandoned or diminished in number of inhabitants. An extremely high growth rate occurred in Ashdod, Beer Sheva and Dimona. In many of the development towns the population is not greater than 10,000 and in several of them there are even fewer than this number of inhabitants. In several of the new towns such as Ashdod, Beer Sheva, Dimona, Upper Nazareth and Qiryat Shemona, growth was encouraged via the government together with the extraordinary investments as witnessed by the industry in Beer Sheva, the harbour in Ashdod, the nuclear plant in Dimona, and the industry in Upper Nazareth. More than 20, 000 inhabitants are needed in a town in order for it to reach a take-off point and only Beer Sheva, Ashdod, Dimona, Ashqelon, Qiryat Gat, Lod and Ramla achieved populations of this size. The higher rates or urban growth happened in the southern part of the country more so than in the center, and in the center more so than in the north. Even the number of large development towns is greater in the south than in the central part of Israel or its north.

In the past number of years only a part of the immigrants have been directed to the new towns, while the rest could be absorbed only in the large towns. Country of origin, level of education and socio-economic status are the main reasons for that trend. In the first decade of statehood, 1 million immigrants arrived, but only 17.5% of them were directed to the development towns. As more immigrants came from Western countries, fewer went to development towns. It can be assumed that the rate of immigrants that will live in these towns in the

future will be not more than 25%-30%. The development towns can expand only with improved infrastructure, level of services and by becoming more
attractive. Each town has its own attraction power
dependent upon its geographical location, years of
existence, the factories and installations located
in it and the amount of initiative its population
has in shaping the town and its services. In several of the new towns there is a danger of a negative rate of migration where the percentage of those
leaving will be higher than the percentage of those
moving into the town. It appears that the development towns in the southern part of the country have
a much greater magnetic force than those in the
north. This can partially be explained by the pull
of Beer Sheva and Ashdod. In all of the development
towns there are tremendous vicissitudes in those
coming and leaving demonstrating that they have
still not crystallized socially and economically.
The demographic composition found in the development
towns today was mainly influenced by the immigration
structure. This is witnessed especially in development towns where a stratum of poorer people remained.
Immigration to Israel brought with it a high percentage of uneducated people without professions who
were unaccustomed to a modern, urban way of life.
Ninety-five percent of those arriving in development
towns were new immigrants, in medium-sized towns
approximately 80% were new immigrants and in the
larger towns about 60%. In the agricultural settlements established after 1948 the percentage of new
immigrants was above 95, especially in the Moshavim.
In contrast to that was the small percentage of new
immigrants living on Kibbutzim because absorption
was difficult without a strong ideological background. The majority of immigrants was thus concentrated in the new Moshavim or in new development
towns. The larger a town was, or the longer a
Kibbutz had been established, the lower the percentage of immigrants living there.

The distribution between veteran inhabitants
and newcomers in the settlement is also very interesting. The larger the development town or settlement the higher the number of veteran residents.
In the small towns and young Moshavim the rate of
new immigrants is high irrespective of geographical
region. During the urban process integration of
newcomers with veterans was impossible. The arrival
of large waves of immigration necessitated immediate
settlement so that no time existed for social integration processes. An even more influential fact

151

was that it was quite difficult to separate people from the same homeland and community because of the danger of isolation connected to the immigration and resettlement periods. Integration was more successful in the younger towns such as Arad and Karmiel where a population composed of one third veterans, one third Europeans and one third Asian-Africans was mixed together. Practically speaking it was quite difficult to guide demographic development in the new towns as there was no reign over the sources of immigration and those arriving with capital were free to go where they pleased.

In the past number of years a greater interest in the structure and quality of life of the new towns has arisen. A new wave of rehabilitation has appeared in many of them. Qiryat Gat, for example, experienced a renewal with the construction of new neighbourhoods built for veterans. In Arad, a careful social selection was done of those wanting to live in the town so that a suitable group of veterans was chosen to live with new immigrants. Even the construction style was greatly improved. More compact and higher housing was built, the CBD was improved,institutions were constructed. industrial projects were promoted establishing an employment base and even private enterprise was permitted to develop in this town. Today, new towns are recognized as important factors in settlement pioneering. Town and village are equal in importance and are given the same treatment by governmental authorities. Although the new towns have been greatly criticized their imprint on Israel's landscape is so strong that they will influence the urban layout for many years to come.

NOTES

1.   E. Spiegel, <u>New Towns in Israel</u> (Karl Kraemer Verlag, Stuttgart-Bern, 1966).
2.   A Hebrew term for a part of the rift valley on the eastern side of the Negev, between the Dead Sea in the north and the Gulf of Elat in the south.
3.   An institution in the Ministry of Agriculture, which is in charge of the administration of the land owned by the country.

Chapter Eleven

ASHDOD

The building of the town of Ashod and its harbour is one of the greatest urban projects ever undertaken in Israel from a planning and an engineering perspective. Ashod is the only one among the new towns in Israel which from the beginning, was planned for a population of 350,000 inhabitants on an area of 4,000 hectars, with a harbour that will handle a capacity of 4 million tons.

CONSIDERATIONS OF THE HARBOUR'S LOCATION

The construction of the harbour was connected to many considerations taken by various governmental institutions. The discussions focused on two main questions:

1. Was there a need to construct a new deep water harbour in addition to Haifa, or was it possible just to enlarge the harbour of Tel Aviv?

2. If it was decided to build a new harbour where should it be located?

In the development plan of Tel Aviv the idea of building a harbour there was considered. Although at the beginning of the 1930s the Jewish public was enthusiastic about constructing a Jewish harbour separate from Jaffa, this project was never undertaken because the proposed and only possible harbour location was too close to the border of these two towns. After the establishment of the State the demand for a second deep water harbour rose again due to the comparatively distant location of Haifa's harbour to the central economic activities which took place around Tel Aviv. The issue of a second

deep water harbour was also of great importance because of the policy advocating the development of
the Negev as Israel's main objective. Because of
this policy there was a need to locate a deep water
harbour at some distance south of Haifa.

At that time there was a proposal to build the
second harbour in Tel Aviv. The advantages of locating the harbour in Tel Aviv were that together
with its satellites it contained more than 40% of
the Jewish population in Israel, the city and its
surroundings had become the largest center of industrial, institutional and economic activity, and was
located in the center of the citrus plantation distribution, the main branch of export in the country.

Among the deliberations about locating the harbour in Tel Aviv was the declared governmental policy regarding the distribution of the population. In
order to undertake this policy it was necessary to
take two steps simultaneously. To buffer the growth
and the high proportional weight of Tel Aviv's population and to increase population rates in the development towns located in the north and south. It
became apparent that from such a starting point,
there was little chance that the harbour would be
built in Tel Aviv and therefore a search for a better location began.

Later on other serious reasons for not building
the harbour in Tel Aviv were raised as follows:

1. The locating of a deep water harbour near
   the large population concentrations of
   the country could be dangerous from a
   security point of view.
2. The limited land reserves around the envisioned harbour area could not meet the
   demands it would have. Therefore, houses
   would have to be demolished via land
   acquisition which would be very costly.
3. A modern harbour not only needs areas
   loading, unloading and storage, but also
   transportation routes - highways and railways. All of these transportation arteries did not exist in the proposed harbour location.
4. Tel Aviv is one of the highest priced
   areas for land in the country so that
   again harbour establishment would be very
   costly.
5. Despite Tel Aviv's proximity to the citrus plantations and accessibility to the
   proposed harbour site, the traffic on the

transportation arteries would be much
greater with a harbour there, making life
for the populous more difficult and diminishing accessibility in due time.

During the search for a new location there was a
proposal to establish the harbour in Ashqelon, but
because of its proximity to the Gaza Strip it was
rejected. Another proposition was to locate the
harbour at the mouth of the Soreq River not far from
Tel Aviv where the land prices were quite low. Due
to particular security problems this idea was also
rejected.
     Serious security reasons on one hand, and plann-
ing and geographical ones on the other brought about
the rejection of the above mentioned proposals and
made it that much more important to consider a new
proposition of locating the harbour at the mouth of
the Lakhish River a few miles north of the ancient
site of Ashdod-Yam (Maritime-Ashdod). The surrounding area was at that time undeveloped and desolate,
the location fit into the distribution of population
idea, it was close to the citrus plantation areas
and not far from Tel Aviv. In addition, the area
had two advantages which were on unrestricted amount
of inexpensive land suitable for housing and from a
security perspective it was 25 miles (40 kms.) north
of the Gaza Strip and about the same distance south
of Tel Aviv. Its main detraction was its remoteness
from the existing infrastructure of roads and settlements.
     In the middle of the 1950s with a decrease in
immigration it was feared that the proposal to build
this new town would not be implemented. In 1953, a
specific problem arose when the electric company was
looking to find a location for a new power station.
The decision to locate the power station on that uninhabited coast of Ashdod-Yam, along with the pav-
ing of an access load to and from the plant, together with the need to build a neighbourhood for
the company workers, was the first step towards establishing a new urban settlement. In 1957 the decision to build a deep water harbour in Ashdod was
made and in 1961 construction of Ashdod began with
the promise that it would become one of the largest
towns in Israel.

THE CONSTRUCTION OF THE TOWN

The town of Ashdod **was pl**anned on a strip of dunes 7 miles (11 kms.) long and 1-2 miles (2-4 kms.) wide. Its eastern border parallels the agricultural land extending east of the Wadi Lakish which divides the town into two parts. In the north lies the harbour and the industrial zone, to the south, the residential area. Experimentation was done in the planning of Ashdod in order to prevent it from developing the typical structure of a small new town. A plan for a large town was prepared dividing it into neighbourhoods with a modern road network. The sand dune topography was suitable for this purpose as the higher locations were favourable for residential areas and the lower ones for roads. The coastline was for recreation and bathing beaches, while the flat area to the north of Wadi Lakhish was designated for industry and the harbour.

The town was planned on the basis of a gridiron road system which clearly limited the size of the neighbourhood units and their connection from one to the other. Traffic traveling at fast speeds for long distances and slower inner neighbourhood traffic was to be separated according to the plan. The major north-south road passing through the town connects it with Tel Aviv, the harbour and the CBD. main east-west road is the town's connection to the Negev. (Figure 11.1)

The major road network divides the town into 16 residential neighbourhoods where in each one 3,000 - 5,000 apartments were built. Neighbourhood activity is planned from an internal perspective. A commercial center, public open space, gardens and pedestrian walks are contained in each neighbourhood. The CBD is planned for the geographical center of Ashdod at the junction of the two major routes passing through the town.

The principle behind the outline scheme of Ashdod is maximum separation between urban activities at their various levels. In the towns - by the distinction between the residential areas on one hand and the harbour, industry, commerce and services on the other. In the residential areas - by a separation between dwellings, local commerce, shops, schools and open space.

Town construction according to the outline scheme began in 1960. A high standard of construction was undertaken in comparison to what had been done in other towns for the following groups: Good quality, compact buildings of 3-4 storeys for new

156

Figure 11.1: Outline Scheme of Ashdod

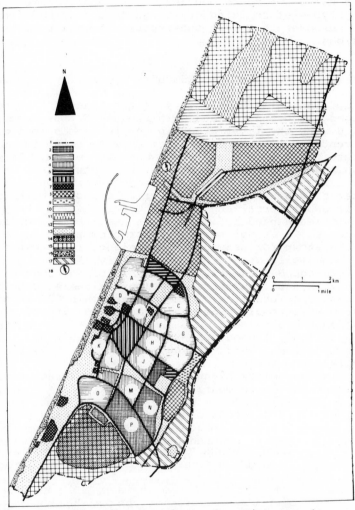

1. Town Planning Boundary 2. High Density
3. Mid-Density 4. Low Density 5. Commercial
   Zone 6. Central Business District
7. Institutions 8. Industrial Zone 9. Storing
   Area 10. Harbour Installations 11. Seepage
   Area 12. Zone for Potential Industry
13. Public Open Space 14. Potential Residential
    Area 15. Afforestation 16. Beach
17. Agricultural Area 18. Power Installation

157

immigrants, buildings of a higher standard for the veteran who were to live in Ashdod and a third type of housing for young couples. As a result there are many types of building styles in Ashdod with different purposes that were constructed at various time periods.

THE CBD AND THE NEIGHBOURHOODS

Ashdod initially developed with the construction of neighbourhoods A, B, and C in the north. Because A and B were the first areas in the town, most people concentrated in them and services were established before the main CBD of Ashdod was even built. As a result these neighbourhood service areas today function as the main centers of Ashdod even though other neighbourhoods were later constructed with their own internal and smaller CBDs. All of the facilities needed by its inhabitants are located in Ashdod so it is not necessary for them to go to another town for services. The higher rank town for very specialized services is Tel Aviv. As neighbourhoods A and B presently fulfill all of the town's needs, in the future the question will arise concerning the functions of the planned main CBD in a system where smaller neighbourhood CBDs already provide enough services.

In 1961, Ashdod numbered 6,200 inhabitants, in 1965 - 23,400 in 1968 - 32,000, and in 1981 - 66,000 people lived there.

In the policy planning of the town three main mistakes should be mentioned.

1. By developing neighbourhoods A and B in the north, they were too remote from the major planned CBD. Therefore these neighbourhood CBDs took on a higher level of functions than what was projected for them.

2. The initial lack of a main CBD caused an over-construction of the neighbourhood CBDs and the distribution of overloaded functions in these sub-centers emptied out the functions of the main CBD.

3. In order to develop the secondary system of roads only the main roads which became the axes for public transportation, pedestrians and for the development of commerce. Such development was in contrast to the planned function of these roads

which was as bypass arteries only. It
appears that the immediate and intensive
development of the main CBD and the settling of a few hundred families there, is
necessary to counterbalance what has occurred in the neighbourhoods.

THE HARBOUR

The local and regional reason for constructing the
harbour was, as stated above, for the export of citrus from vast hinterland comprising the entire
southern lowland in the country. It was also assumed that minerals from the Negev would be exported
from this harbour rather than having to be sent the
considerable distance to Haifa.

By 1958, all of the plans for the harbour were
completed, and by July 1961 the cornerstone was laid.
The harbour was to be constructed in two stages according to the original plans, but piers and other
installations were built earlier to facilitate the
urgent need to export citrus, potash, and phosphates.
By 1966, most of the other installations were completed.

The harbour has both local and national influence. Locally, it provides employment for the people of Ashdod while being a center which will attract future growth. Nationally, the harbour allev-
iates some of the pressures on Haifa's port, reduces
the distance of the transportation routes from the
south, and promotes the distribution of the population.

Today, approximately 40% of the citrus export
passes through Ashdod. With the assistance of auto-
matic conveyor belts, phosphates and potash are exported through this harbour. Special tanks are
located there to transmit chemicals in a liquid
form. Vehicles are imported via Ashdod's harbour
which has large storage areas. Large refrigeration
units have promoted meat imports. At the present,
the harbour has reached the stage where it is pre-
paring to load and unload container units which are
used in the most modern harbours throughout the
world.

THE INTERRELATIONSHIP OF THE HARBOUR AND THE TOWN

The separation between the harbour activities and
the residential areas was to facilitate a link be-

tween the harbour and its industries which would not
pass through the residential areas. From a municipal perspective, the harbour and its hinterland belong to The Harbour Authority of Israel and function
as a self-contained unit. Many industrial plants
were built around the harbour which must import
their raw materials and which export their completed
products in the same manner. The Harbour Authority
leases land to those factories which have strong
ties to the harbour.

Close to 40% of all employment in Ashdod is
directly or indirectly connected to the harbour. The
percentage of employment in industry there is also
approximately 40%. In the future it can be assumed
that Ashdod will be an industrial town and that the
harbour activities will be only secondary. The harbour's influence on the town in the future will not
be as strong.

Of the two main functions that Ashdod was planned to fulfill - supplying a harbour and industry,
only the first was accomplished. Industrial development is at its beginning stages but it has a
bright future because Ashdod and its surroundings
have the largest amount of reserve area for industry in the central part of the country. Several
years ago Ashdod and its harbour were connected to
the metropolitan area of Tel Aviv by a highway   12
miles (20 kms.) long, but today the harbour serves
all of the needs of the largest metropolitan area in
the country.

THE FUNCTIONS OF THE TOWN

The harbour and industrial functions of Ashdod are
national and not regional in nature. In the future,
the town itself will not have any national functions
and Ashdod will be the center of its agricultural
hinterland only. The town, with its present population of about 70,000 is able to supply all of the
services to its inhabitants such as commerce, health
education, etc.

In an attempt to analyse the geographic and
demographic situation of Ashdod, it must be noted
that it is located in the center of a region that
within a radius of less than 12 miles (20 kms.) a
quarter of a million people live and where many
small and medium towns exist. Undoubtedly, their
growth will lag behind the development of Ashdod
which will be the largest urban center along the
southern coastal strip. During the initial stages

of its development Ashdod was unable to free itself from the gravity of Tel Aviv, but today, after developing harbour functions, industry and housing for close to 100,000 people, along with a network of main roads surrounding the town, it has become a center within its own right.

Despite Ashdod's urban development problems, the town today appears on the map of Israel as one of the most successful development towns in terms of geographic location, national and regional functions and because of the rate of its population growth.

Chapter Twelve

ELAT - A GATE TO THE SOUTH

Elat was established in 1954 because Israel needed a
harbour in the southern part of the country as a
gateway to Africa and the Far East. Here, like in
Ashdod, the town also grew as a result of the harbour's functions. Through Elat's harbour goods were
exported to the East such as copper from Sinai,
phosphates from the Negev and Arad region and even
citrus and cement from the central part of the country. Crude oil imported from the Persian Gulf and
tropical agriculture products from African countries
came through Elat. The government of Israel decided
to build a harbour on the Gulf of Elat and to establish a town of 50,000 inhabitants there because its
geographical location enabled the Suez Canal to be
bypassed which was of great economic importance to
the country.

THE TOWN'S LOCATION ON THE BACKGROUND OF ITS GEO-
GRAPHICAL CONDITIONS

Elat is not a favourable nor convenient location for
a town and although it lies on the coast of a gulf,
climatic conditions make living in the town difficult. Temperatures are high in the summer reaching
an average of $38\,^{O}C$ ($100^{O}F$) in July and August. The
climate is very dry, almost without any precipitation, no water sources exist there and an agricultural hinterland is lacking. Geographical conditions
such as these are not conductive to permanent settlement as people are not attracted to live in such
a setting. In the past, settlement had developed
there north of the Gulf of Elat, this time it occured on the north-eastern corner near where Aqaba is
located today.
     Due to their proportional height, the mounts of

Edom and Moab received more precipitation than other
mountains in the Negev so that the wells along the
foot of these two mounts had much more water relatively speaking. Water resources are therefore found
at the eastern part of the Arava and closer to Aqaba
rather than to Elat. The ancient historical site of
this area is Tel Khleifa which lies near the water
sources at the eastern part of the Arava. The north
eastern corner of the Gulf, Aqaba, situated near the
water sources, therefore has better conditions than
Elat. Political reasons necessitated the location
of a town at the southern edge of the Negev on the
Gulf even though the geographical conditions were
much worse in comparison to the Jordanian side of
the Gulf.

It is better to locate a town on a generally
flat topography having solid ground for housing
foundations, space for further development and geographical proximity to the main economic and social
centers of the country. These conditions do not
exist where Elat is located. Its coastal plain is
very narrow and to the west the topography is steep
and borders the granite cliffs. The soil on which
Elat is founded is no more than a conglomeration of
granite stones which structurally speaking is not
suitable for housing foundations. The granite topography also is difficult to build on due to the
hardness of this stone. Elat's geographic distance
from other parts of the country is a negative factor.
In the urban development of a country a new town
should not be erected at a distance of more than 150
miles (250 kms.) from the nearest town, Beer Sheva,
which is what happened in this case. This jump is
too great from the national sprawl of towns and
makes it quite difficult to supply services to the
area such as water, electricity, transportation, etc.

THE STRUCTURE OF THE TOWN

Elat's internal structure can be described as follows: The natural center of the town is on the
northern part of the Gulf which is the meeting point
of the land and sea as well as the coast and mountains. Most of the living accomodations were erected near the center which is even the junction of
the roads not far from the airport. The harbour of
Elat has no outstanding physical characteristics
and actually, the eastern coast is a much more convenient location for a harbour because of the east-
west circulation of sea water. On the western coast

a commercial port was built and to the south of it a
port for oil deliveries. The airport was built on a
flat area not far from the town center. Today, this
is an impractical location for the airport because
the town has grown and the airport creates too much
pollution. Thus, in the near future it will be relocated north of the town.

The residential areas of Elat sprawl from the
town center to the northwest in segments. Industry
and tourism are two functions which later came to
Elat and that had to be located further inside the
town. The harbour attracted industry while repuls-
ing hotels which therefore were located to the north
of the Gulf, while the industrial areas were located
on the hinterland of the commercial and oil port.
The main road connecting Elat with the south was constructed close to the coast creating a buffer zone
between the industrial area and the harbour. As the
mountains are so close to the industrial area, upon
expansion it sprawled to the south longitudinally.
South of the oil port is a coral nature reserve
which attracts many tourists and to the south of
that a long, narrow bathing beach. Throughout the
years the pressure on Elat's coastal strip has increased as it has taken on many more activities,
some of which are adverse to the others. Due to its
geographical conditions Elat sprawled for some distance and experienced no crystallized build-up.

Today, the town is dissected by main arteries,
has few public open spaces and its sub-centers are
small. Tourism activities and hotels are concentrated on the northern part of the Gulf because the
area there is alkaline-based and therefore unsuitable for housing foundations. The harbour was located south of the town because of the dangerous
northern winds and the strong north-south water cur-
rents. On the northwestern corner of the Gulf the
CBD was built because of this central location,
while neighbourhood units were constructed on the
western hill slopes at a 5% - 7% gradient because
this was the most convenient and economic method for
initial development. Clusters of housing extended
upwards on the detritus which covered the alluvial
fan coming out of the mountain. Concerning the
housing type in Elat, it has no special structure
which could characterize a desert town. Housing
standards accepted in other parts of the country
were merely brought to Elat. It can be noted that
close to the CBD of Elat the houses are low-rise
while in the periphery they are higher. Air condit-
ioning is an integral part of the housing system

there in order to overcome the difficult climatic
conditions.

POPULATION

In contrast to a place like Ashdod, the population
increase in Elat has not been rapid. By 1960 the
number of inhabitants in Elat was 6,200 and a gradual increase brought the population to no more than
20,000 residents by 1982. The rate of population
replacement in Elat is the highest in the country.
For many years the town's image was as a place for
temporary dwelling used in order to make money with
a high emigration rate, and demographically speaking,
a town where there are 20% more men than women,
small families and a low rate of elderly. The main
employment source is the Timna Copper Mines 13 miles
(20 kms.) north of the town and the rest of employment is found in hotel services and the harbour.

PLANNING AND DEVELOPMENT IN THE TOWN

After the above described sprawl of the town occured
due to the lack of experience in building under desert conditions, a new approach arose concerning the
future form of Elat. Now there is a trend to build
Elat on better topographical conditions such as on
the flat mountain extending southward from the town
rather than along the coastline. (Figure 12.1). This
is being done in order to create better atmospheric
conditions for residential living, but until the
town grows population-wise and is better developed
economically, people will not be willing to live
further from the original CBD. Future neighbourhoods will be built at an elevation of 360 feet (120
meters) above sea level in contrast to industry
which must be developed at a lower level close to
the coast and harbour and perhaps even where the
first houses of Elat were built. (1) The
airport will be relocated to Timna and hotels and
recreation sports will have to find new sites on the
mountains west of the town in order to prevent their
concentration and congestion along the northern
coast of the Gulf. The present planning approach of
Elat attempts to make the maximum amount of building
improvements in the town on its geographical background and according to what has taken place there
previously.

Figure 12.1: Elat - Existing and Proposed Land Uses

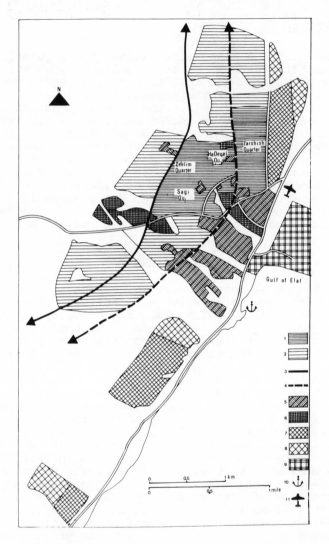

1. Residential Area 2. Future Residential
   Area 3. Lower Building Level 4. Upper
   Building Level 5. Commercial Zone
6. Institutions 7. Industrial Zone
8. Future Industrial Zone 9. Hotels and
   Recreation 10. Harbour 11. Airport

NOTES

1.   M. Turner, Eilat, <u>Preliminary Study for the Town Expansion to 50,000</u> (Ministry of the Interior, Jerusalem, 1968).

Chapter Thirteen

ARAD - A NEW TOWN IN THE DESERT

Arad is one of the new towns that was built in Israel in pursuance of the policy of population dispersal and settlement of frontier regions. More than 30 such towns have been built since the establishment of the state, but Arad differs from the rest as regards the character of its surrounding region, its planning, its buildings, the composition of its population and the basis of its economy, and it represents a new conception of urban development in a desert region. Arad is therefore an interesting subject for a case study of an attempt to create an urban center in the desert, this being a problem common to Israel and to many developing countries.

The object of this chapter is to examine the planning conception that was realized in Arad, and to describe some of the experiments tried out during the construction of the town. We shall also attempt to evaluate the results obtained, in the light of the expectations of two decades ago.

PLANNING PRINCIPLES

Most of the development towns in Israel were established on the assumption that the agricultural potential of their surrounding area would provide the main source of livelihood for the new town-dwellers. However, after a number of these towns had been built, it was found that the agricultural potential was smaller than expected, and would be insufficient to support an urban population of some hundreds of thousands of inhabitants. The difficulty was particularly acute in arid regions, where the agricultural potential is practically nil. Both in Israel and abroad very little is known on the subject of the development of desert regions, the more

168

so as extremely large expenditures of capital are
required for land amelioration and for the desal-
ination of sea-water.

Arad first appeared on Israel's map of urban
settlement in the early sixties, when the agricultural potential as a basis for urban employment had
been exhausted and attention turned to the development of mineral resources. The basing of a town's
economy on local natural resources is related to a
new conception which had made a somewhat belated
appearance in Israel. According to it the new town
is in no way inferior to the kibbutz as a legiti-
mate means for the realization of pioneering ideals.
The rise in the status of the towns is linked to
the gradual change in the social structure of Israel
and to the character of its urban population. While
in the past no socio-urban ideology had been developed, there is today a growing interest in the quality of the towns and in their role within the state.
No effort was made in the past to encourage and to
develop an urban way of life, but since the establishment of the state, and particularly after the
failure of some of the development towns, thinking
on this subject was revised and led to the conclus-
ion that modern and unconventional urban development may be the key to the settlement of frontier-
regions.

Arad marks therefore a new stage in urban development, which attempts to correct the mistakes
made in the past. Its distinctive features are:
urban integration between old-timers and new immigrants, building suited to the desert climate, provision of immediate employment to new immigrants,
furthering of private initiative independent of the
socialist-economic establishment, selection of potential settlers, economy based on a nucleus of old-
timers, development of cooperative enterprises, and,
generally, recognition that the new town is a legit-
imate pioneering means for the development of a
desert frontier region.

LOCATION

The immediate incentive for the creation of the new
town was the need to settle a waste and arid region
and to provide a dormitory town for the workers of
the Dead Sea Works, who were then living in Sedom
under very trying climatic conditions - mean summer
temperatures of 32°C (90°F) and maximum temperatures
of over 40°C (129°F). Beer Sheva was not suitable,

as its distance from the Dead Sea (ca. 44 miles   10
kms.) is too great for commuting to work.   Dimona, founded in 1956, is only 50 miles (80 kms.)
from Sedom, but it has already developed its own industries, which provided full employment to the new
immigrants who had settled there.   It became therefore necessary to found a new town not far from the
Dead Sea, which would possess the geographic conditions suitable for a permanent urban settlement.

The site for the new town was chosen on the
watershed between the Mediterranean and the Dead Sea
14 miles (22.5 kms.) as the crow flies from the Jordanian border, about 25 miles (40 kms.) from Beer
Sheva and 15 miles (24 kms.) from Sedom.   The site
lies about 1,500 ft. (500 m.) above sea-level, while
the Dead Sea, 10 miles (16 kms.)to the east, is
1,176 ft. (329 m.) below sea-level, a drop of nearly
2,676 ft. (892 m.).   The average summer temperatures
in Arad are lower than in Beer Sheva ($19^{\circ}C$ - $21^{\circ}C$)
($66^{\circ}F$ - $70^{\circ}F$), and are mitigated by westerly winds.
The relative humidity does not rise above 40%. The
average yearly precipitation does not exceed 6.8
inches and there is no vegetation, apart from low
bushes.   There are no natural water resources, and
water from the National Water Carrier is pumped to
Arad from Beer Sheva.

Not far from Arad are a number of mineral de-
posits: phosphates, coloured marble and glass sand
between Arad and Dimona, natural gas near Rosh Zohar,
potassium and bromine salts in the Dead Sea.   The
mineral springs at Hamei Zohar and 'En Boqeq, on the
shore of the Dead Sea about 13 miles (21 kms.) from
Arad, add to the tourism potential of the region.
Arad's dry climate has been found to be beneficial
for the treatment of asthma and various types of
allergy.   This area is also of archaeological interest - not far from Arad are a number of sites associated with the history of the Jewish people, such as
Masada, Har Qanna'im, Rosh Zohar, Tel Arad and Tel
Beer Sheva.

The agricultural potential of the region is extremely poor.   There is some loess to the west of
Arad, but no water for its irrigation.   Only a few
areas are suitable for pasture.   About fifty thous-
and Bedouins live between the Beer Sheva plain and
the Judean desert, some of whom may find employment
in service industries in and near Arad.

The site lay outside the existing regional road
network, and it was necessary to build new roads
connecting Arad with Beer Sheva, Dimona and the Dead
Sea.   After the Six Day War (1967) the road to

170

Hebron was opened and improved and a new road was built to the north, by passing Beer Sheva.

THE TOWN PLAN

The plan of Arad covers an area of 3,000 acres sufficient for the population goal of 50,000 in the year 2000. The present population is 11,900, concentrated mainly in three or four residential quarters. The plan envisages six main residential quarters, forming a rectangle around the central business district (CBD). Each of these quarters is planned for about 4,000 inhabitants, a total of about 25,000 for the six quarters. (Figure 13.1)

The linear CBD runs in a south-east to north-west direction. North and west of it are areas that will contain the principle public buildings and it will be the administrative, economic and social centre of the town. It is planned on a raised and slightly undulating terrain.

Sub-centres have been planned for the residential quarters, each containing four or five shops. In the CBD there are already food, furniture and clothing shops, banks, etc. The sub-centres contain mainly food shops and haberdasheries. Other kinds of shops that opened in the sub-centres had to close down for lack of customers. A floor for offices was added above the shops of the CBD, but most of the space was occupied by shops and other businesses, since the demand for these greatly exceeds the supply. Many of these shops are of a high standard, such as expensive delicatessen and furniture shops. This reflects the high standard of living of many of the inhabitants, but it is not a healthy sign for the economy of a new town still in the early stages of its development.

Around the rectangle of the inner town are planned two or three residential quarters, that will house about 20,000 inhabitants. To the east will be a low density quarter of one-family villas, and still further east, an area for hotels. A large industrial zone is planned in the south-west corner of the scheme. Between the six inner and the two or three outer residential quarters will be a public open space. The boundaries of the diverse quarters have been laid out to accord with the irregular topography of the area.

Figure 13.1: Arad – Outline Scheme 1967

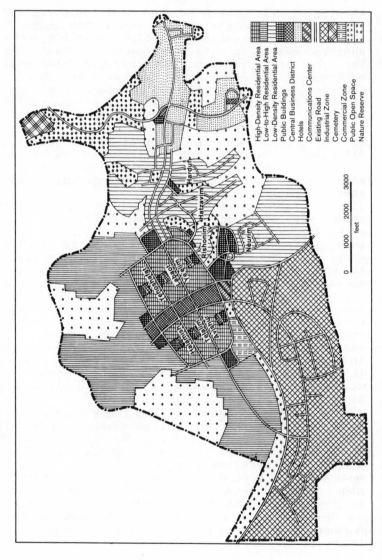

High-Density Residential Area
Low-to-High Residential Area
Low-Density Residential Area
Public Buildings
Central Business District
Hotels
Communications Center
Existing Road
Industrial Zone
Cemetery
Commercial Zone
Public Open Space
Nature Reserve

0   1000   2000   3000
feet

BUILDING THE TOWN

The planners of Arad had the rare opportunity of
being able to start from scratch to create a town
that would be both functional and attractive. The
plan calls for high density and compact building,
interspersed with open spaces. The buildings will
be places so as to afford maximum protection from
the wind and dust of the desert. Projecting storeys
and roofs will provide shaded pedestrian passageways.
The compact plan of the residential quarters will
make for short walking distances between home and
shop. The intention is, in fact, that inhabitants
should be able to dispense with the use of vehicular
transport, while limiting the walking distance to
1,500 ft (500 m). The town is being built quarter
by quarter, so as to provide from the start the conditions for an urban way of life.

The first quarter to be built in Arad was
Rishonim, which consisted of temporary asbestos
sheet houses. It was built in 1962-63 to house the
first 210 families who had been selected to form the
social and economic nucleus of the town. The quarter was built on the main road, before work had started on the comprehensive town plan. Today this
quarter has a not very attractive appearance, and
there is a tendency among its inhabitants to leave
it for one of the newer and better quarters.

In the years 1963-66 the Ye'elim quarter was
built, consisting of patio and multi-storey brick
buildings. This was the first permanent quarter of
the town, and it housed about 900 families. Here
were made the first attempts to adapt the building
to the desert conditions. For example, two and
three-storey houses were surrounded by a wall that
served as a windbreak. The buildings were placed
at a suitable angle from the North, so as to receive more sunlight in the winter and less in the
summer. The window surface was kept to 5% of the
wall surface, instead of the usual 20%. Ventilating
flues were provided to lower the summer room temperature, and an average difference of 3°C was in fact
measured between street and room temperature. On the
other hand, there were some drawbacks to high density building, such as a common stairhall for as many
as 28 apartments, poor acoustics and lack of privacy.
A more successful building type consisted of rows of
buildings placed on columns, with sheltered pedestrian passageways.

The third stage started in 1966 with the building of the Avishur quarter, for a population of

about 2,000. The buildings here have several
storeys and are prefabricated. Buildings are
either long or L-shaped, and there are children's
playgrounds surrounded by windbreak walls. In the
same year a start was also made with the building
of 60 villas in the Hazavim quarter in the eastern
part of the town. This quarter is situated on a
raised spur, and its streets are parallel to the contour lines. The Ne'urim quarter, south-west of the
CBD, was started in 1970. It contains multi-storey
buildings, either brick or prefabricated, and also
two-family prefabricated buildings. Particular pains
were taken to give this quarter a pleasing appearance, and it is considered today the prestige quarter of Arad, attracting both new settlers and inhabitants of the older quarters. Most of the new immigrants from Soviet Russia who settled in Arad, live
here. All other quarters, Telalim and Labaot, which
are part of the rectangle around the CBD were constructed later on.

        Little was known regarding the types of build-
ings, materials, etc. which are best suited to the
desert, and a method of trial and error had to be
followed. Where satisfactory solutions were found,
and this was by no means always the case, they were
not always fully implemented. Building was not sufficiently governed by micro-climatic considerations,
little was known about the influence of the wind,
and not much more about the behaviour of various
building materials in an arid climate. As a result
of the experience gained in Arad up to this day, it
would appear that the most suitable buildings are
long and compact blocks, built on columns, with
shaded pedestrian passageways, and few indows facing
west. The most favourable orientation is towards
the north-west, two parallel buildings with this
orientation being joined by two buildings at right
angles to them, forming a closed square.

        For the CBD too, no ideal solution has been
found. From a functional point of view, it is not
sufficiently well adapted to the local climatic conditions, and it does not differ greatly from the
business districts of other towns. Its plan is too
open, and insufficient shade is provided.

        In spite of the above shortcomings, a survey
carried out locally showed that the inhabitants of
Arad are, on the whole, satisfied with the CBD.
Business has thrived as a result of careful planning
of the kinds of shops and other businesses required
at various stages of development of the town. Although the CBD began to function only in the year

1969, it already plays an important part in the life of Arad. Its sphere of influence extends to the whole of the town, and there is some overlapping with the spheres of influence of the neighbourhood subcenters. The further away a quarter is from the town center , the greater is its dependence on its local subcenters.

POPULATION AND EMPLOYMENT

Contrary to other development towns, settlement in Arad was, from the very start, a controlled process. At the time of its foundation in 1961, Arad numbered 100 inhabitants, and subsequent growth was slow: in 1965 there were 1,320 inhabitants, in 1967 - 2,000, in 1969 - 3,430, in 1970 - 4,350, and in 1983, the population numbered over 11,900. The settlers are mainly Israeli-born, and come from Kibbutzim, Moshavim and from other towns. Among the newer settlers there are a number of new immigrants from eastern Europe and from the affluent countries of western Europe and America, but about 60% of the inhabitants in all town quarters are Israeli-born. In the Ne'urim Quarter there is a concentration of immigrants from Soviet Russia, but in all other quarters there is no marked predominance of any one community.

As a result of the constant desire of the inhabitants to improve their living conditions, there is a certain amount of internal migration between the town quarters, mainly from Rishonim to Ne'urim, Hazavim and Avishur, and from Ye'elim to Avishur and Ne'urim. The existing quarters of Arad form a kind of hierarchy: Rishonim - Ye'elim - Avishur - Ne'urim - Hazavim. The movement of inhabitants from one quarter to another is a positive feature, as the aspiration to achieve a higher social and economic status may be satisfied within the town itself, without having to move elsewhere.

Another of Arad's characteristics is the large proportion of commuters. Over 2,000 persons travel every day to and from Arad, the main commuter goals being Beer Sheva, the Dead Sea and the Arad Chemical Industries complex. Among the workers coming daily to Arad are Bedouins employed in the local factories and in various services. Most of the travel is for the purpose of work, while shopping and study account for relatively few journeys. A break-down of the town's commuting shows that, apart from very specialized services, Arad is not dependent on Beer

Sheva.

Arad's economy is based mainly on industry, and the industrial district is large compared with that of other Israel towns.

In 1981, the percentage of employed persons in Arad reached 43%, compared with the national average of 26%. The three important centers of employment are: The enterprises located in the industrial district, the Dead Sea Works and the Arad Chemical Industries. A survey of all industries shows that chemicals take first place, followed by building materials and food products. Most of the chemical industries are located outside the town, as they have to be near the sources of raw materials, and also for ecological reasons.

HOTELS AND TOURISM

Arad's altidude of 1,500 ft (500 m.) above sea-level, its proximity to medicinal springs, the wild desert landscape and the dry climate are assets that should favour the development of a hotel and tourist industry. However, since the Six Day War, several new factors have had an adverse effect on this industry. They are: 1. the opening of the road from 'En Feshkha to 'En Gedi, which provides easy access to the Dead Sea by way of Jerusalem; 2. the opening of the road from Hebron to Beer Sheva, which enables tourists to reach the northern Negev by way of Jerusalem and Bethlehem, without stopping at Arad; 3. the aerial ropeway to Masada, which enables visitors to reach this site from the Dead Sea, and not, as previously, by way of Arad; 4. the opening of new hotels on the Dead Sea shore. All of these have contributed to lowering the occupancy ration of Arad hotels by 65%. As a rule, visitors spend the night in Arad only when there is no vacant room in the other hotels of this region.

An employment survey of the recreation and hotel industry has shown that Arad's main attraction to visitors is its dry climate which is especially favourable for sufferers from asthma. The care of asthmatic patients is a better source of income than tourism, and it is interesting to note there are a number of asthmatics among the owners of industrial and other enterprises, who chose to settle in Arad on account of its beneficial climate. Arad's tourism and hotel industry was at the beginning largely in the hands of persons who have no expert knowledge in this field, and this may be one of the reasons for the unsatisfactory state of the industry, which had been envisaged by the planners as forming the main economic basis of the town.   This role has instead been taken by the various branches of industry which have been mentioned above.

Chapter Fourteen

TOWNS IN JUDEA AND SAMARIA

From the war of 1948 until the Six Day War in 1967,
Judea and Samaria were cut off from Israel by the Israel Jordanian Armistice lines.   The two regions
forming an integral part of cis-Jordanian Palestine
have thus been deprived of their contacts with the
adjacent Coastal Plain and Gaza Strip as well as
their outlet to the Mediterranean.   Their sole remaining contacts were with the Kingdom of Jordan.
   In order to adapt to these enforced and unnatural political conditions both the rural and urban
settlement structure had to undergo far-reaching
changes, which it is intended in this chapter to
describe and analyze against the physical, economic
and social background of the area.

PHYSICAL BACKGROUND

Judea and Samaria form part of Palestine's central
massive, Judea comprising the Hebron and Jerusalem
mountains and Samaria covering the area from Jerusalem to Jenin.   Both together cover an area of
about 2,200 sq. miles (5,700 sq. km).
   Mount Hebron forms a wide crest with two syn-
clines on both sides, the lowland in the west and
the desert in the east.   Rising to a height of 3,000
ft. (1,000 m.) it runs in a north, east-south west
direction. Hebron is located on the flat crest which
continues to the north, declining gradually to 2,100
ft. (700 m.) in the vicinity of Jerusalem. To the
west a tectonic fold line provides a gradual 1,500-
1,650 ft. (500-550 m.) high slope.   In the east another fold forms the transition from the crest to
the Judean desert.
   The mountains of Samaria fall off gradually
from south.   They extend from the hills of Jerusalem

up to the Jezreel Valley in the north, and border on
the Jordan Valley in the east and the Coastal Plain
in the west. In contrast to the compact Hebron
mountains, whose average height is 1,650 ft. (550 m)
are dissected by rifts and valleys underlining the
topographical differences between one section and
another.

GEOGRAPHICAL LAYOUT OF VILLAGES

In Mount Hebron the layout of the rural settlements
follows a linear, concentrated pattern, in line with
the geographic structure. Owing to the strong
effects of the desert, the rainfall in the eastern
part is down to 4-12 inch (100-300 mm.), with sparse
vegetation, little soil and springs but few and far
between. Human settlement accordingly does not extend beyond a line running about 3 miles (5 km.)
east of the watershed. In the south, too, the influence of the Negev is making itself felt, and settlement tends to dwindle on the fringes of the desert penetrating into the Hebron mountains. The villages on the mountain crest run parallel with the
watershed, but are located at some distance from it,
where soft stones are available for building, rather than in the fertile soil of the crest proper.
To the west a further series of villages is located
along the tectonic fold line running parallel with
the mountain. This location, besides the topographical advantage, also offers them access to water
sources. (1)
    The largest villages with a population of 3,500
-5,000 tend to be located in the south east, while
the villages in the central part of Mount Hebron
usually have only 500-1,000 inhabitants each. The
larger size of the outlying villages is probably due
to the need of the farm population to ward off mar-
auding desert nomads and the gradual settlement of
bedouin in the more prosperous villages where they
have since merged with the farmers.
    In Mount Hebron we thus find a compact settle-
ment pattern, along well defined axes corresponding
to the geographic layout and the agricultural potential of the region. (Figures 14.1 and 14.2)
    No such compact layout is found in Samaria,
where the settlements are dispersed practically over
the entire region, in line with its dissected topographic structure. They are located on hilltops,
domes and ridges dominating the surrounding countryside and offering a good strategic position. The

Figure 14.1: Distribution of Settlements in Judea
and Samaria 1947

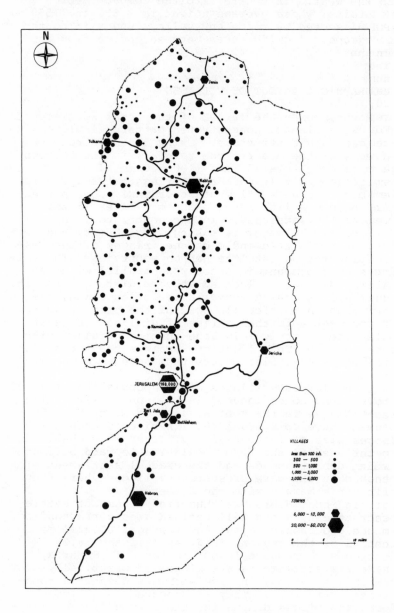

Figure 14.2: Distribution of Settlements in Judea
and Samaria 1967

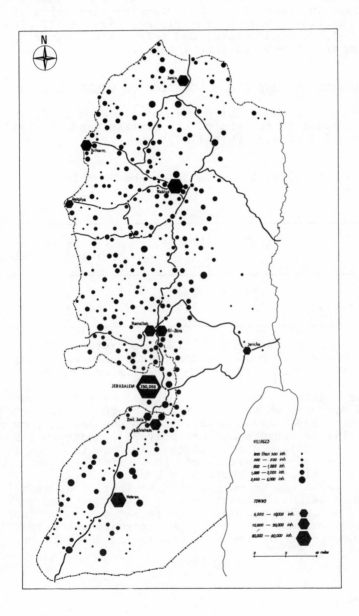

valleys with their rich alluvial soil are generally
uninhabited, being left free for intensive cultivation. The numerous springs which are the outdome
of the fault lines characteristic of the Samarian
mountains facilitate the extensive dispersion of the
population. Most of the villages are small, with
500-1,000 inhabitants, and only a small minority
number 3,000-5,000 inhabitants.

CHANGES IN NUMBER AND LOCATION OF VILLAGES

Table 14.1 shows the number of villages in Samaria
and Judea at the end of the British Mandate (1947)
and of Jordanian rule (1967).

Table 14.1: Villages in Judea and Samaria

	1947*	1967**	Increase Total	Percent
Judea	54	132	78	144
Samaria	210	264	54	25
Total	204	396	132	50

* Based on Mandatory Village Statistics, 1945
** Based on Population Census of Judea and Samaria,
   1967, conducted by the Israel Army Command.

The figures show a total increase of 132 villages or
50 percent, which is, however, unequally divided between Judea and Samaria, the one showing an increase
of 144 percent as against only 25 percent in the
other. Although most of the increase in Judea is
made up of small villages, their impact on the overall settlement structure is considerable.
     From the sub-district distribution as seen in
Table 14.2 it appears that in Judea both the Hebron
and Jerusalem sub-districts received a major increment, whereas in Samaria the increase was primarily
concentrated in the northern Jenin sub-district.

Table 14.2:   Villages in Judea and Samaria by Sub-
District

Sub-District	1947	1967	Increase Total	Percent
Nablus	91	97	6	6.5
Jenin	29	55	26	89
Tulkarm	34	42	8	23.5
Ramallah	56	70	14	25
Jerusalem	34	66	32	94
Hebron	20	66	46	230
Total:	264	396	132	50

On comparing the village dispersion at the beginning
and at the end of this period it becomes evident
that a maximum effort was made in the intervening
nineteen years to settle the Judean region, especially along the former southern and south-western
border with Israel as well as on the fringes of the
desert, in the eastern sections of Mount Hebron and
the Jerusalem Hills. In Samaria the distribution
was less lop-sided, though here, too, more new villages were founded near the armistice lines in the
north and west than in the east. The older villages
near the armistice line underwent considerable demographic and physical changes. Cut off from their
lands in the Coastal Plain, they began to cultivate
the less fertile foothills and being unable to sell
their produce either to Israel in the west or to
potential markets in the east, in the absence of
proper communication and transportation facilities
their production and standard of living declined.
Villages assumed an inner-directed, eastward orientation. In many of them the reasons of early location on hilltops disappeared. There is evidence
showing disintegration of the clustered villages.
Many villages even create new neighbourhood unit or
sprawl to other sites which are not always connected
with water resources. Subsequently, the emigration
of young men to the oil principalities on the Persian Gulf led to a renewed influx of funds, stimulating construction and enlarging the built-up area
of the initially impoverished villages. The build-

ing of new and expansion of existing roads along the border, primarily for defence purposes, also enhanced the status of the villages located there. However despite deliberate settlement efforts, geographic factors continued to play a predominant role and only few new settlements sprang up along the threshold of the desert and the shores of the Dead Sea, as well as in the Jordan Valley with its problematic soil conditions and paucity of water sources. (2)

CHANGES IN RURAL POPULATION

Below in Table 14.3 is a comparison of the rural sub-district population in 1947 and 1967.

Table 14.3: The Population of Judea and Samaria by Sub-District

Sub-District	1947*	1967**	Percentage Increase
Nablus	62,500	152,400	144
Jenin	49,000	78,300	60
Tulkarm	35,000	72,300	106
Ramallah	50,700	88,800	75
Jerusalem	39,400	88,400	124
Hebron	47,000	118,300	151
Total:	283,600	598,500	111
Judea	86,400	206,700	139
Samaria	197,200	391,800	99

*   Estimate based on Mandatory Village Statistics, 1945, rounded off to nearest hundred.
*** Figures of Population Census, 1967, conducted by the Israel Army Command, rounded off to nearest hundred.

Thus, the rural population went up from 283,600 in 1947 to 598,000 by 1967, an increase of 111 percent in 20 years. The increase was more marked in Judea

(139 percent) than in Samaria (99 percent), apparently as a result of the internal migration of refugees and sedentary tendencies among the nomadic population. Whereas in 1947 the population was more or less evenly spread over the different sub-districts, two of them, Nablus and Hebron, are found to predominate by the end of the period, with a respective increase of 144 and 151 percent. The population has thus tended to concentrate in the two principal nodes in the north and the south as well as along the armistice lines.

It should further be noted that in mandatory times the villages showed a distribution that the majority having 500-1,000 inhabitants and only a small minority either less than 500 or more than 3,000. Now, on the other hand, a disproportionately high share has only 100-300 inhabitants.

An analysis by population growth groups shows that most of the villages existing in mandatory times experienced a population increase (Table 14.4 and Figure 14.2). The highest proportion went up by 100-200 inhabitants (22 percent). Next comes villages which increased by up to 100, 200-300 and 500-1,000 inhabitants (17 percent). An extraordinary growth of 1,200-2,000 inhabitants occurred in sixteen, and of 2,000 and more in nine villages.

Table 14.4: Rural Population Growth in Judea and Samaria, by Growth Groups and Sub-Districts

Sub-Districts	Up to 100	100–200	200–300	300–400	400–500	500–1,000	1,000–2,000	2,000	Total Villages	per cent
Nablus	19	27	19	11	6	9	6	0	97	26.5
Jenin	6	5	10	6	5	10	2	1	45	12.
Tulkarm	5	11	5	3	2	8	2	0	36	10.
Ramallah	14	11	11	8	4	8	1	0	57	15.5
Jerusalem	9	12	11	7	6	16	1	4	66	18.
Hebron	9	15	6	14	2	11	4	4	65	18.
Total	62	81	62	49	25	62	16	9	366*100	
Percent	17	22	17	13.5	7	17	4	2.5	100	

*Thirty villages which were abandoned or whose population decreased were not included.

Geographically, most of the villages whose population grew by up to 100 inhabitants are located in
Central Samaria. These are small villages whose
growth is apparently due to natural increase. In
Judea some of the new settlements along the armistice line belong to this group. In Samaria an increase by 100-200 inhabitants took place mainly in
villages facing the Jezreel Valley and the Coastal
Plain, along the armistice line and in Judea on the
south-western slopes of Mount Hebron. Apart from
the natural increase, the population of these villages was apparently boosted by the Jordanian government, for security reasons. The villages whose
population grew by 500-1,000 inhabitants had also
previously been of a substantial size as were those
growing by 1,000-2,000 or more which in addition are
located on the fringes of the desert, in the midst
of the fertile agricultural lands of Samaria or in
the vicinity of a major city.

THE GEOGRAPHICAL LAYOUT OF THE TOWNS

On the whole the towns in Judea follow the watershed
from Hebron to Bethlehem and Beit Jala via Jerusalem
to Ramallah and El-Bire. They are located on the
mountain crest, each constituting a service, administrative, agricultural, marketing and commercial
center for the surrounding villages. While Jerusalem has the central function of being the capital
city of both Judea and Samaria, Hebron is the main
center of the southern Judean mountains while Bethlehem and Beit Jala, on the one side, and Ramallah
and El-Bire, on the other, form secondary centers
which are economically and otherwise dependent on
Jerusalem. Thus Judea has a linear urban lay-out
characterized by a functional division between the
various towns.
      In Samaria, on the other hand, the towns have
developed primarily on the edge of the mountains
facing the Coastal Plain and the Jezreel Valley or
as intra or interregional communications centers.
The urban system is largely focused on Nablus, with
Jenin as a subsidiary center in the north, Tulkarm
in the west, and Qalqilye in the south-west.
      None of the towns of Judea and Samaria is par-
ticularly big, and their share in the population is
not very considerable. A comparison of their population figures in 1947 and 1967 is given below.
(Table 14.5)

Table 14.5: The Urban Population of Judea and Samaria

	1947*	1967**	Percentage Increase
Jenin	4,000	8,346	109
Nablus	23,250	41,537	78
Tulkarm	8,000	10,157	27
Qalqilye	(5,850)***	8,922	52
Ramallah	5,000	12,030	141
El Bire	(2,920)***	9,568	228
East Jerusalem	65,000	65,857	–
Bethlehem	9,000	14,439	60
Beit Jala	3,700	6,041	63
Hebron	24,600	38,091	55
Jericho	3,000	5,200	73
Total	154,320	220,188	42

* Estimate based on Mandatory Village Statistics, 1945, rounded off to the nearest hundred.

** Population Census, 1967, conducted by the Israel Army Command.

*** Village in 1947.

**** Comprising those parts of Jerusalem annexed in 1967 to "Greater Jerusalem".

From this breakdown it may be seen that:

1. The urban population grew by a mere 42 percent compared with a 111 percent increase of the rural population, so that the index of urbanization, which has reached 87 percent in Israel, is still very low with a marked predominance of the rural areas.

2. As before, all the towns are very small, with the biggest of them - Hebron and Nablus - having a population of about 40,000.

3. Although two villages, Qalqilye and El-Bire, were promoted to urban status, their population was less than 10,000.

4. In Judea the towns grew less than in Samaria while the villages grew more, apparently because of their more tenuous economic and social relations with Trans-Jordan, compared with the far closer links maintained by the Samarian towns.

5. The urban growth was due more to the migration of refugees or rural-urban migration than to the natural increase of the town population.

6. East Jerusalem remained static except for the urban spread to the surrounding villages and to Ramallah and El-Bire.

7. Jericho experienced an extraordinary growth thanks to its location on the road between Trans-Jordan and Jerusalem and its winter resort function.

CHANGES IN THE INTERNAL STRUCTURE OF THE TOWNS

Most of the towns of Judea and Samaria experienced changes in the orientation of their urban sprawl and municipal boundaries as a result of the armistice lines sealing off Jordan from Israel. An analysis of the building trends revealed by some of them during 20 years may serve as an illustration of the general development. (Figure 14.3)

EAST JERUSALEM

Under the British Mandate, East Jerusalem was a commercial and economic center for the residents of

Figure 14.3: Urban Sprawl of Four Towns in Judea
and Samaria (1947-1967)

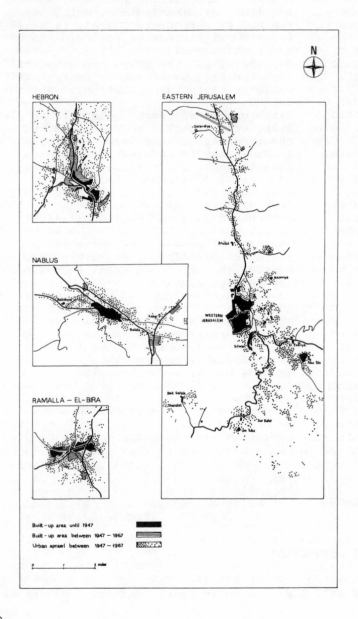

Judea, Samaria and Trans-Jordan and provided an outlet to the Mediterranean via the roads leading through it to Jaffa and Haifa. (3) With the annexation of Judea and Samaria by the Hashemite Kingdom,
it became an economic backwater. All its supply
lines were centered on 'Amman which drew its own
goods from the ports of 'Aqaba and Beirut. The loss
of the city's economic predominance also affected
its orientation. Since to the east and south-east
the topography was not amenable to urban development, most of the development took place in a north-
erly direction along the mountain crests and on both
sides of the Jerusalem-Ramallah road. Since communications with Bethlehem were impaired there was little development towards the south of the city.

Considerable efforts were invested in improving
housing conditions and the standard services in the
Old City which has always been the main residential
quarter of Jerusalem's Arab population. The lack of
adequate commercial and industrial facilities in the
eastern section of Jerusalem led to the rezoning of
areas in the northern part of the city which had
formerly been designed for residential purposes. In
view of the altered conditions the government of
Jordan set about replanning the Jerusalem region
fixing its boundaries along a circular line stretch-
from the Qalandia Airfield in the north to the village of Sur Bahir in the south, so as to comprise an
area of 32,500 acres.

East Jerusalem under Jordanian rule therefore
had to adapt to the artificial boundaries hemming
in its natural expansion. Turning its back upon
its natural economic base in the west, it had to
spread out towards north, south and east. The main
planning concepts were dispersion along the mountain
crest, the development of new settlement nodes on
the flat outrunners of the central ridge and their
connection by means of a main road along the north-
south axis bypassing the Old City, and the development of an eastern traffic artery to Trans-Jordan(4)

HEBRON

At one time Hebron had consisted of the inner core
of the Old City and some few buildings around it,
all straddling the main highway. At the beginning
of the century further developments were carried
out to the north-west along the highway to Bethlehem
and Jerusalem. The new, more spacious and taller

buildings also enhanced the town's economic activities. The main expansion, however, took place during the nineteen years of Jordanian rule when the city received a population increment of about 35,000. Its standard of living rose, not least because of the influx of funds from emigrants returning from the oil principalities. About 1,800 new houses were built in this period, about 500 of them in the surrounding agricultural area. Most of the development still was along the Jerusalem highway, over a stretch of 3 miles (5 kms.) and at a depth of 600 ft. (200 m.) either way. To the south-east, however, the city expanded by only about 1 mile (1.5 kms.), having been cut off from Beer Sheva, the marketing center of the bedouins.

NABLUS

The original core of Nablus, the second largest city in Judea and Samaria after Jerusalem, is a compact, unplanned warren of buildings hemmed in between two mountains. The influx of refugees from the Coastal Plain provided a considerable impetus for expansion while at the same time the city lost its western zone of influence. It therefore had to develop an eastward orientation and strengthen its economic and social ties with 'Amman. The regional road leading to the east was expanded and the town began to spread out in a new direction previously barren by the presence of an ancient tel, a power station and a prison. During six years alone, from 1961 until 1967, over 1,000 houses were built, many of them with money earned in Quwait. The building boom also spread to the refugee camps and the suburbs on the Nablus-'Amman and Nablus-Jerusalem highways.

RAMALLAH

Until 1947 Ramallah was densely built up, especially along the road to El-Bire and about half a mile (800 m.) to the north and to the south of it. Again, with the growing wealth of the population earned in foreign fields, new and better spaced buildings went up and the satellite town of El-Bire began to be developed. As buildings sprawled over onto formerly agricultural areas these were retroactively annexed to form part of the municipal boundaries. Though the new developments are totally unplanned they show

192

a certain orientation towards Jerusalem, especially its northern neighbourhoods which have begun to merge with Ramallah into a continuous built-up strip along the mountain crest.

These few examples are enough to indicate that the towns of Judea and Samaria responded in different ways to the region's severance from its natural outlets and surroundings, each according to its specific regional functions and geographic conditions. It may, moreover, be noted that they were all affected by the exogenous economic factor of emigration to the Arab oil principalities. Throughout urban growth was sporadic. No attempt was made to adopt a modern approach to land uses, zoning and the construction of modern, functional neighbourhoods. The towns developed without an appropriate industrial base or adequate public institutions. Many of the residents still have an agrarian background, being landlords and farmers. Physical expansion thus did not go hand in hand with the development of urban functions and occupations. Moreover, the city boundaries were mostly determined haphazardly through the incorporation of rural areas on which buildings happened to be put up, so that the towns tend to sprawl out at low density.

From the above-mentioned details, it may be concluded:

1. During the nineteen years (1948-1967) of Jordanian rule in Judea and Samaria rural growth exceeded urban growth, as is evidenced by the number of new villages and the rural population increase. In spite of some urban development reflected in the growth of the urban population and of the built-up areas, there is as yet no perceivable process of urbanization.

2. The impassable armistice lines between Israel and Jordan have resulted in changes in the rural urban settlement structure of Judea and Samaria, necessitated by the new artificial conditions. A large number of new villages was founded along these lines, border settlements underwent a major expansion, as did villages located along new security roads, and hilly areas were cultivated instead of the fields in the Coastal Plain which were no longer accessible. In the towns the built-up areas were reoriented in line with the new foci of attraction

while a building boom was set off by
residents forced through lack of local
employment to emigrate to the Arab oil
principalities and investing their earn-
ings in this way.
3. Since the Hashemite Kingdom of Jordan
did almost nothing to stimulate the economy and develop local resources, looking
upon Judea and Samaria merely as a strategic front buffer zone, development has
been largely dictated by the dominant
geographic characteristics of the area.
In the absence of new water sources,
mineral exploitation and industrial development, the region had to contend with
the desert conditions in the east, the
artificial boundary in the west, north
and south, and its own inhospitable topography. The resulting modified settlement pattern was thus unfavourably effected by the armistice lines on the one
hand and the lack of economic progress on
the other.

JEWISH SETTLEMENT SINCE 1967

From 1967, a consensus existed in the Israeli government on the need for new settlement in Judea and
Samaria, albeit with different approaches. One,
hoping for an eventual territorial compromise with
Jordan, proposed to restrict settlement mainly to a
security chain in the practically uninhabited Lower
Jordan Valley. The opposing view demanded Jewish
presence throughout the historical region, thereby
describing also the hill tops as indispensable for
defence.

        The first initiative came in September 1967,
with the renewal of the Etzyon Block on the Hebron
Hills by youth whose parents had fallen in defence
of the settlements in 1948. As a result, by 1967,
the kibbutzim Kefar Etzyon, Rosh Tzurim, Migdal Oz,
the Moshav El'azar and the semi-urban center Allon
Shevut were established. In 1968, Jews went to
Hebron to renew that age-old community and, from
1971, built their new urban center, Qiryat Arba, on
the city's eastern outskirts.

        From 1968, kibbutzim, moshavim and outposts
were founded in the Lower Jordan Valley. Today
they include more than 20 settlements in a chain
from Bet She'an Valley in the north to the northern

part of the Dead Sea in the south. A parallel chain
was created further west, on the empty eastern
slopes of Samaria and Judea. It contains today
about 10 settlements, as well as the semi-urban
center of Ma'ale Efrayim. Between Jerusalem and
Jericho, in the Judean Desert, the town of Ma'ale
Edumim was established, for more than 10,000 families, and an industrial center nearby, called
Mishor Edumim.
     Elsewhere in Judea and Samaria, more than 100
big or smaller settlements had been established, on
rocky sites or on public property elsewhere. After
a temporary break during and following The Camp
David deliberations, settlement activities continue
till today. New urban and semi-urban centers, especially on the western flanks of the Samarian Hills
have been established in the last five years, as
Ariel, Qarnei Shomron, Alfei Menashe, Emanuel and
Yaqir. Most of them don't have, meanwhile, local
branches for employment, and their inhabitants commute dayly to Greater Tel Aviv, where they can find
work. In 1982, the Jewish population in all the
different kinds of settlements counted about 25,000.

NOTES

     1.   E. Efrat, Judea and Samaria, Guidelines
for Regional and Physical Planning (Ministry of
the Interior, Jerusalem, 1970).
     2.   Ibid.
     3.   H. Kendall, Jerusalem - The Holy City
Plan, Preservation and Development during the Brit-
ish Mandate 1918-1948(London, 1948)
     4.   E. Efrat, Changes in the Town Planning
Concepts of Jerusalem 1919-1969 (Environmental
Planning, The Israeli Association for Environmental
Planning Quarterly, 1971), pp.53-65.

Chapter Fifteen

CHANGES IN THE URBAN SETTLEMENT PATTERN OF THE
GAZA STRIP

THE GEOGRAPHICAL BACKGROUND

We can distinguish three geographical sub-regions,
running parallel to the coastline. They are, from
west to east: sand-dunes, agricultural land and
sandstone ridges. These sub-regions greatly influence the anthropogeographical formation of the
Gaza Strip, and the development of the settlement,
the economy and the communications in this area.
    The dune belt in this region is similar to
that west of the Judean Plain. It reaches an average width of 3-4 miles (5-7 kms.) and is continuous
save for one marked gap near Deir el-Balah. The
dunes are from 30-60 ft. (10-20 m.) high, and rising in some places to as much as 150-180 ft. (50 to
60 m.). Patches of cultivated land are to be found
within the confines of the dune belt, particularly
in the flat portion of the Strip. Parallel to the
coastline is the Coastal Depression, which contains
few cultivated patches.
    The agricultural belt in the central part of
the Gaza Strip is the southern continuation of the
Depression, which extends in a north-south direction parallel to the coastal plain of Israel. The
agricultural soil found in this area has been de-
posited throughout the ages by streams in wadis,
such as Wadi Besor, Wadi Sahaf and Wadi Shiqma,
whose catchment area lies in the western Negev.
    The sandstone ridges framing the Gaza Strip on
the east reach a height of 210-240 ft. (70-80 m.)
In the past they probably formed a continuous barrier, which was later breached by streams, thus
creating a number of separate ridges. This geo-

graphical formation has a bearing on the water resources and the soil quality of this region. The
streams reaching the Gaza Strip from the western
Negev follow a winding course until they breach the
dunes and flow into the sea. The longer course and
the slower flow velocity cause an increase in the
seepage rate from the streams into the soil. This
is also affected by the composition of the soil itself. In the north of the Strip we have mainly dark
brown soil, in the centre - light brown soil and
loess, and in the south - light brown soil and sandy
regosols.

As we progress southwards, the proportion of
sand to loess in the soil increases, until, south of
Rafah, we find only sand. This soil composition ac-
counts for the formation of shallow ground water,
which can be tapped near the surface, especially in
the region of the Depression, or where it borders
on the sands. The ground water potential of the
Gaza Strip is fairly high, and it is not surprising
that over one thousand wells supplied water for irrigation. Between the years 1948-1967 the sinking
and operating of wells in the Strip was not subject
to government control, and excessive pumping caused
intrusion of sea water and the salination of wells.

The composition of the soil in the Gaza Strip
also determines the geographical distribution of the
varieties of agricultural crops. In the north, with
a high concentration of dark brown soil, there are
mainly citrus plantations, and also some field crops
in the central region there are field crops, with
few citrus and other plantations, while in the south
where the soil contains loess with sandy regosols,
we have water melons, field crops and dates, as well
as other crops resistant to a certain degree of sal-
inity. As we progress southwards, the grazing increases.

DISTRIBUTION OF SETTLEMENTS IN THE GAZA STRIP

Although the Gaza Strip is subject to the temperate
influence of the Mediterranean Sea, it must be classified with the semi-arid zones. The 8 inch (200mm)
isohyet, which is generally taken to mark the limit
of the Zone of Aridity, passes through the center
of the Jordan Valley and south of the Hebron hills,
while in the Gaza Strip it turns southwards to
Rafah, due to the moderating influence of the sea.
This circumstance has enabled settlements and population to spread further south, even beyond the

usually accepted boundary of the Zone of Aridity.

The land uses and the settlement pattern of the Gaza Strip are determined by its physiographic structure, which is characterized by sands in the west, alluvial soil in the center and sandstone ridges in the east. The sands are, on the whole, not suitable for farming, and did not attract agricultural settlement, and the same can be said of the sandstone ridges with their thin soil layer. There remains the central part of the Strip, where most of the rural settlements and agricultural activities are concentrated. Owing to these geographical conditions, the population in the Gaza Strip has tended to concentrate in the agricultural areas, along the main communications axis and around focal points that enjoy some special local advantage. The population did not spread across the whole width of the Strip, but tended to follow the line of the historical Via Maris. Such a population distribution in selected focal points along a linear axis is characteristic of desert and semi-arid regions, and can be observed in other parts of Israel, along the Beer Sheva-Arad-Sedom, the Beer Sheva-Dimona-Mitzpe Ramon-Elat, and the Sedom-Hazeva-Elat axes, which are of importance to the economy and the communications of the country.

Another distinguishing feature of the settlement pattern in the Gaza Strip is that, while in the rest of the coastal region Arab settlements were built on relatively high land and on sandstone ridges, leaving the low-lying land for farming use only, settlement in the Strip has concentrated in the plain in the midst of the agricultural area. One reason for this is the absence of swamps in the Gaza Strip, which were common in the northern plain. Another reason may be the ancient main highway passing through the Depression which stimulated commerce and provided possibilities of employment, in times of peace as well as in thimes of war.

POPULATION DISTRIBUTION IN 1945

Toward the end of the British Mandate in Palestine, there were only two urban concentrations in the Gaza Strip; Gaza, with 34,250 inhabitants, and Khan Yunis with 11,200 inhabitants. The remainder of the population lived in 15 small to medium-sized villages, located on both sides of the coastal road linking Palestine and Egypt, and at a distance of not more than 1-2 miles (2-4 kms.) from the main road or the railway. Five of these villages numbered less than 2,000 inhabitants, and ten between 2,000 and 5,000 inhabitants. (Figure 15.1)

The five largest villages were: Jabaliya, Deir el-Balah, Bani Suheila, 'Abasan and Rafah. The population of the Gaza Strip numbered 69,700, of which 65.2% lived in Gaza and Khan Yunis. The population distribution was thus to a marked degree nodal and concentrated, as is usually the case in border regions and desert fringes.

The two towns, Gaza and Khan Yunis, occupied a more or less symetrical position in relation to the groups of villages. Gaza, in the north of the Strip, and Khan Yunis in the south, constituted two focal points in the heart of farming country, and they were based on a plentiful supply of water and on their location at the junction of main roads with the railway line. Gaza was the focal point for connections of Jaffa and Beer Sheva, while Khan Yunis played a similar role in respect of North Sinai and Egypt.

Four out of the five large villages were strung out, at more or less regular intervals of 6-9 miles (10-15 kms.), along the main communication axis of the Strip. The smaller villages were grouped in four areas: north of Gaza, south of Gaza, east of Khan Yunis and in the vicinity of Rafah. The inhabitants in the first and second groups earned their livelihood from the cultivation of citrus and field crops. The third group contained mainly concentrations of Negev and North Sinai Bedouin, who had settled on the fringes of the region. In the fourth group lived villagers whose cocupation was connected with the army camps at Rafah.

It can be seen that the population was concentrated around focal points, most of them rural, whose location was determined by the nature of the soil, the main communication arteries and the sources of livelihood. The settlements formed a clearly graded hierarchy - a large number of small villages, a smaller number of large villages, one small town, Khan Yunis, and the main town of the region, Gaza. The formation of such a hierarchy of settlements was the result of the heterogeneous agricultural and economic background, which led to the development of a wide range of settlement types.

Figure 15.1: The Gaza Strip - Distribution of Towns and Villages (1947, 1977)

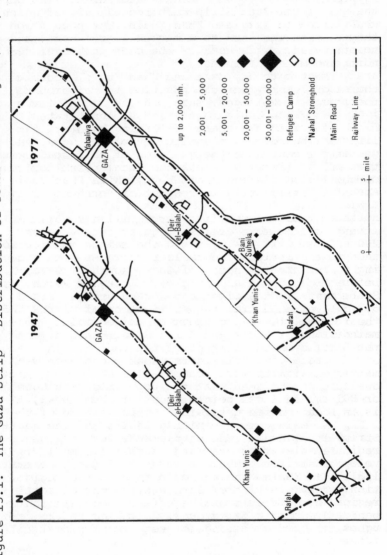

THE GAZA STRIP IN THE YEARS 1948-1981

The Gaza Strip, as a demographic unit, is a product of Israel's War of Independence. In May, 1948, the Egyptian army advanced along the coastal road into the Strip, the object being the conquest of the coastal plain. In the initial stages of the war they succeeded in penetrating far beyond the narrow coastal strip, and occupied extensive areas in the northern Negev. Israeli counter-attacks reduced the area under Egyptian occupation, and at the time of the signature of the armistice agreement, in 1949, there remained a narrow strip, 28 miles (45 kms.) long and 10 miles (17 kms.) wide.

The consolidation of the Gaza Strip as a political and administrative unit brought about changes in the settlement pattern and in the distribution of the population. To the former inhabitants of the Strip, numbering 69,700 in 1945, were added Arabs who had abandoned their villages in the Judean Plain and Bedouin who had left their camps in the northern and central Negev. The number of inhabitants of the Strip was suddenly increased by over 200,000 newcomers, most of whom were without means, and sought asylum, work and a place to live. According to the 1967 census, 207,250 (58.6%) were born before 1948 within the boundaries of what became the State of Israel. Out of the total population of 353,376, 283,714, or 80.2%, were refugees. 75.5% of the refugee population lived in camps, while the remainder were absorbed in the towns and villages of the Strip.

The rapid influx of population brought about a marked increase in the proportion of urban to rural dwellers. At the time of the 1967 census, 252,803 or 80% of the total population lived in towns, which is an extremely high figure.

Only about one sixth of the inhabitants of the Strip are farmers. Although conditions in this region favour agriculture, there has been little development in this field between the years 1948 and 1981. The existence of a relatively large population, in excess of the absorptive capacity of the region, was made possible by the high degree of urbanization and by the fact that for most of the refugees, the main means of support was the aid administered by the United Nations.

The growth of the towns and villages in the Gaza Strip has been remarkable. First place is taken by the town of Gaza, by virtue of its being the main urban center of the Strip: its population, which numbered 34,250 in 1945, has more than trebled, and today reaches ca. 115,000. During the same period, Khan Yunis has grown 160% from 11,200 to 29,700; Jabaliya by 200%; Deir el-Balah by 320% and Rafah by 350%. The whole population in the Gaza Strip counts today to 480,000 inhabitants.

In the course of the last 35 years, the population distribution of the Gaza Strip has undergone substantial changes. The number of settlements has greatly increased and today reaches 27. Gaza has kept its place as the largest town in the Strip, followed by Khan Yunis. The large villages have grown about threefold, with the exception of Abasan, whose growth was slower on account of its distance from the main routes of communications. The small villages, too, increased in size and, on the average- their population has doubled during the same period. On the whole, it can be said that the hierarchy of the Gaza Strip settlements has not changed basically, although their number and size have increased.

The refugee camps, which were established in 1948, added a new element to the population and settlement pattern of the Gaza Strip. Each camp covers a large area and houses 10,000 -40,000 refugees. The camps were originally eight in number, four large camps - Jabaliya, Esh-Shati, Khan Yunis and Rafah, and four smaller camps - Nuseirat, El-Bureij, El-Mughazi and Deir el-Balah.
Two large camps were built in the north of the Strip, and looked to Gaza and the surrounding agricultural land as a source of livelihood. Another two camps were located in the south, one near Khan Yunis and the second near Rafah, and were intended to supply labour to the nearby army camps. Smaller refugee camps were established in the central part of the Strip, where there had been no large urban settlements.

The refugee camps were a notable addition to the population of the Gaza Strip. They were built at the time as a temporary measure, in a haphazard pattern of narrow intersecting streets, and closely packed one-storey houses. The camps were generally located near existing Arab settlements or in abandoned army camps, and they constituted a manpower reservoir for agriculture and services in the Strip. Up to this day the camps have remained a foreign body which did not integrate with the municipal structure of the towns. The incertitude regarding the political future of the Strip tends to perpetuate this state of affairs; the camps are not abolished nor are they given the status of permanent settlements. The number of refugees who live today in the Gaza Strip is 260,000. About 170,000 of them still live in the camps.

After 1967 a new type of settlement made its appearance in the Gaza Strip, and all the others - in towns or villages. While prior to 1948, there had been only one Jewish settlement in the whole of this region, namely Kefar Darom, there are today nine: the rebuilt Kefar Darom, Neve Deqalim, Katif, Netzer Hazani, Gane Tal, Gedid, Gan Or, Bedolah and Morag. These are all strongholds which were established for defence purposes between towns and near main traffic arteris. They did not grow in response to local geographical conditions, and are spaced at more or less regular intervals between Rafah and Khan Yunis, between Khan Yunis and El-bureij and between El-Bureij and Gaza. They are all small units, numbering very few settlers, and they do not materially affect the settlement pattern of the Strip. They count today not more than one thousand inhabitants.

It can be seen that the Gaza Strip, an artificial geographical entity, which for 19 years had been bounded by the armistice line (the Green Line), and since 1967, is subject to Israeli military rule, has changed but little in its internal structure. The region has few soil and water resources, no minerals, and is generally poor. Its economy was formerly dependent on the limited agricultural potential, and any addition to the population could only be based on urban employment in industry or services, and on outside aid. There has been no basic change in the hierarchy of settlements of the Strip. Growth is concentrated mainly in the larger urban centers and in the refugee camps, which, as we have noted above, are artificial settlements receiving assistance from outside. The lack of substantial investment, the maintaining of the refugee camps in their stagnating state and the high natural increase of the population, which is in the neighbourhood of 35 per thousand, have all contributed to intensify the social pressure of the inhabitants on their surroundings, which in turn has formented extremist nationalistic sentiments.

A number of steps were taken since 1967 by the Israeli military government of the Gaza Strip with a view to modify the artificial structure that had been created in the past. The chief of these was to build new and planned residential quarters for

the inmates of the refugee camps. Other steps included the improvement of the road network, the setting up of new administrative and health institutions, and the raising of the level of agricultural
employment.

GAZA - THE MAIN URBAN CENTER

The town of Gaza, by virtue of its size and its
regional and historical importance, is the dominant
geographical feature in the Strip. The town is surrounded on all sides by sands and citrus groves.
The municipal boundary encloses an area of 2,750
acres, of which 550 are built up. The population
numbers 152,000, not counting the 28,000 persons
living in the Esh-Shati refugee camp, which has
lately been incorporated into the municipal area of
Gaza.
     The town contains several distinct parts,
which reflect its historical development and certain
political circumstances. The old historical town
was built largely during the Ottoman period, over
the remains of an ancient settlement. The buildings
are mainly in Mameluke style, and Turkish influence
is also evident. There is a central square, from
which springs the main street, 'Omar el-Mukhtar.
This is the main longitudinal axis along which the
town has developed. On both sides is the principal
business center, with rows of shops, some of farely
modern construction. Gaza is situated near the main
communications axis of the Strip and in an agricultural region. It has thus the advantages of easy
accessibility and economic basis.
     During the thirties and forties of this century
the development of Gaza was guided by the interests
and the policies of the mandatory government. A new
and spacious residential quarter, Rimal, was built
on the sands west of the town. It contained de-
tached houses built in European style, with plots of
¼ acre or larger. This development was not due to
any local initiative. Arabs preferred, as a rule,
to live in the area of the sandstone ridges or on
agricultural land. The British, on the other hand,
gave priority to building on the sands, in the proximity of the sea, so as to enable maximum use to be
made of the sea-shore, including the development of
a port, even if only for the export of citrus and
other local produce. This also accorded with the
general European town planning conception that towns
should not be built on land suitable for agriculture.

The policy of the mandatory government was to transfer the center of gravity of the town to an axis leading to the port, whose economic basis would thereby be strengthened, and to achieve a gradual detachment from the old center.

During the same period, the Zeitun and Judeide quarters were built, expanding the town towards the south, the south-west and the east. The growth of these quarters was to a large extent due to the activities of foreign institutions, such as hospitals, who were in need of unoccupied land suitable for building. The Jewish Quarter of Gaza, where about 50 Jewish families had lived until the 1929 riots, also expanded in the same direction. Two other quarters - Turkeman and Tuffah, sprang up in the southern part of Gaza, around the nucleus of old dilapidated houses dating from the last century. They were now slum areas, with mud houses, and were in the nature of semi-urban settlements for the Bedouin of the area. Today, most of Gaza's automobile repair shops and service stations are concentrated here. The villages of Jabaliya and Nazla, northeast of Gaza, are gradually expanding in the direction of the town.

An additional urban element of Gaza is represented by the Esh-Shati refugee camp, which was established in the fifties as one of the eight camps in the Strip. It is situated at some distance north of the town. Esh-Shati has recently been incorporated in the Gaza municipal area, in view of its influence in all matters relating to manpower, employment policy services, finances and administration. The camp inmates consider themselves as temporary residents and make no attempt to take part in the life of the town. The Gaza Municipality, for their part, was never interested in accepting the refugees as an integral part of the town. The Esh-Shati inhabitants do not build outside the limits of the camp, but add rooms to their already crowded quarters isolated from the rest of the population. There is no intermarriage with residents of Gaza, and in the secondary schools there are separate classes for refugee and for Gaza children. The wide gulf separating the refugees from the established Gaza residents is typified by the building at Rimal, not far from the Esh-Shati camp, of an exclusive quarter of villas for the Gaza rich.

In the development of Gaza we can recognize the same elements which characterize most Middle-Eastern towns: situation near a communications cross-roads, environmental advantages, a compact

town plan. Had it not been for the intervention of
the government, which imposed a linear development,
Gaza's original pattern would have remained unchanged until this day. After 1948, the town turned a-
way from the armistice line and directed its development in a western direction, while at the same
time spreading along a north-south axis. In Gaza,
as well as in other towns of the Strip and the West
Bank, the refugee population has not been integrated within any municipal framework, and there has
been practically no absorption in the local population.

Chapter Sixteen

TOWN PLANNING IN THE LAND OF ISRAEL

CONSTRUCTION SINCE THE BEGINNING OF THE 20th
CENTURY

Although Jewish urban settlement began in The Land
of Israel in the middle of the 19th Century, the
actual building of the country started with the beginning of Zionist settlement in 1882. Until World
War I, construction was undertaken by the Ottoman
Authorities who had no concept of town planning in
regular town building. Since the beginning of this
century only three town plans were known, none of
which were prepared by Jews: the town plan of Beer
Sheva from the year 1903, the town plan of Acre
from 1906, and the plans for the German Colonies in
Jerusalem, Jaffa and Haifa. These plans were quite
basic and showed land use by very simple lines.
The erection of Ahuzat Bayit near Jaffa in 1909 and
the beginning of the first Jewish town of Tel Aviv
were not done with the use of a town plan.
     Town planning in the Land of Israel had a great
potential as many favourable characteristics existed in the landscape which would have facilitated
planning, especially the traditional Arab architecture which is a variation on the Italian Mediterranean style. Although the Hebrew Technion, which
opened in 1925, began instruction in the fields of
engineering and architecture, the profession of
town planning found no expression in daily life.
Construction during the Zionist period attempted to
adapt the Mediterranean-Oriental style which was
not always suitable for the Jewish immigrants and
which did not fit into Zionist ideology. Oriental
construction clearly distinguished between lavish
dwellings and those which are simple, while the
trend in Jewish and Zionist housing is not to dif-
ferentiate between the living quarters of different

classes. In fact, the Zionists encouraged unit housing for all. In the Middle Eastern countries there are distinctions between rural and urban housing with towns having a special status and features, but Jewish construction did not emphasize functional urban construction and viewed everything from the perspective of labour class needs so that the differences in the building of housing projects in the town or countryside were not obvious at all. Even until today most of the Jews in Israel do not live in private houses of their own but rather in apartment houses or in housing projects, while the Arabs for the most part live in their own private dwelling units, a self-understood elementary need for them.

CONSTRUCTION DURING THE MANDATE PERIOD

The transition from Turkish to British rule brought with it a new approach to town planning. The British, in contrast to the Turks, combined an urban culture of the highest standard, with a romantic attachment to the Middle East. Immediately after the conquest of the country from the Turks, the Mandatory Government began to tackle the problem of a plan for Jerusalem, and between the years 1919 and 1930 a number of plans for the city were prepared. Although they may seem today somewhat improvised and naive, these plans constituted at the time a novel and positive approach to town planning problems. The Government also founded the Pro-Jerusalem Society, whose aims included the preservation of the beauty of the city and the furthering of its planning and development. At that time, Zionist settlement was still in its early stages, and any initiative that the Jewish authorities may have taken in the field of building and town planning, was directed towards the rural sector. As for the Arabs, their attitude to town planning was mainly one of indifference, as long as their material interests were not involved.

The urban planning policy of the Mandatory Government was influenced by the classical Garden City movement. There was a tendency to subdivide large plots and to safeguard the economic interests of the individual and the community. There is no doubt that such an approach weakened the position of the government as regards long range planning. Furthermore, the government did not itself become a landowner, either within or outside the towns. In

spite of the authorities' wide knowledge and experience in town planning, their attitude to fundamental problems of urban development was peculiar.
They did not seem to mind narrow streets in densely
built-up quarters, provided the streets were shaded,
as is customary in the Middle East. They did not
realize the need for a hierarchy of urban streets,
or a width sufficient to cope with modern traffic,
and they had no idea of the traffic technology that
would take into account future developments.

As regards the Jewish sector, the question of
where and when to build centered at first on the
possibility of buying urban property. Land purchases from Arabs were effected through private middlemen. Later on, it was the deliberate policy of the
Mandatory Government to put obstacles in the way of
Jewish urban development. Land speculation increased, and greatly profited Arab landowners, many of
whom became very wealthy as a result of Jewish land
purchases.

The Mandatory Governments principle contribution to the development of the towns was the creation of the town planning commissions, whose main
function was to establish the administrative machin-
ery for building control. The control was decentralized, and based on local, municipal and district
commissions. The Mandatory legislation which gave
legal sanction to the functions of these commissions
was enacted in the year 1936, at the peak of Jewish
immigration from Europe. This immigration created
an enormous demand for residential and public, as
well as for commercial and industrial building. However, Jewish initiative in building development was
often hampered by the official instruments of control and inspection.

Jewish interests were in continuous conflict
with the town planning authorities of the Mandatory
Government, who favoured a low building density and
objected to the rapid development of urban land.
Palestine was visualized as a British colony, to be
administered in the interests of its political potential within the region, where the emphasis should
be laid on tranquility rather than on dynamic development. The Zionist movement, on the other hand,
strove towards an intensive and accelerated development of the country, mass immigration, building and
economic expansion. This policy was to be proved
correct by the political changes which the country
underwent in that period.

The British Mandatory Government was aware of
the problems relating to town planning, and knew how

to develop towns and quarters according to established European practice, but it applied this knowledge only to those areas in whose development it had a special interest. On the whole, it can be said that the Mandatory Government did not leave any special imprint on the country's development. It only acted in selected urban centers and was guided by considerations of security, strategy and economics. Thus, the government was interested in developing Haifa as a major port in the eastern Mediterranean, and hence encouraged large investments in the construction of the harbour and the adjoining industrial areas. It was also interested in stressing the importance of Jerusalem as the center of the administration, and this found expression in the construction of public buildings and residential quarters for British officials. Other localities in which the government had a special interest were Beer Sheva, the regional capital of the Negev, Yaffa, the second port of the country and Gaza, the port in the southern part of the coastal plain. If the other towns developed during the same period some had administrative or security functions, like Ramla, others were communication centers like Lod, or holiday and recreation centers like Nahariyya and Netanya. There were also other medium-sized towns that appeared on the map of the country during Mandatory times, including some in Judea and Samaria, which had grown out of large villages whose development had received preferential treatment.

During the Second World War the Mandatory Government also gave economic aid to some Jewish settlements that had developed industries, and this greatly furthered their urban growth. However, no serious effort was made during the Mandatory period to plan an overall scheme of towns on a regional basis, and to improve upon their existing historical distribution.

THE DEVELOPMENT OF THE URBAN PATTERN IN ISRAEL

With the establishment of the State of Israel, Jews assumed full responsibility for the planning and building of the country's towns. The 1936 Town Planning Ordinance remained in force, with some amendments until it was replaced by the Planning and Building Law of 1965. The large waves of immigration which reached Israel soon after the establishment of the State, had to be absorbed in the existing towns. The planning concepts and the land uses on which Mandatory town planning schemes were based, proved to be quite inadequate to cope with the new situation, which called for rapid and large scale building. The new national approach to planning, and the need to absorb within a relatively short time a large number of immigrants while ensuring a desirable geographical distribution of the population, had an immediate influence on the towns. The urgent need for new large scale housing caused the towns to expand at a pace incompatible with orderly and gradual development. The Mandatory planning and building laws had but little influence on this dynamic process, and the quality of the buildings put up at that time was not of a high standard.

At the time of the establishment of the State, there was still no clearly defined urban policy on the part of the Jewish settlement agencies, whose main activity was connected with agriculture. However, there was beginning to emerge a general concept of what should be the aim of such a policy, namely: the rapid absorption of immigrants, which could only be made possible by the foundation of new towns; creation of an urban hierarchy which would regulate the interaction between large towns and villages by establishing urban settlements of various sizes, the dispersal of the population in the interests of security and defence of the borders and the still unsettled parts of the country.

After seventy years of planning and directing the intensive agricultural settlements of the country, the settlement organizations gradually began to turn their attention to the towns, and realized the important role they could play in the rapid population of the various parts of the country. However, owing to the hesitant approach to the subject, no immediate steps were taken to build new towns, and the first urban activity was limited to settling new immigrants to abandoned towns such as Lod, Ramla, Bet She'an and Beer Sheva. When there was no more room in these towns, temporary transit camps were set up near the old established settlements in the coastal plain. Some of these were later dismantled, others contributed to the growth of settlements such as Rishon LeZion, Rehovot and Hadera, which eventually received the status of towns, and some as Or-Aqiva and Yehud, even developed into independent settlements.

The next step consisted in the founding of small development towns, such as Sederot, Ofaqim, Ramat Yishay and Netivot, followed by larger towns,

211

such as Bet Shemesh, Qiryat Malakhi,Qiryat Ono.
Dimona and Maalot. Only later, towards the end of
the fifties and the beginning of the sixties was
it decided to build still larger towns, such as Ashdod or Beer Sheva, and settlements of a definately
urban character, such as Arad or Karmiel. In all,
dozens of urban centers of all kinds have been
founded since the establishment of the State, in
addition to new suburbs in Tel Aviv and Haifa. In
the near future, these may become the nucleus of a
more intensified development of the coastal plain,
thereby changing the traditional urban pattern of
the country.
        The new immigrants gradually filled the various
types of the towns. The gradual nature of this process had a decisive influence on the country's
urban development. It is well known that immigrants
tend to remain in the places of entry in their new
country, in this case, Tel Aviv and Haifa. These
two cities absorbed the largest number of immigrants
while only a relatively small number reached the
interior, including Jerusalem. The concentration of
large numbers of newcomers in the urban centers of
the coastal plain, resulted in this region under-
goind a marked economic development in the fields of
industry, agriculture and services, and the whole
chain of settlements from Nahariyya in the north to
Ashqelon in the south, became a center of attraction
for additional immigrants. Most new immigrants had
been town dwellers in their country of origin, and
it was, therefore, natural that in their new country
too, they should gravitate to the towns and to urban occupation. The result was an every growing
concentration of immigrants in the towns, a considerable increase in the population of the coastal
plain, the development of suburbs around the large
cities and the transformation of small settlements
int town. (Figure 16.1)
        The development of the towns in the hilly re-
gions of Judea, Samaria and Galilee was limited because of the special topographical conditions and
the distance of these towns from the main centers of
population and economic activity. Their main functions have always been connected with the supply
of services to the neighbouring farmers. They have
also been centers of communications and of religious worship, but they never attracted large scale
industry.The hill towns have therefore retained
their original character, and no comprehensive urban pattern has evolved in this region.
        As a result of the policy of urban development

212

Figure 16.1: Existing Town System 1983

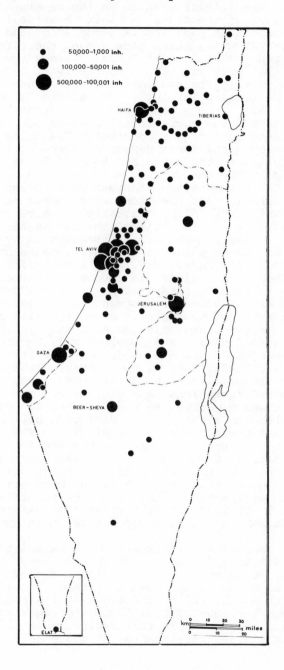

followed since the establishment of the State, there
have been significant changes in the geographical
distribution of the towns in their relative importance. A dominant position is occupied by the conurbation of Tel Aviv, which grew around the first all-
Jewish town in The Land of Israel. Since the early
twenties Tel Aviv with the aid of private enterprise
began to develop its economic infrastructure and it
became the focal point for the population of the
coastal plain. The process of urbanization eventually reached the agricultural suburbs of Tel Aviv,
which became part of the conurbation reaching today
from Herzliyya and Ramat HaSharon in the north to
Rishon LeZion in the south and to Bene Beraq and
Givatayim in the east.

It is in the nature of urban development in the
Land of Israel, that the older settlements and the
development towns in the coastal plain have the advantage over towns in Galilee, the Judean hills or
the Negev. The pace or urban processes is more
rapid where there exists a well developed economic
and agricultural background, favourable climatic and
topographical conditions and proximity to the sea or
to the main traffic arteries. Any initiative to artifically direct urban development to the eastern or
southern parts of the country or to the hill regions
will encounter greater difficulties than is the case
in the coastal plain, and progress will be slower.
Qiryat Shemona or Bet She'an do not grow at the same
pace as Herzliyya, Rehovot or Nahariyya, which enjoy more favourable geographical conditions.

The two exceptions to the above general rule
are the towns of Jerusalem and Beer Sheva. Jerusalem, although situated in a difficult hilly terrain, has since the establishment of the State,
grown into a large city owing to the economic and
administrative support given it by the Israeli
Government, and in spite of adverse political conditions. After the Six Day War, the boundaries of
Jerusalem were extended and it is now possible to
envisage a continuous metropolitan area extending
from Ramallah in the north to Bethlehem in the
south.

The population of Jerusalem at the end of 1981
reached 415,000, including 100,000 non-Jews, this
being more than the population within the municipal
boundaries of any other town in Israel. It is estimated that at the end of the eighties the population
will reach 450,000-500,000, 340,000 of them Jews.
There is room within the residential areas of Jerusalem for 650,000 inhabitants, at reasonable dwell-

ing standards.

The development of Beer Sheva also exceeded expectations, in spite of its position on the edge of
the desert. Its favourable geographical location to
the north of the Negev and in the center of a plain,
and the fact that it was built around an existing
urban nucleus, contributed to Beer Sheva's developing at a more rapid rate than urban centers such as
Elat, Mizpe Ramon, Yeruham, and even Arad. To the
above advantages should be added the communication
routes which passed through Beer Sheva in the past,
and which are being efficiently used today.

As can be seem from the above, the geographical
pattern of Israel towns is still in a process of
transition and has not yet crystallized into a def-
inite form. On the one hand, there are signs of a
certain degree of maturity, such as the Tel Aviv
conurbation, Haifa with its industrial complex
along the Bay, and Jerusalem, a capital city built
in the hills. On the other hand there are many
examples of settlements whose character is as yet
undefined, and it is not clear if they are fully
fledged towns, small towns or large villages. Most
development towns founded since the establishment of
the State, belong to this category. In recent years
many of the older settlements in the coastal plain
have undergone a process of progressive urbanization.
The same applies to a few new settlements, such as
Ashdod, Ashqelon, Upper Nazareth and Dimona, which,
in spite of being new, have already acquired a de-
cidedly urban character.

RURAL BUILDING

In contrast to the lack of town building during the
Mandate period, rural building developed extensively. In   Land of Israel, the Jewish village developed late, comparatively speaking, to other
countries in the world and therefore it was established on a new set of fundamentals. The village
was based on a combination of professional knowledge, clear cut functions and on a social and ideological background. The specialization of building
villages reached its height during those years so
that different housing types were implemented in the
various settlements as the Moshavah, Kibbutz and
Moshav. In each form of settlement building type
and lay-out were different and were suited to the
ideology of its inhabitants.

Rural building had different technical problems

similar to those of the town. Accessibility to the
nearby village without having to pass directly
through it was one concern. In addition, the problems of contact between the dwelling unit and the
public institutions of the settlement existed, as
well as building for the purpose of security. The
entire rural sector reached a high standard of
building and was shaped by the features that
characterized the various settlement forms according to the ideologies of their founders.

TOWN DESIGN

Estheticism does not play a very large role in town
planning in Israel. When town building was initially begun, it was possible to promote estheticism.
Regional planning which was much more developed than
town planning strove to prevent the destruction of
open space, but on the town level almost nothing was
done in this direction. The desire to beautify
towns is a function and expression of a culture and
the urban mentality of its people. It appears that
this urban mentality is very weak in Israel. Housing there has been too experimental to be considered beautiful. In addition, building is very expensive causing most towns to delay implementation
of their outline schemes. Towns located along the
coast, and especially those in the hilly areas need
special esthetic designs. In Israel, there are many
archaeological and historical orders which should be
integrated into town building. Preservation of open
space and the development of gardens are quite expensive under the climatic conditions of Israel and
must be calculated very carefully.
     Israel also has some significant urban orders
worthy of reconstruction efforts such as the Old
City of Jerusalem, the Old City of Acre, the Cape
of Jaffa, the mountainous Safed, the Mea She'arim
Quarter in Jerusalem, the village of En Kerem. In
contrast to these areas are the new towns created
between 1950 and 1963 which lack any interesting
characteristics. They do not have squares, meeting
places, impressive monuments, towers and architectural elements which beautify a town.
     The approach towards the space and technology
of housing has gone through many changes throughout
the last 150 years. In the past, the architectural
style of a single building was stressed and later
the functional aspects of building became much more
important. It is very strange that in the surround-

216

ings of the Mediterranean, an area noted as the originator of building for esthetic purposes, that such changes in approach could occur. Today, functional building is much more important than architecture, and social problems have begun to influence building more than function has.

SELECTED BIBLIOGRAPHY

Amiran D.H.K. (1973) The Development of Jerusalem
        1860 - 1970, in Urban Geography of Jerusalem,
        Massada Press, Jerusalem, A companion Volume
        to the Atlas of Jerusalem, pp. 20-52.
                        (1973) Elat, Seaside Town in the Des-
        ert of Israel in Amiran D.H.K. and A.W. Wilson
        (eds), Coastal Deserts, their Natural and
        Human Environments, University of Arizona
        Press, Tuscon, Arizona, pp. 171-177.
Amiran D.H.K. and A. Schachar (1969), Development
        Towns in Israel, The Hebrew University, Jeru-
        salem.
                                        (1964), The Towns in
        Israel; The Principles of their Urban Geogra-
        phy, Geo. Rev. 51, pp. 348-369.
                                        (1960), Estimates of
        the Urban Population of Palestine in the
        Second Half of the Nineteenth Century, Israel
        Exploration Journal, 10, pp. 181-183.
Ben-Arieh Y. (1976), Legislative and Cultural Fact-
        ors in the Development of Jerusalem 1800-1914,
        Jerusalem, pp. 54-105, in D.H.K. Amiran and Y.
        Ben Arieh (eds.), Geography in Israel, The
        Israel National Committee.
Berler A. (1964), Urbanization Process in Israel,
        Ekistics.
Berman M. (1965), The Evolution of Beer Sheva as an
        Urban Center, Annals of the American Assoc-
        iation Geographers, pp. 308-326.
Brutzkus E. (1969), Regional Policy in Israel, Min-
        istry of the Interior, Jerusalem.
Clement R. (1974), Eilat, The Southern Gateway,
        Israel Magazine, Vol.6, No.3, pp. 32-39.
Cohen E. (1970), The City in the Zionist Ideology,
        Institute of Urban and Regional Studies, The
        Hebrew University, Jerusalem, 1, 62 pp.

Dash J. and E. Efrat (1964), The Israel Physical Master Plan, Ministry of the Interior, Jerusalem, 91 pp. + plates.

Efrat E. (1978), Optimum Versus Reality in Israel's Town System, Geojournal, Vol. 2, 6, pp. 507-520.

_____ (1979) Settlement Pattern and Economic Changes of the Gaza Strip 1947-1977, The Middle East Journal, Vol.31, pp. 349-356.

_____ (1977) Industry in Israel's New Development Towns, Geojournal, Vol. 1, 4, Wiesbaden, pp. 41-46.

_____ (1977), Le Development Urbain en Israel, Connaissance d'Israel, Cirel, Charleroi, Belgique, 1, pp. 89-104.

_____ (1976), Changes in the Settlement Pattern of the Gaza Strip: 1945-1975, Asian Affairs, London, Vol. 13, Part II, pp. 168-177.

_____ (1976), Geographical Influences on the Physical Planning of Israel's Coasts in D.H.K. Amiran and Y. Ben Arieh (eds.), Geography in Israel, The Israel National Committee, Jerusalem, pp. 158-161.

_____ (1974), Arad - A New Town in the Desert, Geoforum, Pergamon Press, pp. 81-86.

_____ (1973), Geography of Jerusalem, in Jerusalem, Israel Pocket Library, Keter Publishing House, Jerusalem, pp. 216-220.

_____ (1971), Changes in the Town Planning Concepts of Jerusalem 1919-1969, Environmental Planning, The Israeli Association for Environmental Planning Quarterly, pp. 53-65.

_____ (1970), Judea and Samaria, Guidelines for Regional and Physical Planning, Ministry of the Interior, Jerusalem, 156 pp.

_____ (1964) The Hinterland of the New City of Jerusalem and its Economic Significance, Economic Geography, 40, 3, pp. 256-260.

_____ (1964), Patterns in Urban Development of Modern Jerusalem, Tijd. Voor Econ. en Soc. Geog. pp. 223-229.

Gavish D. (1976), Changes in the Rural Land - Use on the Urban Fringe of Tel Aviv in D.H.K Amiran and Y. Ben Arieh (eds.), Geography in Israel, The Israel National Committee, Jerusalem, pp. 218-238.

Gonen A. (1976), The Suburban Mosaic in Israel, in D.H.K. Amiran and Y. Ben Arieh (eds.), Geography in Israel, The Israel National Committee, Jerusalem, pp. 163-186.

219

_____ (1975), Locational and Ecological Aspects of Urban Public Sector Housing: The Israeli Case in G. Gappart and H.M. Rose (eds.), The Social Economy of Cities, Urban Affairs, Annual Review, Vol.9, Beverly Hills, pp.283-289.

_____(1972), The Role of High Growth Rates and of Public Housing Agencies in Shaping the Spatial Structure of Israel Towns, Tijd. voor Ec. en Soc. Geog., pp. 410-410.

Gouldman M.D. (1966), Legal Aspects of Town Planning in Israel, Institute for Legislative and Comparative Law, the Hebrew University, Jerusalem, 187 pp.

Gradus Y. (1976), Factor Ecology in a Controlled Urban System: The Case of Metropolitan Haifa, Israel, Geografiska Annaler, Vol.5B, 1, pp. 59-65.

Gradus Y. and E. Stern (1980), Changing Strategies of Development: Toward a Regiopolis in the Negev Desert, Journal of the American Planning Association, Vol.46, 4, pp.410-423.

Greiczer I. (1978), Spatial Patterns and Residential Densities in Israeli 'Moshavot' in Process of Urbanization, Geojournal, Vol.2, No. 6, pp.533-538.

Grossman D. (1981), The Relationship between Settlement Pattern and Resource Utilization: The Case of North-eastern Samaria, Translations of the Institute of British Geographers, N.S., Vol.6, pp.19-38.

Karmon Y. (1976), Eilat, Problems of a Port on a Desert Coast, in D.H.K. Amiran and Y. Ben Arieh (eds.), Geography in Israel, The Israel National Committee, Jerusalem, pp.106-137.

_____ (1971), Israel, A Regional Geography, Wiley & Sons Interscience, London, pp.74-94, 161-267.

_____ (1963), Eilat, Israel's Red Sea Port Tijdsch. voor Econ. en Soc. Geog., pp.117-126.

Kendall H. (1948), Jerusalem - The Holy City Plan, Preservation and Development during the British Mandate 1918-1948, London.

Kipnis B.A. (1976), The Functioning of a New Town as a Regional Center, A Case Study in Northern Israel in D.H.K. Amiran and Y. Ben Arieh (eds.), Geography in Israel, The Israel National Committee, Jerusalem, pp.239-254.

Lichfield N. (1971), Israel's New Towns: A Strategy for the Future, 3 Vols, Ministry of Housing, Tel Aviv.

Orni E. (1975), Städtebau und Bevölkerungslenkung in Israel, Geographische Zeitschrift, pp.63, Heft 3, pp.195-216.
_____ (1970), Städtische Siedlungen Israels, Geographische Rundschau, 5, pp.165-174.
Orni E. and E. Efrat (1980), Geography of Israel, Fourth Revised Edition, Israel University Press, Jerusalem, pp.193-364.
Romann M. (1978), Jerusalem Since 1967: A Profile of Reunited City, Geojournal, Vol.6, 2, pp.499-506.
Shachar A. (1976), New Towns in a National Settlement Policy, Town and Country Planning, pp. 83-87.
_____ (1975), Patterns of Population Densities in the Tel Aviv Metropolitan Area, Enviroment and Planning, A, Vol.7, pp.279-291.
_____ (1973), The Functional Structure of Jerusalem in Urban Geography of Jerusalem, Massada Press, Jerusalem, A Companion Volume to the Atlas of Jerusalem, pp.76-90.
Schachar A. and G. Lifshitz (1980), Regional Influences in Israel, Environment and Planning, Vol.13, pp.463-473.
Shapiro S. (1973), Planning Jerusalem: The First Generation 1917-1968, Urban Geography of Jerusalem, Massada Press, Jerusalem. A Companion Volume to the Atlas of Jerusalem, pp.139-153.
Sharon A. (1973), Planning Jerusalem, The Old City and its Environs, Weidenfeld and Nicolson, Jerusalem, 211 pp.
Shattner Y. (1954), Haifa: A Study in the Relation of City and Coast, Israel Exploration Journal, Vol.4, 1, pp.26-46.
Shmeltz V.O. (1973), The Evolution of Jerusalem's Population in Urban Geography of Jerusalem, Massada Press, Jerusalem, A Companion Volume to the Atlas of Jerusalem, pp.53-75.
Sofer A. and Y. Bar-Gal (1976), Urban Elements in Non-Jewish Villages in the North of Israel in D.H.K Amiran and Y. Ben Arieh (eds.), Geography in Israel, The Israel National Committee.
Spiegel E. (1976), New Towns in Israel: Urban and Regional Planning and Development, Praeger,N.Y.
_____ (1966), New Towns in Israel, Karl Kraemer Verlag, Stuttgart-Bern, 192 pp.
Stern E. (1981), Relative Population Change Determinants and Redistribution Policy-The Israeli Example, S.A. Geographer, 9(2), pp.101-109.

Turner M. (1968): Eilat, Preliminary Study for the
    Town Expansion to 50,000, Ministry of the
    Interior, Jerusalem, 102 pp.
Waterman S. (1975), Early Post-State Planning in
    Israel - The 1949 Plan for Acre, Horizons,
    University of Haifa, pp.IX-XVIII.
    _____ (1971), Pre-Israeli Planning in Pales-
    tine - The Example of Acre, Town Planning
    Review, 42.

INDEX